Understanding Latin America

A DECODING GUIDE

Understanding
Latin America

A DECODING GUIDE

Alfredo Toro Hardy
Venezuelan Scholar and Diplomat

World Scientific

NEW JERSEY • LONDON • SINGAPORE • BEIJING • SHANGHAI • HONG KONG • TAIPEI • CHENNAI • TOKYO

Published by

World Scientific Publishing Co. Pte. Ltd.
5 Toh Tuck Link, Singapore 596224
USA office: 27 Warren Street, Suite 401-402, Hackensack, NJ 07601
UK office: 57 Shelton Street, Covent Garden, London WC2H 9HE

British Library Cataloguing-in-Publication Data
A catalogue record for this book is available from the British Library.

UNDERSTANDING LATIN AMERICA
A Decoding Guide

ISBN 978-981-3229-94-5

Desk Editor: Sandhya Venkatesh

Typeset by Stallion Press
Email: enquiries@stallionpress.com

Printed in Singapore

**To Gaby, who structures and complements my life,
with all my love.**

To Ceci, Fer and Diego, always close to my heart.

FOREWORD

Addressing the profound tendencies that define a highly heterogeneous region, such as Latin America, is a complex task. To be able to do so, while simultaneously explaining the similarities and commonalities that exist within the region, is even more difficult. To that it should be added the important achievement of recreating a historical journey spanning several centuries, in a coherent, clear, thorough and pleasant manner. Alfredo Toro Hardy's excellent book, *Understanding Latin America: A Decoding Guide*, provides a key to this region and to its historical cycles and current challenges. It also opens a prospective window into the near future.

Ambassador Toro Hardy leads us to comprehend the crossing between the meaning of our historical roots and the tendencies that have defined each of the junctures that have marked new cycles in Latin America. Similarly, he introduces us to the ways in which, throughout history, the external actors have influenced or fought to exert their influence over Latin America.

The complexities of this topic begin with the very denomination of the region. This part of the world has been designated and referred to in different ways and through different concepts: Pan–Latin, Latin America, Pan–America. One part has been called Luso–America and the other Hispano–America, this being the result of the Treaty of Tordesillas which divided the region between Portugal and Spain. Because of the racial characteristics of its people, it has also been called Indo–America in some parts, while being referred to in others as Afro–America, although there is no one meaning that can capture its wide miscegenation and multiculturalism. The French expression of *Latin America* is the one that best adjusts to its global recognition.

Politically, the region has enjoyed cycles of both convergence and divergence. Latin America has been indelibly marked by the weight of the sword and of the cross, being this the symbiosis that resulted from a colonization in which military power and the Catholic Church acted together. This political, cultural and institutional brand was broken in some countries as a result of the independence wars. In others, though, it remained as part of the process of elite consensus building. A second major political trend was the great difficulty of integrating the different colonial territories into a single state. Fragmentation reined after the wars of independence, and with it, came the rivalries and conflicts between the new states. This marked the 19th and 20th centuries, and remains to this day as a problem in certain cases. A third trend is the difference and antagonism between liberals and conservatives. This differentiation produced long wars and widespread polarization. This dichotomy persists under various forms. However, perhaps the most genuine product of this region has been *populism*. Its warlords and their populist tendencies have plagues all their political systems at some point in history, as clearly emphasized by Ambassador Toro Hardy.

As far as the international insertion of Latin America is concerned, this has been an area in which the weight and the influence of the United States has marked one of the central historical tendencies. As Alfredo Toro Hardy highlights, in chapters six and seven of this book, there has not been a singular hegemonic policy by the United States. On the contrary, such hegemony has been exerted through different policies that have oscillated between the extremes of military intervention and the search for partnership and collaboration. There have also been periods in which the region has fallen into oblivion. But these tendencies have been marked by geographical differences as well. The major weight of the United States impact in the region has been felt in Mexico and the Caribbean Basin.

In the post–Cold War 21st century, many global trends have changed. This expresses itself in Latin America through the presence of new international actors, most significantly China. This country does not seek to dispute the American hegemony, but aims at ensuring ever more meaningful cooperation ties and investment opportunities. America's withdrawal from many international economic scenarios, mainly in the Asia–Pacific region, has generated new opportunities for China in its relations with Latin America. This is especially true in relation to South America, where China has become the main trading and investment partner. From a broader perspective, though, the economies of India and the Asia–Pacific region, namely Japan, South Korea, Malaysia, Singapore, Australia and New Zealand, along with China, occupy increasingly relevant places in terms of their economic relationship with Latin America.

Today, heterogeneous Latin America is characterized for being a peaceful zone, free of nuclear weapons and all types of weapons of mass destruction. It is also a democratic region. Electoral democracy works and is respected by its people. However, deficiencies and weaknesses with regards to greater social inclusion and citizen participation remain. Another characteristic of Latin America is its "middle–income region" nature, perhaps even high–middle income, which results in societies with high levels of inequality. This particular characteristic, in this day and age, hinders its possibilities of being considered as a recipient of international cooperation funds. Likewise, the region is characterized by the abundance of natural resources, making it very attractive for countries in the Asia–Pacific region, particularly Japan, South Korea, and China, although for different reasons in each case. It is undoubtedly true that the Asia–Pacific region is playing a defining role in the future of the region. Finally, it should be emphasized that the concept of integration has been embedded into the DNA of the region since its independence, entrenched within the psyche of its founding fathers. Today, this is expressed in the form of the *Community of Latin American and Caribbean States* (CELAC its name in Spanish), in the consultation process within this community, which was built under the motto of *United in Diversity.*

The region is also characterized by large deficits and inadequacies, most notably two: (1) the high level of inequality, being the region with the highest economic and social polarization indices in the world and (2) the high degrees of violence expressed in the region, particularly in areas without an effective presence of the Rule of Law.

The vision of the future, as well as the forthcoming challenges and options for Latin America, have allowed Ambassador Toro Hardy to highlight the great tendencies that the region will face in the years ahead. The author emphasizes the impact of the fourth industrial revolution, the fluctuations in commodity prices, and the governance needs brought about by globalization, among others.

There are no easy answers to these challenges. The risks are many and overcoming them will imply, as noted by Alfredo Toro Hardy, addressing challenges in education, technology, and political governance. Only international cooperation, regional association, and a shared vision of global tendencies will allow Latin America to find the partners it needs to advance jointly on the path towards prosperity and harmony.

In short, where can Latin America be placed within the international system? This solid, comprehensive, and suggestive book tells us that we are part of the "West". However, it also indicates that this identity should be nuanced by the complex crossing between the historical trends and the challenges present in the 21st century. The differentiated developments, the weight of the United States, the emergence of Asia–Pacific actors, the Robotics Revolution, the new demands in the field of research and development, all complicate our vision of the future. This book allows us to understand the great tendencies in motion while raising new questions about the future of Latin America.

We welcome the fundamental and significant contribution made by Alfredo Toro Hardy in *Understanding Latin America: A Decoding Guide.*

Francisco Rojas Aravena,
Rector
United Nations University for Peace

FOREWORD

I thank Ambassador Alfredo Toro Hardy for requesting me to write a foreword for this important and timely book.

Ambassador Toro Hardy is one of Venezuela's most senior and distinguished diplomats. He is currently serving as Venezuela's Ambassador to Singapore. Prior to coming to Singapore, he had served as his country's Ambassador to the United States of America, United Kingdom, Brazil, Spain, Chile and Ireland.

Ambassador Toro Hardy is also a scholar and public intellectual. He has taught at the Simon Bolivar University in Caracas, Princeton University in the United States and at universities in Brazil and Spain. He is the author of 18 books and the co–author of 13 books.

I have described this book as important and timely. I would like to explain why. I have always believed that there is tremendous potential in the relationship between East Asia and Latin America. I was one of the officials who helped Singapore's former Prime Minister, Mr Goh Chok Tong, in conceptualising the proposal to establish the Forum for East Asia–Latin America Cooperation (FEALAC) in 1998. The rationale for the proposal was to bring together two dynamic regions of the world and to harness economic and other opportunities. FEALAC was established in 1999. Given the protectionist sentiments in the US and in some parts of Europe, the time is opportune for FEALAC to champion free trade and globalisation.

East Asia should be of great interest to Latin America because the rise of China, India and ASEAN represent the three biggest growth stories of this century. China has already become a major economic partner of Latin America. India and ASEAN can do much more.

At the same time, Latin America should be of great interest to East Asia. It is a region well–endowed with natural resources and with talented people. It is a region seeking to diversify its connections beyond North America and Europe.

There are some obstacles to overcome. The first is distance. The second is language. Not many Asian business people can speak Spanish or Portuguese. It is true, of course, that English is widely spoken by the elite in Latin America. The third obstacle is culture. I once asked a Mexican friend why a trade negotiation between Mexico and an Asian country had failed. He said it was because of culture. He explained that the Asian country's representative was very cold–blooded and transactional. He said that, in the Mexican cultural box, we must first become friends before we negotiate. Asians need a cultural guide to Latin America.

Ambassador Toro Hardy's book seeks to fill this void. It is therefore most important and timely. I have enjoyed reading the book and gained many new insights about the countries of Latin America from it. I wish the book success.

Tommy Koh
Ambassador–At–Large at Singapore's Ministry of Foreign Affairs.
Chairman of the Board of Governors of the Centre
for International Law and Rector of the Tembusu College
at the National University of Singapore

ABOUT THE AUTHOR

Alfredo Toro Hardy is a Venezuelan Diplomat, scholar and public intellectual. He graduated in Law from the Central University of Venezuela with master degrees from the University of Pennsylvania and the Central University of Venezuela, and postgraduate degrees from the University of Paris II and the Ecole Nationale d'Administration, ENA.

He is one of his country's most senior career diplomats, having served as Ambassador to Washington, London, Madrid, Brasilia, Santiago de Chile, Dublin and, currently, Singapore.

As scholar he was Director of the Diplomatic Academy of the Venezuelan Ministry of Foreign Affairs and Associate Professor at the Simón Bolívar University in Caracas, where he was Director of the Centre for North American Studies and Co-ordinator of the Institute for Higher Latin American Studies. He has been a member of the Advising Committee of the Diplomatic Academy of London, a Fulbright Scholar and a Rockefeller Foundation Bellagio Center Resident Scholar. He has also been a member of the Bellagio Center Nominations Committee. A Visiting Professor at Princeton University, he has also taught at the universities of Brasilia and Barcelona and has lectured extensively at universities and think tanks in the Americas, Europe and Asia.

Author of 18 books and co-author of 13 more on international affairs, he received the "Latino Book Award" (best book by an author whose original language is in Spanish or Portuguese) twice — at the ExpoBook America fairs celebrated in Chicago and Los Angeles in 2003 and 2008, respectively. He has published nearly 30 papers in academic magazines, including the *Cambridge Review of International Affairs*. He is a weekly columnist for Venezuela's leading newspaper *El Universal and* contributes frequently to written media from Latin America and Spain.

INTRODUCTION

Booming volumes of trade, foreign direct investment and loans, prove the thriving nature of economic relations between Asia and Latin America. Indeed, according to the Asian Development Bank Institute: *"Latin America is firmly on the economic radar of Asia in the post-global financial crisis world economy"*,[1] and yet, Asian knowledge about Latin America is surprisingly scarce.

In Asia, little is known about the idiosyncrasies of Latin Americans, or about their cultural identities and social values. Differences between Brazilians and Spanish Americans, or amid the diverse Spanish American countries, are not sufficiently understood. Even less is known about the amplitude of the Iberian heritage of such countries, or about the miscegenation and acculturation processes that took place between their different constitutive races. There is no clarity regarding the Western nature of Latin America or about its cultural affinities with Latin Europe. Nor is there sufficient understanding about the links existing between the Latin population of the United States and the inhabitants of Latin America.

In the end, even in the eyes of cultivated Asians, Latin America is like a blurry tableau. Devoid of defining lines, particularities and nuances, a generic and imprecise image emerges. Without context — cultural,

---

[1] Wingnaraja, G (28 January 2015). Will Asian investments follow trade with Latin America?, *Asia Pathways*, Asian Development Bank Institute. https://www.asiapathways-adbi.org/2015/01/will-asian-investment-follow-trade-with-latin-america/. Accessed on 10/06/2017.

historic and idiosyncratic backgrounds — no amount of news coverage or analytical tools can provide an adequate understanding of the region. Furthermore, news coverage tends to be insufficient, stereotyped, and focused on a series of unrelated crises and events. If anything, news contributes to an even more blurry picture.

Profoundly involved in economic relations, yet with unfamiliar partners, Asians find themselves at a manifest disadvantage vis–à–vis North Americans or Europeans, when dealing with Latin Americans. Unlike the concrete, centuries old, and continuous relations of the United States and Europe with the region, Asians are newcomers. Insufficiently knowledgeable newcomers. Thus, there would seem to be an inverse correlation between the amount of business existing between Asia and Latin America, and the limited grasp that Asians have of their Latin American interlocutors.

The amount of such business undoubtedly tells a story of economic interest and commitment on the part of Asians. In 1990, only 0.6 percent of Latin America's total exports came from China, while that country was listed as number 17 for Latin American exports. In 2000, China was number 12 within Brazil's export markets, and ranked number 35 within Venezuelan export destinations.[2] In 1999, trade between China and Latin America represented only US$8.3 billion.[3]

However, in 2011, China was the origin of 14 percent of all Latin American imports, represented nine percent of total Latin American exports, and close to 15 percent of South American exports. Similarly, by 2011, China became the number one export market for Brazil, Chile and Peru, and was rapidly becoming number one for Argentina, Cuba, Uruguay and Venezuela as well.[4] Furthermore, in the decade between 2003 and 2013, trade between China and Latin America increased at an

---

[2] El Sistema Económico Latinoamericano y del Caribe (17 al 19 de octubre, 2012). La Crisis en la Zona del Euro, su impacto en el proceso de integración europeo y en las relaciones birregionales entre América Latina y el Caribe. Líneas de acción desde la perspectiva latinoamericana y caribeña. Caracas: SELA.

[3] CEPAL (Junio, 2012). La República Popular China y América Latina y el Caribe: Diálogo y Cooperación ante los Nuevos Desafíos de la Economía Mundial. Santiago de Chile: CEPAL.

[4] Ibid.

amazing average of 27 percent per year, rising to an unprecedented US$289 billion in 2013.[5] In other words, in a span of scarcely fourteen years, the bilateral trade between China and Latin America multiplied more than 35 times.

Not surprisingly, China easily surpassed Latin America's two historic trade partners in the Asia-Pacific area: Japan and South Korea.[6] These two countries, which had been actively trading with the region since the seventies, are currently in a significantly lower position compared to China. Latin America's trade with Japan amounted to US$44 billion in 2015, and with South Korea US$48 billion in 2013.[7]

Another reshuffling is now taking place. In the same way China has left those two countries behind in the past decade, India is currently in the process of surpassing them as well. In 2015, India's bilateral trade with Latin America reached US$45 billion, ahead of Japan and slightly behind South Korea. Nonetheless, between 2000 and 2013, trade between Latin America and South Korea grew at an annual rate of 13 percent, while India's trade with Latin America grew at an annual rate of 25 percent between 2005 and 2015.[8] Before the end of this decade, India is expected to surpass South Korea.

Trade between Latin America's Pacific Alliance (Chile, Colombia, Mexico and Peru) and the Association of Southeast Asian Nations (ASEAN) members reached US$16.8 billion in 2013[9] — also an unprec-

---

[5] Devlin, R and Kahn, T (2016). Latin American Trade with India and China, in Roett, R and Paz, G (eds.) *Latin America and the Asian Giants: Evolving Ties with China and India,* p. 151. Washington D.C.: Brookings Institution Press.

[6] It is important to note that these statistics also include non-Latin American Caribbean countries. However, Latin American nations represent the clear majority of such amounts, with non-Latin American Caribbean countries assuming a marginal position.

[7] Inter-American Development Bank (2016). A Virtuous Cycle of Integration: The Past, Present, and Future of Japan-Latin American and the Caribbean Relations. Washington D.C.: IADB, p. 33.; ECLAC (April 2015). Economic Relations between Latin America and the Caribbean and the Republic of Korea: Advances and Opportunities. Santiago de Chile: ECLAC, p. 23.

[8] ECLAC, *op. cit.*, p. 23; Roett, R (2016). Latin America Looks to Asia, in Roett , R and Paz, G (eds.), *op. cit.*, p. 32.

[9] Faure, A (2017). The New Trans-Pacific Partnership (5 April 2017). *The Diplomat.* www.diplomat.com/2017/04/the-new-transpacific-partnership. Accessed 27/04/2017.

edented amount. All in all, the Asian Development Bank Institute highlights that in 2014, trade between Asia and Latin America reached a historic high of over half a trillion US dollars, and it is projected to increase to 750 billion by 2020.[10]

Foreign Direct Investment and loans have also played a very important role in deepening economic relations between Asia and Latin America. Large flows of Asian capital have followed the remarkable increase of trade between the two regions. According to the Asian Development Bank Institute, the annual average greenfield investment from Asia to Latin America between 2003 and 2013, was US$14.1 billion, mostly coming from China, Japan, and South Korea. Conversely, Latin America's annual average greenfield investments to Asia was only US$1.2 billion.[11]

China has played the leading role in foreign direct investment in Latin America. Between 2010 and the end of 2014, such investments accounted for US$106 billion. However, that amount is expected to increase more than twofold in the next few years. Indeed, in the first ministerial meeting of the Forum of China and the Community of Latin American and Caribbean States, held in Beijing in January 2015, President Xi Jinping pledged US$250 billion of Foreign Direct Investment to the region, for the five–year period of 2015–2019.[12]

Chinese loan commitments to Latin America have been as significant as its direct investment, totalling more than US$130 billion during the period 2005–2013. The largest part of that amount was dedicated to infrastructure and energy projects in commodities producing countries.[13] In fact, since 2005, China has lent more to Latin America than the World Bank, the Inter–American Bank and the US Export and Import Bank combined.

Institutions such as Asia-Pacific Economic Cooperation (APEC) and the Forum for East Asia Latin America Cooperation (FEALAC), have

---

[10] Wingnaraja, *op. cit.*

[11] Ibid.

[12] Dollar, D (January 2017). China's Investment in Latin America. Washington D.C.: Brookings Institution, p. 1. https://www.brookings.edu/wp-content/uploads/2017/01/fp_201701_china_investment_lat_am.pdf. Accessed 18/02/2017.

[13] Guajardo, J (2016). A Latin American Perspective on China's Growing Presence in the region, in Roett, R and Paz, G o*p. cit.*, p. 69.

become useful tools to foster trade and investment between the two regions, which every day becomes more relevant.

However, Asian knowledge of Latin America has not kept pace with the economic critical mass it has attained. This gap creates important vulnerabilities for Asians as they are in an obvious comparative disadvantage with their competitors in that part of the world. How can Asians engage in intense business relationships and expect to continue along a path of growth with the region, yet remain unfamiliar with the idiosyncrasies of their trade partners?

This book aims to provide what seems to be missing: a context, regarding Latin America. The following pages deal with Latin America's history, culture, identity and idiosyncrasies. As such, these dimensions can become a guide for understanding regional attitudes, meanings and behavioural differences. Furthermore, the book does not only focus on history or in abstract dissections of the Latin American character, but also analyses the present economic situation of the region while it tries to forecast its future.

Although the book has been written with an Asian audience in mind, and hence has an emphasis on trying to be as instructive as possible, it is in no way limited to Asian readers. On the contrary, it seeks to become a tool for decoding what Latin America is all about, and, as such, it can be useful for all kinds of readers interested in knowing more about the region.

CONTENTS

Foreword vii
Foreword xi
About the Author xiii
Introduction xv

Chapter 1: Why Latin America? **1**

Latin America and the Caribbean 1
Mexican Conservatives 3
Napoleon III and his Mexican Adventure 4
Two Sides of the Same Coin 5
Maximilian's Tragic Story 6
Why did the Term Survive? 8
Courting France, Bashing Spain 9

Chapter 2: What is Iberian America? **13**

The Treaty of Tordesillas 14
Spaniards and Portuguese 16
Romans and Moors 16
New Lands, Old People 20
The Indians 22
Shattering Experiences 25
African Slavery 28
Acculturation, Miscegenation and White Predominance 31

Chapter 3: Brazil and Spanish America 35

From Reconquest to Conquest 36
Global Reach, Loose Grip 38
One Enlightenment, Two Results 42
Napoleon and the Two Different Routes of Iberian America 44
Spanish American Wars of Independence 48
Brazilian Stability and Spanish American Turmoil 51
Latin American Convergence 56

Chapter 4: Spanish America: One or Many? 59

The Glue that Holds the Group Together 60
More than Five Centuries of Shared Experiences 64
From Dreamers to "Caudillos" 65
Liberals and Positivists 67
Ariel 69
Enfranchising the Middle Classes 70
Cold War and National Security Doctrine 72
From the Washington Consensus to the Left Tidal 75
Geography and Ethnicity 78
Three Hispanic Americas 80

Chapter 5: Where do Latin Americans Belong? 85

The Black Legend 86
On the fringes of the fringe 90
Soul Searching 92
The Big Debate 94
The Main Question 100
The Latin American Periphery 103

Chapter 6: Latin America and the United States: A Dichotomy 105

Nuances 106
Rules and Self-Rule 108
Bullion and Manufacturing 110

Modernizing Christianity or Christianizing Modernity 112
Pyramids, Protestants and Hidalgos 114
Identity and Institutions 116
Economy and Individualism 118
Spaces for Democracy, Spaces for Work and Wealth 120

Chapter 7: Latin America and the United States: A History in Seven Chapters 123

The Monroe Doctrine 124
Manifest Destiny 127
Empire 129
The Good Neighbourhood 132
The Cold War 134
Trade and Security 138
On the Losing Equation 144

Chapter 8: The Revenge of the South 147

Crossed by the Border 148
Crossing the Border 151
Cubans and Others 152
Latino Activism 156
From Political Power to Soft Power 159
Gross Numbers and Republican Myopia 163

Chapter 9: When China Arrived from Nowhere 169

Latin American Style Industrialization 171
The Eternal Infancy 173
A Fatidic Duo 176
Genghis Khan's Hordes 178
Redeeming Virtue 181
The Maquila System 184
A Tale of Two Giants 187
The In Between 193
The Paper Giant 194

Chapter 10: Latin America's Options 199

Caught in the Middle 199
Commodities Widening Horizons 202
The New Export Frontier 207
Latin America and the Global Chains of Value 209
The Fourth Industrial Revolution 211
The Incoming Tsunami 214
Shortcomings and Comparative Advantages 219

Conclusion 221
Bibliography 237
Map of Latin America 245

CHAPTER 1

WHY LATIN AMERICA?

Latin America is made up of non–Anglo or Dutch components of the Americas formed in the common mould of the Catholic religion, Latin cultural heritage and the romance languages. Iberian America and Haiti would naturally fit into this description. The former because of its Spanish and Portuguese ancestry, the latter because of its French ancestry.

However, if we were to take the argument to its logical conclusion, we would have to include not only the French speaking province of Quebec in Canada, but also France itself by its overseas territories in the Americas. Indeed, such territories are not considered to be colonies but integral parts of the French state.

Nonetheless, when the term Latin America is used its meaning is more restricted as it merely covers the Iberian American countries; Brazil and Hispanic America. The latter includes countries in North America (Mexico); Central America (Guatemala, El Salvador, Honduras Costa Rica and Nicaragua); the Isthmus (Panama); the Caribbean Sea (Cuba and Dominican Republic) and South America (Venezuela, Colombia, Ecuador, Peru, Chile, Bolivia Argentina, Uruguay and Paraguay). In total, nineteen republics.

Latin America and the Caribbean

As it happens, however, the denomination Latin America is frequently associated with the notion of the Caribbean. As a result, the combined term of Latin America and the Caribbean has been coined. More than being a cultural or historical notion, it is simply a geographical expression derived from the contiguity of the two areas. Given that, nonetheless, the two of them have as a common denominator the fact of being the only developing economies within the Western Hemisphere, this lax expression took hold.

The non–Latin American Caribbean countries can be divided into three groups according to their mother tongue. The English–speaking Caribbean comprising Trinidad and Tobago, Jamaica, the Bahamas, Guyana, Belize, Saint Lucia, Grenada, Saint Kitts and Nevis, Dominica, Montserrat, Saint Vincent and the Grenadines and, finally, Antigua and Barbados. The Dutch–speaking Caribbean which is formed by Suriname and the French–speaking Caribbean by Haiti. The three of them have distinct cultural and historical backgrounds and traits.

Except for Belize, Guyana and Suriname, located in Central or South America, the rest are island nations. Curiously enough, the continental countries of Guyana and Suriname are not even located in the Caribbean basin but facing the Atlantic Ocean. Hence, they are not strictly Caribbean nations.

Apart from Haiti which obtained its independence at the beginning of the nineteenth century, when most of Latin America did so as well, the rest had access to independence within the decolonization process of the second half of the twentieth century. When compared to the Latin American countries, these other nations tend to have much smaller GDPs and populations. The richest Caribbean nation would be Trinidad and Tobago whose GDP compares to Bolivia and Paraguay, two of the poorest of the Latin American nations.

As each of these Caribbean countries became independent, they began to interact with the Latin American nations within the framework of hemispheric and regional organizations. Finally, during the XXI Summit of the so–called Group of Rio, in February of 2010, it was agreed to create a new association with the aim of integrating these two regions in a systematic way. That gave birth to the Community of Latin American and Caribbean States, which was formally launched in Caracas, Venezuela, in December of 2011.

The organization comprises 33 states which is equivalent to all the Western Hemisphere except for the United States and Canada. This new group aims at promoting a concerted Latin American and Caribbean position in the fundamental global issues of the day, while strengthening the economic links among its members.

Nonetheless, the term Latin American and the Caribbean, even if practical for joining together two contiguous regions which have in common their developing status, has no real common identity. The members of the Community of Latin American and Caribbean States have four clear cut cultural and historical identities. One of those identities is the Iberian American one, which holds together Spanish America and Brazil.

But if the term Latin America tends to be confusing, as it does not reflect in an obvious manner the clear–cut Iberian American identity that it is supposed to reflect, why then is it used? What is the purpose of this ambiguous term of Latin America?

To answer this question, we must go back to 1861. Latin America was a term coined that year in an article published by French scholar L.M. Tisserand in the magazine *Revues des Races Latines*. Neither the article, which referred to the Iberian countries of the Americas as part of the Latin civilization, nor the term were neutral in content.

More to the contrary, they subscribed to the so–called Pan–Latin thesis whose main ideologue was Michel Chevalier and whose aim was French power projection on the other side of the Atlantic. Moreover, its immediate objective was to provide intellectual legitimacy to Emperor Napoleon III's imperial ambitions over Mexico and other parts of Hispanic America.

This needs some historical context.

Mexican Conservatives

Since its independence from Spain, Mexico was divided between the Liberal and Conservative political movements. The latter had always aspired to a monarchical form of government.

Agustin de Iturbide, the general that represented the leading force behind Mexico's separation from Spain, had aimed at an independent Mexico under a constitutional monarch of the royal house of Spain. To such an end he had reached an agreement with the rebel chieftain Vicente Guerrero, who headed the pro-independence forces. The result being the so–called Plan of Iguala, which offered the independent crown of Mexico to the King of Spain himself or to any other member of the royal family. Such an offer was flatly rejected by Madrid.

Time and again, however, the idea of a monarchical government under a European prince of royal blood tended to re–emerge among Mexico's

Conservatives. Lucas Alaman, their most notorious representative, periodically mentioned the idea as so did other important members of such movement. As Mexico's continuous instability was becoming an open invitation to the advocates of a "manifest destiny" in the United States, Conservatives pushed again for this proposal.

Not surprisingly, a hopelessly divided and weakened Mexico ended up by yielding lands that were to become the future US states of Texas, New Mexico, Arizona, Nevada, Colorado and California. But even after such a dreadful defeat by the United States, the dead–end polarization between Liberals and Conservatives continued.

In the 1850s the Liberals gained control of the country and began a series of Reform Laws aimed at curtailing the ascendancy of the Church and the power of the Army. This process culminated with the passing of the 1857 Constitution, which provoked a military revolt by the Conservatives–the Reform War.

In December 1860, the Liberals won this war and in March 1861 Benito Juarez, who had headed this faction under the title of Provisional President, was duly elected President of Mexico. The defeated Conservatives again saw the idea of a monarchical regime, under a European prince of royal blood, as the natural solution to their problems.

So, it was that they proceeded to lobby (some of the Conservative members had begun to do so since the beginning of the civil war) French Emperor Napoleon III. Their objective was that a European prince under his stewardship and military support would become Monarch of Mexico.

Napoleon III and his Mexican Adventure

This proposal was music to Napoleon's ears, who after his country's military success in Indochina aimed at expanding his Empire. Not surprisingly he wanted to follow in the footsteps of his famous uncle. According to his reasoning, consolidating a French stronghold in Mexico would fulfil several converging purposes.

Among these were the following: creating a barrier to the encroachment of the United States hegemony in the region; ensuring free access to France's increasing trade with Hispanic America; creating the appropriate conditions for establishing other French puppet monarchies in the area;

fulfilling the dream of his wife, Empress Eugenie, to expand French imperial influence in the Americas; guarantying the security of the French colonies in the Caribbean and exploiting the rich Mexican mines.

Significantly, the gates of Mexico and Hispanic America had been just opened to European penetration. Indeed, in January 1861 seven Southern States declared their secession from the United States and formed a new country called the Confederate States of America. The imminent war between the parties implied a sudden stop to the enforcement of the Monroe Doctrine.

This doctrine, issued in 1823 by President James Monroe, formally warned the European monarchies that the United States would not tolerate further colonization or the creation of tributary monarchies in the Americas.

Furthermore, Napoleon III was convinced that such a war would be won by the South, which implied that Mexico's northern neighbour would not be a powerful United States of America but a weakened Confederate States of America.

In other words, ambition and occasion made such endeavour an inescapable one. On 9 October 1861, Napoleon wrote to Count Flahaut, his Ambassador in London, that if Mexico could be regenerated under the influence of France, they would have erected an impenetrable barrier against the encroachment of the United States. A few months later in a letter to General Elie Frederic Forey, dated 3 June 1862, the Emperor emphasized that France had the historic mission to restore the strength and prestige of the Latin race that lived on the other side of the Atlantic.

Two Sides of the Same Coin

The aims, barrier and restoration, represented two sides of the same coin. They formed the basis of Napoleon's Pan–Latin project in the Americas: counterbalancing the growing Anglo Protestant power by developing a Latin Catholic one. A Latin power that would be, of course, subject to the tutelage of France.

The nature of the Latin link that existed between France and the Hispanic part of the Americas derived from their common Roman heritage. A heritage also shared by Brazil. The latter, though, even if considered a fundamental part of "Latin America", represented a totally different proposition in terms of France's imperial designs. With an Emperor from the Royal House of Braganza ruling the nation and with Great Britain leading its international trade, Brazil was off limits for Napoleon's grand plans.

Such common heritage dated back to ancient times. The original Latins inhabited central Italy in present day Lazio. Through the conquest of Rome, the rest of Italy became "Latinized". In other words, the term Latin lost its ethnic meaning to acquire a cultural one.

As the Roman Empire spread to what were to become Spain, Portugal, France and Romania, they too became Latin spaces. Roman law was to become a fundamental part of that sphere.

Circa 313 A.D., Roman Emperor Constantine decriminalized Christianity, pushing the ascendancy of the religion which was to become shortly after the official creed of the State. Hence the origins of the Roman Catholic Church.

Vulgar Latin was the language spoken by the ordinary citizens of the Roman Empire, distinct from cultivated Classical Latin. It covered the vernacular dialects that evolved into the Romance languages. That is languages like Spanish, Portuguese or French.

The Pan–Latin thesis that emerged during Napoleon III's reign, aimed at emphasising the commonality existing between the "Latin Race" of the Americas and Europe. Both peoples, on both sides of the Atlantic Ocean, shared religion, culture and Romance languages. As such the Latins of the Americas were called to become a natural ally of Latin Europe in their struggle not only against the "Anglo–Saxon" world but also against "Teutonic" and "Slavic" Europe.

Maximilian's Tragic Story

To build a barrier against Anglo–Saxon America and restore the Latin race in the Americas, Napoleon needed to begin by creating a tributary regime in Mexico. Maximilian of Habsburg, brother of the Austrian Emperor Francis Joseph, was the chosen French puppet for the Mexican throne. In Napoleon's words:

> "The Prince who may mount the Mexican throne will always be forced to act in the interests of France, not only from gratitude but even more

because his country's interest will be in accordance with ours, and he will not be able to maintain himself without our influence". [1]

So, after consolidating the conquest of the country by French troops and overthrowing its legitimate President Benito Juarez, the crown was offered to the Austrian prince on 10 July 1863. According to the Miramar Treaty, signed between Maximilian and the French Empire, the future Mexican Empire, under the former, had to reimburse and pay all the military costs of the French invasion and presence in Mexico. Maximilian was finally enthroned in May 1864, though it was to be a short lived and tragic reign.

A combination of factors dictated the end of this Latin adventure. First, Napoleon III underestimated the stubborn resistance of the Mexican forces under Juarez. Second, the choice of Maximilian was not a suitable one as his liberal ideas were much more in tune with those of his adversary Benito Juarez than with those of his Mexican Conservative allies. Third, the American Civil War ended with the defeat of the Confederation on 2 June 1865. This re–established the Monroe Doctrine and provided the basis for an open threat of war by the United States–50,000 American troops were sent to the border with Mexico and surplus weaponry and ammunitions were supplied to Juarez' troops. Fourth, France itself began to feel threatened by the growing power of Prussia under the able leadership of Bismarck. The 40,000 French troops based in Mexico became increasingly needed in France.

On 5 February 1867, the French troops abandoned Mexico City. Although Maximilian had been advised to follow them, he decided to remain in Mexico under the military support of the Mexican Conservatives. Such an ill–suited match, though, was unable to overcome the growing strength of Juarez' forces, now supported with American arms. Moreover, while the French had overseen the military campaign against Juarez, the top Mexican Conservative generals Miramon and Marquez had been sent to diplomatic exile in Europe. Now back in charge, the two of them had lost much of their former grasp upon the military situation. On 15 May of that year Emperor Maximilian was captured and, following a court–martial,

[1] Ridley, J (1993). *Maximilian & Juárez,* pp. 103–104, London: Phoenix Press.

was executed on 19 June. Two factors motivated the execution: the excesses committed by the French army and a deterrence message against future invaders.

Maximilian's patron, Napoleon III, would also face a crushing defeat three years later. Overwhelmed by Prussian military strength, in a war between the two countries, and imprisoned in the battlefield of Sedan, Napoleon's regime was to be toppled on 4 September 1870, by his enraged fellow citizens.

Curiously enough the term Latin America would survive the defeats of the American Confederation, the Maximilian Monarchy and the Napoleonic Empire. Moreover, it would be accepted as a sign of identity by the same people upon which it was supposed to be imposed as an imperialistic project.

Why did the Term Survive?

Given its tributary connotations, how does this explain the easy assimilation of the term by Iberian American themselves?

It could be assumed that the reason lay in the anti–US stand of the Pan–Latin thesis, especially so because a few decades earlier the United States had taken half of the Mexican territory by force. Nonetheless, that was not the case as the admiration towards the United States political system and entrepreneurial ingenuity, remained high at the time within the Iberian American elites.

On the contrary, the answer, was to be found in the rejection of Spain and everything Spanish, which prevailed within the Hispanic American intelligentsia of the day. But also in the fact that the elites from Brazil and the Spanish American countries were completely fascinated by French culture and civilization.

From the very moment in which independence from Spain was obtained, aspirations towards modernization tended to affirm themselves in contrast to the nation and to the inheritance that it had left behind in the Americas. While Conservatives looked with nostalgia to the good old days of colonial times, Liberals had always looked to the United States, Great Britain and France for inspiration. By the mid–19th century onwards a

Liberal wave covered most of Spanish America. With it came the repudiation of the heritage bequeathed by Spain.

The Liberal period was to be substituted a couple of decades later by a Positivist period which, if anything, was even more critical of the Spanish past in the Americas. Admiration towards France, the United States and Great Britain would also increase under the latter movement. Brazil was also to be engulfed by Positivism and the coup d'état against its monarchical regime in 1889 responded to this school of thought.

As it happened, then, the end of the Napoleonic experiment in the Americas coincided in time with the transitional years between Liberalism and Positivism. As a result, the term Latin America turned out to be agreeable to both movements. Moreover, it was just as agreeable to Spanish Americans as to Brazilians.

Courting France, Bashing Spain

A breathless desire existed among the cultivated people of the region to be like the French or the British. To follow their fashions. To write, paint and compose music like them. To imitate their architectural tastes. To conform to their concept of civilized life. Not surprisingly, Latin American oligarchs, who spent long periods of time in Paris, dreamed of being accepted by its high society.

Hence, a concept like Latin America, which established a direct line of parentage with the matrixes of Western Civilization skirting round Spain, was to be warmly welcomed by Hispanic American elites. But, at the same time, it was equally well received by all of those who were delighted with that new kinship with France. Being considered as the transatlantic cousins of the French was certainly flattering. After all Auguste Compte, the towering figure of the Positivist philosophy, was a Frenchman.

The Argentinian statesman and writer Domingo Faustino Sarmiento, probably the most important member of the Positivist movement within the Iberian American sphere, expressed his admiration for France as follows:

> "Their ideas, their fashions, their literary production are a model and a goal for all other nations. I believe that this which we regard as a desire

> to imitate, is in reality the aspiration of human beings to approach a type of perfection which is inside all of us".[2]

But Sarmiento's bewilderment with France was only equalled by his contempt for Spain:

> "I feel called to struggle against the Spanish race, so incapable of understanding freedom, here as well as in Spain. The Spanish language is an unsurmountable obstacle to the transmission of culture...Spain has never produced a thinker, nor one notable writer, nor a single philosopher...Spain has condemned the descendants of Europeans in America to backwardness".[3]

To express that kind of intellectual contempt for the land that produced such gigantic philosophical or literary figures as Francisco Suarez, Francisco de Vitoria, Miguel de Cervantes, Lope de Vega or Pedro Calderon de la Barca, was certainly going too far. As far as shamelessly bending to France and everything French. But Sarmiento, as mentioned, was just one of the many who shared this sentiment.

Another distinguished member of this Positivist tradition, another Argentinian, Juan Bautista Alberdi, expressed himself in similar terms:

> "Enlightenment should be sought in France, a European meridional nation. We meridionals as well, both in origin and circumstances, fully belong to its intelligent lead".[4]

Curiously enough, in few other places of the Iberian American world would the Positivist movement reach the kind of influence that it had in Mexico, during the several decades of the government of Porfirio Diaz. Franco–Mexican relations reached a zenith during that period, even though General Diaz had been a hero in the fight against the French invaders. Not surprisingly, after being toppled he moved to France, where he

---

[2] Véliz, C (1980). *The Centralist Tradition of Latin America,* p.174. Princeton: Princeton University Press.

[3] ibid. p. 176.

[4] Zea, L (1976). *El Pensamiento Latinoamericano,* p. 169.Barcelona: Editorial Ariel.

spent his last years. So, even Mexico adhered with passion to the notion of Latin America.

Referring to that period, Mexican contemporary intellectual Carlos Fuentes expressed the following:

> "Where could we have looked at in search of models and inspiration? Nineteenth century Latin America found its immediate answer in France and in the city that Baudelaire called 'the capital of the XIX Century'. Parisian influence was felt everywhere from The Hague to Algiers, from St. Petersburg to Cairo. Nonetheless, in Mexico, Bogota or Buenos Aires it filled up the deep void left by Spain. Repudiating Spain meant accepting France as a new temple of freedom, good taste, romanticism and of all the good things that life had to offer".[5]

And so, it was that Iberian Americans suddenly became Latin Americans even though Latin Americans are but Iberian Americans.

[5]Fuentes, C (1992), *El Espejo Enterrado,* pp. 228–229. México: Fondo de Cultura Económica.

CHAPTER 2

WHAT IS IBERIAN AMERICA?

The notion of Iberian America comprises the countries of the Americas which were former territories of Spain or Portugal and where Spanish or Portuguese are the predominant languages. The prefix "Iberian" derives from the two European countries sharing the Iberian Peninsula, located in the foremost western part of that continent.

Iberian America's starting point would be the Treaty of Tordesillas, signed by Spain and Portugal in 1494, dividing between the two of them the lands "discovered" by Cristopher Columbus in 1492. This requires some background.

For the Europeans back then, the Indies was a name that applied not only to India itself, but also to Malacca, the Spice Islands and even, loosely to China and Japan. Sailing had become the way to reach those distant lands since 1453, when Constantinople fell to the Ottoman Turks. That had placed the spice trade entirely in the hands of the Ottomans, who soon raised taxes and increased tariffs to the point of virtually shutting off the spice supply to "infidel" Europe.

Columbus had proposed to reach the East Indies by sailing westwards instead of taking the long sail eastwards. The Spanish Crown, seeing the chance to reach the lands of cloves, cinnamon, pepper, nutmeg and ginger, through what Columbus insisted was a shorter route, decided to finance his expedition. The result is well known.

The Treaty of Tordesillas

When the Portuguese King John II found out about the successful voyage of Columbus, he sent a threatening letter to King Ferdinand and Queen Isabella of Spain. He reminded them that according to a previous agreement between their countries, ratified by a Papal bull, all lands south of the Canary Islands, in the western part of Africa, belonged to Portugal. Hence, King John II announced that he was planning for a Portuguese fleet to take possession of his new lands.

Being substantially weaker than Portugal at sea, Spain could not prevent such undertaking by force. It thus took advantage of the fact that Pope Alexander VI was Spanish and asked him to decide on the matter. As a result, in 1493 the Pope decreed that all lands west and south of a pole–to–pole demarcation line 100 leagues (about 320 miles) west and south of the Cape Verde Islands, in Africa, should belong to Spain. The Papal decision though did not make any mention about Portugal which led the latter to a direct negotiation with Spain.

Because of those negotiations, and given that both parties wanted to avoid a war between them, they agreed to move the boundary line 370 leagues west (about 1,185 miles), giving the Portuguese right to all lands located on the eastern side of that line. Hence, the treaty of Tordesillas became a negotiated compromise between both countries. In 1506, the new Pope Julius II officialised within Christendom, by way of a bull, the agreement reached by the parties.

Needless to say, that the other powers of the day were deeply unhappy with the above. King Francis I of France asked to be shown the clause within Adam's testament (at the Biblical beginning of mankind), that distributed the New World in such a way. Moreover, emerging maritime Protestant countries did not feel constrained by the Pope's bull and did not recognize the partition between Spain and Portugal–neither would Catholic France.

Cosmographer Martin Waldseemuller coined the name America in 1507 in honour of Amerigo Vespucci. The latter was the first to navigate the coasts of what are now Venezuela, Guiana and Brazil, demonstrating that the lands encountered by Columbus were not the Indies easternmost extremities, as it was believed, but a separate and previously unknown land mass. Vespucci himself, in a letter to his patron Pier Francesco de Medici, called it "Mundus Novus", that is, New World.[1]

Spain and Portugal felt empowered to do as they wished in that "America". But as Portugal had deliberately contrived an expansionist strategy, the Spaniards reacted swiftly to the new opportunities. The Portuguese saw these territories as a low priority when compared to its Far East colonial enterprise, and took their time in holding them properly. For the Spaniards, on the other hand, fifty years were enough to discover, explore and subdue these lands. Moreover, for urban–minded Spaniards founding "cities" was a civilizational imperative, which soon produced a whole network of towns and urban settings around their part of the Americas.

According to Mark Williams:

> "While other nations had their explorers, the conquistadors were a unique Spanish archetype, a combination of reckless adventurer, daring idealist, and ruthless overlord. Most of them sprang from a hard and unforgiving part of Spain, which provided traits that helped them survive. The notorious Spanish tendency to improvise rather than to plan also proved invaluable. The audacious exploration of the Amazon, for example, took place without the slightest preparation. Had the explorers insisted on guarantees of success, the project might never have been started".[2]

Larger than life figures such as Hernan Cortes and Francisco Pizarro, and their colossal deeds in the conquest of such immense and powerful empires such as those of the Aztecs or the Incas, had no equivalent in Brazil. With an expedition force of 550 men, 17 horses and 10 canons, and through a series of skilful alliances with indigenous tribes and immensely daring tactics, Cortes ended up defeating the warrior Aztec empire. An empire which had a population of at least seven million people. Similarly, with 110 foot soldiers, 67 cavalry men, three harquebuses and two falconets, Pizarro captured Emperor Atahualpa and brought the Empire of the Incas to its knees. An empire even bigger than that of the Aztecs with 12 million

[1] Arciniegas, G (2001). *Cuando América Completó la Tierra,* Bogotá: Villegas Editores.
[2] Williams, M (2000). *The Story of Spain,* pp.101–102. Málaga: Santana Books.

inhabitants. Nothing remotely similar ever occurred in Portuguese America, where events took shape in a much slower and down to earth manner.

Spaniards and Portuguese

This different approach by the Spaniards and Portuguese had much to do with their respective national traits. The Spaniards were more grandiose and excessive. The Portuguese, more moderate and pragmatic, always remained the exception within the Iberian Peninsula. This explains why while the rest of the Peninsula's kingdoms converged into a single Spanish Crown, Portugal remained an independent kingdom.

Indeed, by the early 13th century there were four well defined Christian kingdoms in the Iberian Peninsula–Portugal, Navarre, Aragon and Castile. While the three latter coalesce into the single Kingdom of Spain, Portugal, which had evolved into independent statehood in 1143 having been a county of Castile, retained its suzerainty.

Nonetheless, Spain and Portugal not only share the same peninsular territory but also an old, rich and complex history. As such, and even if different in many ways, they are very much part of the same civilization.

That civilization would be the result of many centuries of physical co–existence and fusion of cultures among Christians, Muslims and Jews and before that of the interaction with Greeks, Phoenicians, Carthaginians, Romans and Germans. Moreover, Spain and Portugal were part of the same Roman Province, Hispania. So, the term Iberian world has a precise meaning.

Through the centuries, the Iberian Peninsula has been a nerve centre where the most diverse races and civilizations converged. Its original inhabitants though were the Iberians, a people that goes back to ancient times. According to historians they were stoical, quarrelsome, devoted to bulls and horses, suspicious of strangers, superstitious in religion and respectful of their elders. But, above all, they were individualistic and disliked organization.

Romans and Moors

As mentioned earlier, different ancient civilizations converged in the peninsula. However, the Romans were the ones called to exert the greatest influence. They ruled for six centuries, beginning in 218 BC. It was not an easy process though, as it took them two centuries and more than 150,000 lives to subdue local resistance. By contrast, Gaul (France) succumbed to Rome in just ten years.

But once submitted to Roman rule, the Iberian Peninsula was to become Rome's most loyal province. So much so that the inhabitants of Hispania, the name given by Rome to the Iberian Peninsula, were to be the first people outside Italy to enjoy Roman citizenship. Hispania, in short, was the pride of the Roman Empire.

Romans brought with them the Latin language, which was to become the basis for all peninsular tongues, apart from Basque (a pre–Celtic language). The broad cultural baggage with which they bequeathed Hispania's inhabitants also included an advanced legal system and well–developed architectural and engineering knowledge. All of this in addition to providing Hispania with Christianity. In synthesis, language, law, architectural traditions and religion, that remain today, were all part of the Roman heritage.

Conversely, Hispania provided Rome with vast mineral and agricultural wealth, with three of its greatest emperors and with some of its most important names in literature, including Seneca. So loyal was this province that Rome kept only one symbolic legion to control it.

Rome's disintegration opened the German chapter in the Iberian Peninsula with the Goths, the Visigoths and the Suevi converging on its soil. In a short span of time all resistance was overrun. So far Iberian traditions had coexisted with Rome's civilizing impact amid an acculturation process. The same would happen again with the blond barbarians. Indeed, Hispania which was formerly the better assimilated Roman province, would then become the most Germanized area of Europe.

The Iberian Peninsula represented at that point in time the epitome of the Western World. The arrival of the Moors from Africa, in 711 AD, introduced however an important change. From then on, its capacity to absorb and synthetize foreign cultures would work in the opposite direction: distancing it from the rest of Europe. The term Moors has no real ethnographic meaning, simply representing all Muslims, whether Arab or Northern Africa's Berbers, who conquered the peninsula.

This new chapter, which would prolong itself for several centuries, would see this land stamped by a new religion, a new language and a new culture. In just a few years the Moors swept over most of the Peninsula and threatened to invade France as well. Nonetheless they were stopped at their gates by Charles Martel (Charlemagne's grandfather) at the battle of Poitiers in 732 AD.

But not all the Iberian Peninsula was conquered. Due to internal squabbles among rival Moors tribes, some areas in Northern Spain remained free. It was from one of them, Asturias, where the so–called Reconquest began. It was an endeavour of several centuries that would be necessary to reclaim back, mostly on a piecemeal basis, the totality of the occupied territory. Had it not been for these unconquered pockets of resistance in the north, the Iberian Peninsula would have probably remained as a Muslim territory amid a Christian continent.

It is usually said that the Moors remained in Iberian lands for 800 years and, indeed, the truth is that their last stronghold, the small kingdom of Granada, was retaken by the Spaniards in 1492. Nonetheless, for 244 years that was the Moors only possession in the Iberian Peninsula. In 1212, the decisive battle of Navas de Tolosa allowed the recuperation of a substantial part of Muslim territory and, in 1249, Portugal could expel the Moors from their kingdom. But again, this was a long process that consumed all the energies of the Christian kingdoms of the peninsula and marked their psyche with an overwhelming sense of mission.

Militant Christianity; the creation of a war mentality and a war cast; the concept of "hidalgo", which glorified war activities or land ownership (usually obtained through the Reconquest effort), but discouraged business activities and manual labour; always pushing ahead spirit of frontier–these traits would remain invaluable tools for the effort of conquering the Americas.

Chance had it that the Reconquest ended in the same year in which Columbus reached the New World. So, 1492 was to become the natural meeting point between two overwhelming endeavours: Reconquering Spain and conquering the American territory. No other European country would have been better prepared for the latter odyssey, as it simply implied switching its sense of mission from one geographical sphere to another.

But 1492 was also the year in which the Jews were expelled from Spain. That act resulted from the aim of unifying the country by way of homogenizing it. Henceforward, Catholic orthodoxy would become the instrument through which such homogenization was to be obtained. That would put a heavy burden on independent thought and intellectual curiosity. The consequences of Catholic orthodoxy were to be felt for generations to come.

Moreover, expelling the Jews also implied losing the most dynamic sector of society, where not only financial acumen and experience lay, but also where medical knowledge and scientific curiosity were more developed. In 1496, and because of political pressure by the Spanish monarchs, the Jews were also expelled from Portugal. Future insertion into capitalism would be drastically hampered in both cases due to those measures, while the "hidalgo" mentality, at odds with business activities and manual labour, was to take hold in Iberian societies.

In Carlos Rangel's words:

> "It was Latin America's destiny to be colonized by a country that, thought admirable in many ways, was at the time beginning to reject the emerging spirit of modernism, and to build walls against the rise of rationalism, empiricism, and free thought — that is to say, against the very bases of the modern industrial and liberal revolution, and of capitalist economic development".[3]

The impact that the encounter with this New World had in Europe was immense. In Flanders, while reading about it, Thomas More was inspired to write his *Utopia*; while in Poland Nicolaus Copernicus was given the proof that he needed for establishing his thesis on firm ground. The idea of the "Noble Savage" that lived in a free society where oppression was unknown, and which was to be the basis for thinkers of the "Enlightenment" many generations later, was born from that first interaction with the indigenous populations of American lands. Columbus and Vespucci, encountering primitive people, had idealized them to the extent that Vespucci even coined the term of "terrestrial paradise".[4]

The fortuitous encounter with the American territories and their subsequent division between Spain and Portugal put these countries at the forefront of the efforts to bring such lands under European control.

---

[3] Harrison, L.E, (2000). *Underdevelopment is a State of Mind: The Latin American Case,* p.31. Plymouth: Madison Books.

[4] Arciniegas. *op. cit.*

As seen, Spaniards and Portuguese, even if showing distinctive traits, were the offspring of the same historical and cultural process. Furthermore, their respective Romance languages were extremely close. It is worth mentioning, that Castilian was the main language spoken in Spain, while other Romance languages and Basque held a more limited space. Castilian, though, was tantamount to Spanish language.

Hence, when the Iberians from these two countries began their conquering and colonizing efforts in the Americas they came from very similar cultural backgrounds. What they were to find and interact with, in the new lands, would completely change their mental frame and their perception of the world.

New Lands, Old People

The chronicles from the first Europeans arriving into the American lands showed the psychological imbalance brought by the immensity of the American space. There was a violent fracture of the ancestral relation that the Europeans had with their natural environment. But in addition to a totally different geographic scale, there were new animals, new plants, new vegetables, and new meteorological phenomena. Tropical rains, hurricanes, flows, and the disappearance or inversion of annual seasons.

But there was also a different notion of time. The arrival of ships from Spain or Portugal could take months or, in some cases, even years. News coming from home arrived with such delay that past and present intermingled. Every bureaucratic undertaking before the metropolitan authorities required infinite patience. The sense of isolation could become overwhelming. In sum, time was as overwhelming as nature.

Their nourishment habits were also affected by different and unknown food. Potato, tomato, corn, chocolate, chilli, squash and turkey were but a few of the new foodstuff the Iberians would encounter. They were the first to experience what it would become a food revolution in Europe.

But there was much more. They found a new human race. A race with a totally different set of beliefs and cosmogony. A race as alien as if coming from outer space. And if the Iberians who had arrived at the new world could not remain the same after such a totally disruptive encounter, much less would the native inhabitants of the Americas be the same. For the latter, every bit of their identity would be torn apart.

But who were the people that the Iberians encountered? According to long established prevailing scholarly narrative, the natives had arrived from Asia during the Ice Age. Glaciation, indeed, sucked in vast volumes of sea allowing the seabed to be exposed across what is now the Bering Strait. Toward the end of that period a narrow and shallow route between what are now Russia and Alaska, allowed hunters to cross into unknown lands. Thanks to the abundance that they encountered on the new lands, they could multiply prolifically, spreading southward in the search for new hunting grounds.

Well–known British historian Felipe Fernández–Armesto affirms, though, that the truth about the peopling of these lands was much less dramatic. According to him, Asia and America were mutually accessible by land for long intervals over a period of maybe 60,000 years, up to about 10,000 years ago.[5] The standing of this theory derives from elements as the following: the presence of isolated human artefacts dating back more than 30,000 years; the emerging evidence of human occupation in many distant places; a wide range of cultural diversity over a long period of time.

If the former were the case, crossing from one place to the other should have been a much more common feature than previously thought. Some scientists believe, as referred by Charles C. Mann, that the Americas may have been the object of at least five great waves of settlement before Columbus, with the earliest occurring as much as 50,000 years ago.[6]

In every imaginable scenario, though, these newcomers left Asia before the first Neolithic Revolution, which corresponds to the invention of farming and began in the Middle East about 11,000 years ago. Foraging societies in the Middle East grouped themselves into permanent villages and learned to cultivate and breed wild wheat and barley.

If Native Americans left Asia before that event, it is obvious that an independent Neolithic Revolution occurred in the Americas. Such a revolution took place in Middle America (essentially today's Mexico, Guatemala and their surroundings), at a time now believed to have occurred ten thousand years ago, not long after the Middle East's Revolution.

---

[5] Fernandez-Armesto, F (2009). *The Americas: A Hemispheric History. Kindle Ed.*, New York: The Modern Library.

[6] Mann, CC (2011). *1491: New Revelations of the Americas before Columbus. Kindle Ed.*, New York: Vintage Books

The elapsed period between the Neolithic Revolution and the emergence of the city of Sumer, the first civilization in the Middle East, was about 7,000 years. Native Americans navigated the same path probably in less time. The first technologically complex culture of the Americas that of the Olmecs, appeared in what is currently Mexico about 1500 BC.

The Olmecs were the first of many societies that emerged in Middle America. Their cultural, scientific and commercial accomplishments were very important. They created a vast network of trade, invented dozens of different witting systems, traced the orbits of the planets, and gave birth to a 365–day calendar that surpassed in accuracy those of their contemporary Europeans.

But their most relevant creation was the invention of zero, which was a turning point in mathematics. The first historical reference to zero dates to Babylon in the Middle East in 600 BC, appearing first in Europe in the 12th century through the Arabs of the Iberian Peninsula. Nonetheless, an independent creation of zero was recorded in carving in Middle America in 357 AD The Olmecs, the Mayas and other Middle American societies were pioneers in mathematics and astronomy.

But if there is no consensus among historians as to the time and nature of the arrival of Asians in America, neither is there in relation to the precise size of their population at the date of the arrival of the first Europeans. Everybody accepts though that such populations were in the tens of millions of inhabitants. These human groups were diverse and responded to very different ecological environments. They went from nomadic hunter–gatherers to fully sedentary and highly developed civilizations as complex as those of the Old World.

The Indians

As Columbus believed having arrived at the East Indies, there was nothing more natural for him other than to call their inhabitants "Indians". This denomination was to stick, encompassing all the aboriginal populations of the Americas. Classifying this collective population under such a generic term was a big misconception, as they were as different from each other in language and ethnic identity as their European counterparts. Nonetheless, there were common denominators, as all the American peoples lacked metal weapons and tools, did not use the wheel in manual labour (although they had invented it and used it in children's toys) and did not have animals that were suitable beasts of burden as in other parts of the world.

More advanced groups refined gold, silver and cooper for ornamental purposes, but never developed industrial metals such as iron. Thus, they relied on hard and sharp stones for weapons and tools. In that sense, American peoples showed an evident technological stagnation, as the tools and weapons of the Incas or the Aztecs, for example, varied little from those of the peoples who preceded them by more than a millennium.

While there were two poles of developed societies–Middle America and the Andes (basically from current Ecuador to the Northern part of Chile), most of the continent was populated by semi–sedentary and nomadic tribes. In the middle of those groups, sedentary but lesser developed societies could also be found.

Curiously enough, primitive tribes were more difficult to subdue than complex civilizations, as they were too mobile and usually inhabiting extremely harsh terrains. On the contrary, highly centralized and stratified societies would crumble when their leadership was defeated.

Edwin Williamson divides Middle America and Andean regions in four periods: Archaic or Pre–Ceramic (7000–2500 BC); Pre–Classic (2500BC–AD1); Classic (AD1–1000) and Post–Classic (1000–1500).[7]

The Archaic or Pre–Ceramic period marks the beginning of agriculture, with small semi–nomadic tribes using simple techniques of tilling within slash–and–burn agriculture. A rudimentary pottery existed at that time.

The Pre–Classic period saw the development of a settled agrarian economy based on kingship groups living in small villages. Priestly elites appeared in the later stages of the period. Public ceremonies were performed in temples of wood and thatch. Simple pottery and weaving evolved into elaborate decorative styles. The Pre–Classic most advanced civilizations were the Olmecs (1500–400 BC) in current Mexico and the Chavins (900–500 BC) in today's Peru.

The Classic period shows societies more fully developed in terms of ideas, techniques and social organizations compared to those of the

[7] Williamson, E (2009). *The Penguin History of Latin America.* London: Penguin Books.

Pre–Classic but within similar patterns. The state becomes more powerful and is ruled by a king, but the priestly caste retains immense power. A warrior class is rising in status. Cities emerge and ceremonial sites are built of stone as are public buildings and houses of the aristocracy. Sites of Classic civilizations are Teotihuacàn (AD1–750) and Monte Alban (500BC–AD 800) in current Mexico; the Mayas (AD300–900) in today's Mexico and Guatemala; Moches (200 BC–AD 600) in Peru; Tihuancos (AD 600) in Bolivia and Chile and Huaris (AD 1000) in Peru, Ecuador and Bolivia.

According to Williamson, a dark age separates the Classic from the Post–Classic period, characterized by a phase of social collapse and cultural disintegration that seems to have affected the whole of ancient America for unclear reasons. Teotihuacan, Monte Alban and the Mayan sites of Peten were deserted, while later, the Tihuanco and Huari empires fell.

The Post–Classic period marks a more vigorous imperial cycle and even if there are no major innovations in economic productivity or in culture, significant developments in the organization of the state and the society took place. It is a time of aggressive imperialist expansion in which the gods are appeased through the sacrifice of human victims. That implies the constant waging of war to collect new sacrificial offerings. An aristocracy of warriors, priests and bureaucrats, separated itself from the masses through seigneurial privileges, while centralization of power is embodied in an absolute king invested with divine rights.

The Toltecs (AD 1000–1200) and the Aztecs (AD 1427–1520) in Mexico, and the Incas (1438–1533) in Peru, Ecuador, Bolivia and Chile are the best expression of this period. Much less sanguinary and more politically adroit in their conquests than the Toltecs an Aztecs, already by the early 16th century the Incas had assembled the largest empire in the Americas and probably in the world as well.

It is worth mentioning that developed civilizations from Middle America and the Andes never got in contact or knew about each other until the arrival of the Europeans.

But there were other kinds of Indian populations in different parts of the continent. The Arawaks, originally coming from mainland South America, inhabited the larger Caribbean Islands. Their society was sedentary but lacked great complexity. Sedentary and relatively complex social groups could be found in Central America and in north–western South

America in the highlands of modern Colombia and Venezuela. In other areas of South America and in northern Mexico there were semi–sedentary or nomadic peoples with less stratified social structures. These included the bellicose Araucanians of southern Chile or the Chichimecs in what is now southwestern United States.

This last category of primitive tribes was the one found by the Portuguese in Brazil. The largest of them were the Tupis who originated in Paraguay. But there were also the Caribs, originally from Guiana, who were expanding north and south when the Iberians arrived. Being natural sailors they were displacing the Arawaks in some islands of the Antilles and have moved into northern Amazon. They gave its name to what is currently the Caribbean Sea.

Shattering Experiences

Sooner or later all these different indigenous peoples would be confronted by the same shattering experiences: defeat, submission, servitude, conversion and massive human losses. The Iberians, clearly, did not possess any sense of curiosity or sensibility in relation to the indigenous people's thinking, scientific knowledge or culture.

There was a clear pattern in the way in which Spaniards defeated advanced Indian civilizations. First, their daring attacks at the top of the indigenous political structure with the aim of decapitating it. When centralized powers were involved, this was tantamount to blinding the whole. This was the strategy followed with emperors Moctezuma and Atahualpa of the powerful Aztec and Inca empires respectively, a strategy which was to be imitated with minor chieftains.

Second, seeking the military support of submitted indigenous groups who wanted to get rid of their own Indian overlords. These were the cases of the Tlaxcala people in Mexico or the Huanca in Peru, which proved critical to the Spanish conquest of the Aztec and Inca empires. Such alliances expressed the discontent that plagued Aztec and Inca rule and their failure in eradicating the independent military potential of resentful ethnic groups. These allies were easily discarded once they were no longer useful to the Spaniards.

Third, having access to military technological superiority over the Indians. Firearms and the cannon played an important role, but metal weapons, armours and horses were much more important. Armed with sharp stone weapons the Indians were no match for the European war technology.

Submission implied the wiping out of their way of life. In the case of advanced civilizations, whose development in many areas had nothing to envy Europe's own, meant the destruction of their cities, their temples, their codices and their relics. It meant as well the forceful abandonment of their gods and beliefs. Never in history had pre–existing civilizations been subjugated to such a degree after defeat. The empires of the Aztecs and the Incas, which at the beginning of the 16th century were among the most rapidly growing in the world, were simply erased from the earth.

In Charles C. Mann's words:

> "The Western Hemisphere before 1492 was, in the current view, a thriving, stunningly diverse place, a tumult of languages, trade, and culture, a region where tens of millions of people loved and hated and worshipped as people do everywhere. Much of this world vanished after Columbus…So thorough was the erasure that within a few generations neither conqueror nor conquered knew that this world existed. Now, though, it is returning to view".[8]

Servitude was implemented through institutions such as the "encomienda", the "mita" and the "repartimiento" in Spanish America and the "donatary–captaincies" in Brazil. They imposed working in the fields or in the mines of their new Iberian overlords for their enrichment or providing them with tributes in goods. While the Spaniards and the Portuguese emphasised their role of "hidalgos", at odds with all form of manual work, the Indians had to carry the heavy work.

In the case of Brazil, the situation was considerably worse than in Spanish America as Indian slavery was common. Even if the Spanish and Portuguese crowns prohibited the enslavement of Indians, considering them as their vassals, informal slavery was prevalent in Brazil. Inland raids looking to capture Indians to be sold to landowners became one of the most profitable enterprises in Brazil.

Conversion to Christianity meant that beyond raw power was the overwhelming and concomitant power of religion. According to Arturo Arias:

[8] Mann, *op. cit.*, Chapter 1, Loc 748.

> "Catholic priests and Church authorities, themselves formed in the wave of Counter–Reformation measures imposed in Spain by the Holy Inquisition, acted more as cultural censors and as dogmatic enforcers of regulatory social practices than as true missionaries".[9]

The former assertion, though, should be balanced with certain clearly positive elements. Within the Spanish sphere there were important efforts by sectors of the Church to ameliorate the condition of the Indians, with a serious debate taking place within religious and scholarly boundaries in Spain as to the right to subjugate them. The Jesuit missions also played an important role in protecting the Indians and integrating them into a communal production system. On the Portuguese side, such a role was even more significant, as the Jesuits missions became sanctuaries for the Indians against the depredatory impulses of raiders. Jesuit missions covered a vast expansion of land in Brazil and in neighbouring present day Argentina and Uruguay. So much so that the term Jesuits Republic was coined to state the consolidated power held by them.

Nonetheless, the fact remains, that the indigenous people had to absolutely submit and comply with the religious dogmas, teachings and rules imposed upon them. Moreover, overzealous missionaries wanting to expunge memories of paganism, were responsible for the disappearance of valuable old texts and records of knowledge. Only four of the numerous Maya codices, to mention just one example, survived this cultural onslaught.

And then, the massive human losses. If the imperium of the sword and the imposition of the cross were not enough to reduce the indigenous population to despair, there was also the implacable weight of infectious diseases brought by the Iberian newcomers. Diseases against which the Indians had no resistance. Smallpox, influenza, measles, typhus and other European illnesses spread and recurred in several occasions. According to N. D. Cook their population was reduced to around 12 per cent of the original total of about 30 to 40 million in 1500.[10]

John E. Kicza mentions that over a century, successive waves of epidemics reduced the native population of central Mexico by about 95 per

---

[9] Arias, A (2014). Politics and Society. In *The Companion to Latin American Studies,* P Swanson (ed.) p. 27. New York: Routledge.

[10] Restrepo, LF (2014). The Cultures of Colonialism. ibid., p. 51.

cent, while the indigenous population in the Spanish Caribbean had literally been eliminated by 1550, with Central America and the Andean region also being badly hit. Moreover, according to him, without such a demographic catastrophe, modern Latin America would more closely resemble Africa or India, where the European impact, although certainly significant, was not as transformative of native cultural, social and political patterns. [11]

African Slavery

The demographic crumbling of the Indians translated into a lack of workforce that had to be compensated by other means. This led to the introduction in America of its third human protagonist: the African slave.

If the fate of the Indian had been dramatic, that of the African slave was by no means better. They were captured in their own homelands through horrendous manhunts; packed tightly in the filthy holds of slave ships; taken to the other side of the ocean in dreadful crossings; unloaded like animals to be sold as such in huge markets; separated from other slaves from the same geographical origin to facilitate their cultural integration and avoid revolts. All that, before beginning a new life of hard work devoid of gratifications, in which they were even deprived of access to their own language, traditions or beliefs.

Not surprisingly, during the colonial period, the black slave traffic showed little signs of diminishing as deaths exceeded births and constant imports were required to meet labour needs. It must be added, though, that Africans brought with them their own silent revenge: yellow fever. This ailment was to become endemic in the tropical lands of the Americas.

According to Luis Fernando Restrepo, throughout the colonial period about 1.5 million African slaves were imported to Spanish America and 2.5 million to Brazil, most of them during the eighteenth century. [12] Edwin Williamson cites that 132,600 slaves were brought to the Spanish colonies between 1595 and 1640, mentioning that the 18th century produced a surge in that number. [13]

---

[11] Kicza, JE (2004). *The Indian in Latin American History.* Oxford: SR Books.

[12] Restrepo, *op. cit.*, p.56.

[13] Williamson, *op.cit.,* pp. 141–142.

Slaves came from different parts of the West African coasts, between present day Senegal and Angola, with many being captured inland. Hence, their ethnic, linguistic and cultural diversity was huge. In Darcy Ribeiro's words:

> "Negroes brought to Brazil from Western Africa belonged…to hundreds of tribal people who spoke dialects and languages not intelligible to each other".[14]

As aforementioned, to promote their rapid acculturation and prevent riots, slaves from similar origin tended to be separated and sent to different places.

Black slaves were concentrated in areas where the Indian population had fallen beyond recovery. Initially they went to lowlands or coastal regions in Mexico and Peru, but were later disseminated in different places, performing different kinds of jobs. Working at tropical plantations along the Caribbean and the Atlantic coasts was common, but the range of activities was extensive enough to also include gold mining, cattle–ranching or even wheat production. The main destinations for African slaves included Brazil (principally the northeast), Cuba and the rest of the Spanish Caribbean islands and New Granada (today's Colombia, Panama, Ecuador and Venezuela).

From early on, some slaves were freed by their masters or, more frequently, could buy their own freedom with money saved from working on their days off. This situation was more common in Spanish America where, as the general population increased in the second half of the 17th century and the supply of labour improved, the rate of manumission accelerated. By the late 18th century most blacks in Spanish America were free and were to be found working as self–employed artisans, wage–labourers or peasants. Freedom, though, was not tantamount to a better social position and colour prejudice was endemic.

The Church had an ambivalent but pragmatic approach towards slavery. It condoned it as the unfortunate situation of certain races, though it believed that slaves could win salvation through conversion. Hence, the Church saw in the enslavement of "savages" the opportunity for bringing

---

[14] Ribeiro, D (1995). *O Povo Brasileiro,* p.114. Sao Paulo: Companhia das Letras.

them to the knowledge of the true faith and, thus, to salvation. The Church insisted that Negro slaves were human beings with a soul and, as such, had to be treated humanely.

Moreover, Spanish and Portuguese considered slavery as an ancient legal institution, covered by the 10th century legal statute of the so–called "Siete Partidas". Consequently, slaves, even if subjected to compulsory forced labour, had rights. Among them, the right to their life, to their own body, to their reputation as human beings and to marry of their own will.

The former implied a substantial difference in relation to slavery in the United States or in English colonies. Slaves in in the Anglo–Saxon sphere were simply movable property and as such not covered or protected by any legal instrument. Moreover, baptism and religious teaching were seen negatively as they could induce dangerous ideas.

African slaves had a core of beliefs based in the active role of the deceased and in their influence upon the living, in which divination played an important part. A highly ritualistic body of practices is enshrined in these beliefs. At the same time, a group of cultural traits are clearly identified with African heritage.

Curiously enough in Iberian America those beliefs were not a direct import from Africa. Indeed, as emphasis was given to rapid acculturation and conversion into Catholicism, a radical breach with the original cultural background was imposed. As a result, this structure of beliefs conformed what has been labelled as "cultural retention". That is, the autonomous reconstruction in American territory of what slaves retained by way of memory or through the teachings of the elders. As such, their practices, rituals and culture were also influenced by the new environment and the new religion.

African religious practices, as it also happened with the Indigenous ones, were subject to persecution and punishment. Therefore, those practices only persisted in secrecy or through secret adaptation to Catholic practices. This type of adaptation generated a religious syncretism through which Africans and Indians camouflaged their own deities behind Catholic saints. That being the case not only their own body of practices and rituals were influenced by Catholicism, but popular Catholicism in Iberian America was also influenced by those beliefs.

By the mid–17th century, blacks had become a major presence in Iberian America. There was, though, a special category within them: the "cimarrones" or fugitive slaves. These tended to gather in inaccessible or remote areas to escape persecution, sometimes forming rebel communities called "palenques" or "quilombos". Not unfrequently these communities were also joined by escaping Indians or deserting white soldiers.

By 1854 the abolition of African slavery had occurred everywhere in the region. The only exceptions were Puerto Rico and Cuba which remained under Spanish control until the end of the 19th century, and Brazil. In these three cases abolition came in 1873, 1886 and 1888 respectively.

Acculturation, Miscegenation and White Predominance

The human identity of Iberian America resulted from the fusion of the three races — whites, natives of the Americas and blacks — and their respective cultural backgrounds. Several factors derived from that fusion.

Acculturation and miscegenation were a fundamental part of the history of the region. Iberians, Indians and Africans mixed producing what Simon Bolivar called "a smallholding of human race". Immensely diverse roots and cultural identities were amalgamated, generating a final product which was different from the simple sum of its original components. The baroque architectural monuments of Mexico, the Andes or Brazil, or the baroque sculptures at the latter, are amid the most impressive in the world. They are one of the most visible results of such acculturation and could not have been produced in Europe, pre-Columbian America or Africa.

Referring to the syncretism that characterizes artistic expressions within the Iberian American churches, where other religious beliefs were camouflaged under Christian images, Arturo Uslar Pietri says: "Together with the Christian angels, African devils and indigenous semi gods also entered our churches".[15] Moreover as Carlos Fuentes notes:

> "In the same way in which in Mexico the goddess of the Aztecs, Tonantzin, was to be transformed into the brown Catholic Virgin of Guadalupe, in Cuba the African goddess of the sea, Yemaya, would become the Catholic Virgin of Nuestra Señora de la Regla, patroness of the sailors".[16]

---

[15] Pietri, AU (1979). *Fantasmas de Dos Mundos,* p.232. Barcelona: Editorial Seix Barral, S.A.

[16] Fuentes, C (1999). The Buried Mirror: Reflections on Spain and the New World, p.210. Boston: Mariner Books.

The originality of such expressions is no surprise. A literary gender typical of contemporary Latin America, the so called "magical realism", is entirely different to the literary productions of Europe or other parts of the world, reflecting the said amalgamation. The same is highlighted about another literary movement that prevailed a century ago: Latin American Modernism.

Despite the intermingling, there was, nonetheless, a clear white identity within that mixed society, as middle to upper echelons of the social structure preserved their "whiteness" through inbreeding. This was not only the leading sector of the society, but the one that carried with it the hegemonic ideas. During colonial times the white's predominance admitted no doubts, but even after independence their dominant status was preserved.

Iberian preoccupation with racial purity moved to the Americas. In colonial times the so–called "limpieza de sangre" (cleanliness of blood), prevalent in Spain and Portugal to differentiate from Jew or Moors, was reproduced amid the white landowning elite who sought proof of not being tainted by Indian or African blood. Once liberated from their Iberian overlords, whites or mostly whites continued to define the agendas of their countries in their own terms and essentially for their own benefit. Moreover, their disdain for miscegenation was such that in many cases they promoted European immigration as a way of "whitening" their societies.

A rigid social stratification prevailed. In colonial times the same was practically unsurmountable, becoming more relaxed, but never disappearing, after independence. During colonial times a social pyramid existed with the peninsular–born whites at the top. They were followed by "criollos" in Spanish America and "mazombos" in Brazil: that is, Spaniards or Portuguese whites' born in America. At the bottom were the Negros and Indians, with the first being considered as the lowest of the low. In the middle categories, an ambiguous combination of mixtures (the so called "castas"), disclosed a whole spectrum of miscegenation which was accompanied by an equally diversified nomenclature.

The nomenclature of the "castas" included, among others, the "mulatos" (white–black mix); the "mestizos" or "mamelucos" (white–indigenous mix); and the "zambos" or "cafuzos" (indigenous–black mix). Being "mestizo" or "mameluco" was better than being "mulato", which in turn was better than "zambo" or "cafuzo". After independence, social permeability was significantly increased. Nonetheless, race continued to be a very important social consideration.

Consequently, being able to look as a white as possible, or having the economic resources to behave like a white person, became fundamental to ameliorate one's own social standing. It was only after the triumph of the Mexican Revolution, in the first decades of the 20th century, when a Latin American country recognized for the first time the value of miscegenation. From then on, a slow but continuous process towards racial equality, and the recognition of indigenous and African values, was put in motion.

CHAPTER 3

BRAZIL AND SPANISH AMERICA

In the previous chapter, when reviewing the historical similarities in the region, we observed what follows. Two brother European countries with a common background that underwent a similar process once in the Americas. Different indigenous people that were submitted to the same spiral of defeat, submission, servitude, conversion and massive human loss. African slaves that were captured in their own homelands and packed in filthy ships to be taken to the other side of the Atlantic, where they had to adapt to a new environment, a new language and a new religion.

We also observed a similar process of acculturation and miscegenation that gave rise to what was labelled as "a smallholding of human race", and whose final product was different from the sum of its original components. But, simultaneously, a stratified social structure emerged where the white identity prevailed and could impose its ideas and patterns of behaviour.

Such similarities may have led to the belief that Latin America, amid the diversity of its origins, is nonetheless a fairly homogeneous place. That is not the case. Both Brazil and Hispanic America are subject to the same common denominators yet, despite their many similarities, important differences also exist. Exploring the heterogeneous and homogeneous elements that exist between Brazil and Spanish America, is a necessary first step to understand the region.

The history of Brazil displays a process of moderate evolution, devoid of the epic deeds and sudden shocks so typical of Hispanic America. It has been correctly pointed out that the Brazilians fell asleep one night as a colony and woke up to find themselves an independent Empire and, later, woke up again to find themselves a Republic. The history of Hispanic America, on the other hand, looks more grandiose and traumatic.

Such a difference began with conquest itself. The fact that Portugal expelled the Moors in 1249, while it took until 1492 for the Spaniards to do the same, had fundamental consequences.

From Reconquest to Conquest

In Spain, there was a continuum between the reconquest of its own territory from the Moors and the conquest of America: 1492 represented a natural interconnection between the two. That year the former ended and the latter began. As a result, the spirit of mission that animated Spanish life for eight centuries simply moved to the other side of the Atlantic. No other European country without such sense of war and religious mobilization, could have found the energy and the daring do to accomplish what Spain did in the Americas.

In about 50 years, Spain subdued, Christianised, urbanized, populated, and founded universities in those new lands. It also began economic expansion and provided an administrative framework to an enormous and inordinate geographic space filled with unsurpassable rainforests, gigantic chains of mountains, majestic rivers and dreadful deserts.

During that brief period the Spanish "conquistadores" defeated war–oriented indigenous populations through the continent, including the mighty Aztec and Inca empires. Spaniards imposed upon them Christianity; built a wide network of towns and villages; populated those urban spaces and brought education to such populations. In addition, they set the basis for economic expansion and introduced effective administrative organization. As the submission of the indigenous populations was already addressed in Chapter 2, we will focus on the other issues.

The Church played a key role during this initial period, actively evangelizing the Indian populations throughout the Americas. For that purpose, the missionaries had to master not only the different Indian languages but also their meanings and symbols, as it was the only way to create the necessary connections for their own teachings. Accordingly, the missionaries produced the first dictionaries on native languages. The Church also established missions, hospitals and other institutions throughout the region.

Its policing role though cannot be ignored, as it harshly imposed religious conformity. Moreover, after mastering the cultural meanings of the subdued Indians, to use them for their own religious teachings, the missionaries simply discarded that knowledge as an expression of paganism.

Urbanization had been an essential part of the Spanish Reconquest. Indeed, every advance upon the territories of the Moors was consolidated by building cities and towns following a concept of expanding frontiers. Not surprisingly, then, urban–minded Spaniards would bring with them that approach to the Americas. Towns and villages would become the tool for expanding their frontiers in the New World. Subsequently, Spanish towns were strategically located adjacent to native populations, mines, trade routes, rivers or ports. The Spaniards aimed not only at consolidating conquered spaces, but also at integrating the hinterlands into the Atlantic economy.

Populating the conquered lands was concomitant to urbanization, as new towns implied new families. This in turn meant bringing women from Spain. Much has been written about the solitary nature of Spanish conquerors as a leading cause of miscegenation, given that the Indian women were the only females available to them. Undoubtedly this is true, yet only to a certain extent. From the registered 45,327 Spaniards that came to America in the 16th century, 10,118 were women. In other words, there could have been around 20,236 Spanish married people and 25,091 single men. Moreover, during the first quarter of that century, a third of all the arrivals to the colonies were women. This entails, that half of the men may had access to a Spanish wife.[1] Moreover, extensive academic literature refers to the important role played by Spanish women during those early years. [2]

As early as 1538, the Spaniards founded the University of Santo Tomas de Aquino in Santo Domingo (in the Dominican Republic of

---

[1]Maura, JF (2002). Adelantadas, virreinas y aventureras en los primeros años de la conquista de América. *Revista de Literatura Española Medieval y del Renacimiento,* Número 6; Matinez, JL (1983). Pasajeros a Indias, Viajes Trasatlánticos en el Siglo XVI. Madrid: Alianza Editorial; Museo Naval de la Armada Española / Ministerio de Educación, Cultura y Deporte; Exposición (2012). No fueron solos: Mujeres en la conquista y colonización de América. Madrid: Museo Naval, 21 de mayo - 30 de septiembre, 2012.

[2]Morant, I (2006). Historia De Las Mujeres En España y América Latina. Madrid: Ediciones Cátedra and Mujeres hispanas en el Nuevo Mundo: a la vanguardia de los acontecimientos, (Numero 15, 1995). *Revista de Estudios Hispánicos.*

today). It was not only the first in the hemisphere but also among the first 15 of the Spanish world. This institution was followed in 1551 by the founding of the University of Mexico and that of San Marcos in Lima. When these universities came to life, a wide network of schools already existed throughout the region.

In 1545 the 20–year span began in which the major mining discoveries in Mexico and Peru took place. They were to become large–scale operations that would put in motion multiple interconnected economic activities. Workers needed housing and stores, while mines required masonry, winches, ladders and huge amounts of leather. Mules and horses were needed to move the bullion to mints and export points. Plantations and ranches had to be established to provide supplies to mining activities, workers and the emerging adjacent towns and so on amid a flurry of action.

To administer these territories, the Spanish created a centralized political structure. From Spain, the Council of Indies was responsible, while in America two main viceroyalties were created: New Spain (current Mexico) and Peru. These viceroyalties controlled smaller administrative units called "audiencias" (among which were those of Santo Domingo and Santa Fe de Bogotá), which in turn had jurisdiction over governorships and towns. From the beginning, then, a complex bureaucratic system was put in place. Not surprisingly, the Crown became the decisive factor in the Americas enterprise.

Global Reach, Loose Grip

Nothing remotely similar occurred in Brazil during the same period. The fact that Portugal completed its war of reconquest 243 years before Spain, had much to do with it. There was no connection between the reconquest of their own territory and the conquest of their American possessions. Moreover, while in the case of Spain an old sense of purpose was easily switched from one area to another, Portugal had sufficient time to define new priorities that would channel its energy. Naval exploration and international trade represented those priorities.

Beginning with the islands of Azores and Madeira, the Portuguese would keep pushing south through the coasts of West Africa. Along this descendent route they will establish a system of slave and ivory trading posts, without inland colonization. In the late 15th century, they discovered a sea route to the East around the Cape of Good Hope. In 1510, they founded the colony of Goa in the western coast of India. A few years later the Malacca peninsula (current Malaysia), became the strategic base for Portuguese trade expansion with China and South East Asia. Subsequently they seized cities in present day Indonesia where they constructed fortified settlements seeking to dominate and control the spice trade. The Portuguese Empire of the East, with its capital in Goa, included possessions in all the Asian subcontinent, East Africa and the Pacific.

The Portuguese had a global reach unknown to the Spaniards (whose only Asian possession was The Philippines, which became a simple extension of its American Empire through its Galleon Trade with Mexico inaugurated in 1565). But whereas the Spaniards had their American possessions under firm grip, the Portuguese were highly vulnerable in their over expanded territories. According to historian Bernard Vlekke: "…the Portuguese empire in the East was decayed, rotten and tottering, a structure which would collapse if given even a moderate blow".[3] Such a blow was provided by the Dutch through their East India Company, which in a few years seized all Portuguese possessions in that part of the world.

While the attention of Portugal was elsewhere, Brazil was of minor concern for them. As a matter of fact, their first trip to their American "granted" territories happened by accident. In 1500, an expedition headed by Pedro Alvares de Cabral, en route to South Africa, drifted westward and landed somewhere along the Brazilian coast. These lands were soon called by the name of a local dye tree, the "Pau Brasil". For some time, the wood of such a tree would become the only product for export found there. The Portuguese would replicate in Brazil their experience in the western coasts of Africa, with the establishment of isolated trading posts along the coastal areas without aiming at inland penetration.

These first five decades, in which the Spaniards were making deep inroads into their own American territories, were a period of neglect for Brazil. As a result, impoverished Portuguese settlers, left to their own devices, had the time to develop the skills of slave–hunters in the bush. This happened in what is currently the Brazilian state of Sao Paulo.

[3]Brown, SR (2009). *Merchant Kings,* p.25. New York: Thomas Dunne Books.

Through an old indigenous practice of incorporating strangers into their own tribes by way of marriage (the so–called "cunhadismo"), settlers became assimilated into the indigenous population of the area. Taking as many "wives" as possible implied, by extension, widening their network of relations with different local tribes. The result of this process was a polygamist society in which the multiple offspring of the settlers ended up being much closer to their respective Indian mothers' way of life than to their European fathers'.

Speaking the Indian Tupi language and living under primitive conditions, the descendants of Portuguese settlers became a troop of rough adventurers, much closer to plunder than to production. Armed with rudimentary military tools, that were nonetheless superior to those of the Indians, this amalgam of Europeans and Indians transformed themselves into a human hunting society. Their aim was to capture and slave Indians with the purpose to sell them.

After depleting their coastal prey, Portuguese and their offspring began making inland raids that were to become more and more ambitious and predatory. Preceded by banners, they gathered into groups of hundreds or even thousands that for periods of months, or even years, raided the interior territories. They were known as "bandeirantes" (banner holders). The enslaved Indians, for which good prices could be fetched, became the main commodity of this tough community.

The main buyers were the planters of north–eastern Brazil. Indeed, this other pole of Portuguese settling was taking shape further north along the coasts of Brazil, where sugar plantations began to emerge. Planters tended to concentrate in what are today the states of Pernambuco and Bahia. It was undoubtedly a more civilized society where production, and not plundering, was the goal. Eventually, sugar would become Brazil's main export, providing the basis for a refined and cultivated society and allowing such cities as Olinda–Recife and Salvador de Bahia to flourish.

When France proclaimed its right to trade in any part of Brazil not actually occupied, the Portuguese Crown was forced to react. Initially, it sent 400 men in 1530. But that was meaningless compared to the immensity of Brazilian coasts. As a result, the Portuguese Crown created in 1532 the system of "donatary–captaincies", by which twelve captains would receive immense territories for their colonization. The captains were to enjoy civil and criminal jurisdiction over its settlers and have the power to found towns, collect taxes and exploit the land.

As it happened, though, "donatary–captaincies" turned out to be a failed enterprise of colonization. Among the reasons for such failure were the following: apathy by some of the grantees of such concessions; hostility by the Indian tribes; lack of deterrence to the French inroads and inability in to get commercial ventures to prosper. With the single exception of the captaincy of Pernambuco, the rest turned out to be mostly inoperative. So much so, that in 1549 Portugal felt the need to have a direct administrative presence in Brazil to oversee, secure and put order in that territory. To such ends the King appointed his first governor–general with a seat in Salvador de Bahia, which would be the first capital of Brazil. In other words, at a time when Spain held its American possessions under tight control, Portugal was only giving its first steps towards that end.

Nonetheless, with sugar exports generating increasing revenues and Crown authorities guaranteeing a bigger presence through more structured institutions, Portuguese America would end up catching up with Hispanic America. Moreover, between 1580 and 1640 Spain and Portugal would merge under the same Crown: the Spanish one. And even if both colonial endeavours would be run independently, major decisions during that period were to be taken in Madrid.

Brazil would enjoy a period of prosperity in sugar production and trade that would last until the end of the 17th century, followed by a period of prosperity based on gold and diamonds. Hispanic America, on the other hand, would have a period of economic expansion sustained by their silver exports (supported also by gold), eventually complemented with their rich agricultural and ranching exports of the late 18th century.

Both Hispanic and Portuguese colonies, as well as their cargoes, were to be victims of British and Dutch predatory policies. Britain not only periodically raided Spanish ports and cities in the Americas, but between 1762 and 1763 took control of the capital of Cuba, Havana. Dutch incursions were more threatening in nature. After a failed invasion to north eastern Brazil in 1624, the Dutch took hold of a good part of that region between 1630 and 1654. During that time, they mastered sugar production, which they would later develop in their Caribbean territories. This would put in motion the decline of Brazilian sugar exports.

By the end of their respective colonial eras, Brazil and Spanish America were stronger economically than their respective metropolis. During the final decades of Brazil and Hispanic America's submission, Portugal and Spain began to evolve in different directions in relation to their colonies. This would entail strikingly dissimilar consequences.

One Enlightenment, Two Results

In Brazil, conditions were created for the colony to become a unitary state after its independence from Portugal. The opposite happened in Hispanic America, where the terrain was paved for its fracture into 16 different countries after liberation from Spain. Moreover, while in Brazil all factors were conducive to creating the basis for becoming an independent monarchy, Spanish America evolved into the republican system. Curiously enough the resulting opposite directions stemmed from the implementation of similar policies pursued by Lisbon and Madrid.

The Enlightenment movement, which projected itself over most of Europe from the mid–18th century onwards, began to be felt in Madrid and Lisbon in the last decades of that century. Even if the Enlightenment did not penetrate the tissue of their respective societies, particularly in Spain, it promoted more centralized Crown policies. In Portugal, its Prime Minister, the Marquis of Pombal, oversaw those changes. Meanwhile, in Spain a new dynasty whose roots where French, the Bourbons, had arrived in power. The Bourbons brought with them the notions of government that prevailed in France.

When applied to their possessions on the other side of the Atlantic, the centralizing policies of Pombal and the Bourbons produced opposite results. In Brazil, they not only strengthened the unitary character of the colony but also the loyalty of its elites towards the Crown. In Spanish America, much to the contrary, not only did they promote the hostility of its elites against the Crown, but were instrumental in shaping a differentiated sense of identity within the American born white creoles.

A more centralized control of Brazil by Portuguese authorities helped to curtail the centrifugal impulses from certain regions. That was particularly the case in Pernambuco or Minais Gerais, whose elites would prove to be very much in favour of asserting their own identity and evolving in their own separate direction. In 1774, the two main administrative structures in which Brazil had been divided, the vice royalties of Salvador de Bahia and of Rio de Janeiro, were merged. Henceforward, there would be a single Viceroy based in Rio de Janeiro. That curtailed the possibility of the colony evolving into two independent states.

For the Marquis de Pombal, the unitary character of the Empire, comprised by Portugal and Brazil, was fundamental. Hence, he was extremely careful not to alienate the Brazilian elites with his reforms. Subsequently, the benefits of such reforms tended to include the elites from Brazil at every possible step. Posts in the higher echelons of the bureaucracy and in the newly founded militias were opened to Brazilians; local oligarchies could invest in the monopoly companies that he was creating to promote trade; the liberalization of trade brought by his policies was designed to equally favour both Brazilians and Portuguese.

The expulsion of the Jesuits from Brazil, to eliminate the "State within the State" that they represented, was welcomed by the Brazilian elites, which resented the Jesuits' power. The measure helped strengthening not only the links between the Crown and local oligarchies but also the power of the King.

In Spain, as already noted, a new dynasty had arrived into power: The Bourbons. They brought along changes in conceptions and policies in relation to their American possessions. To begin with, the previous dynasty, the Habsburgs, had included their American provinces within a medieval concept of empire, according to which a single sovereign reigned over a constellation of separate entities. Under such conception, their American provinces were an integral part of the Spanish Empire. For the new rulers, the Bourbons, Spain was a European nation state that happened to have dominions overseas. Dominions were to be at the complete service of the metropolis, and whose resources were to be exploited in view of strengthening Spain's position in Europe.

In the 1640s, still under Habsburg rule, Spain had been subject to the centrifugal rebellion of many of the Empire's elites, including the Portuguese, Catalans, and Sicilians. The elites from America, nonetheless, remained firmly loyal to the Crown because they had benefited from Spanish actions or inaction. On the one hand, they had come to occupy most of the posts within the American bureaucracy. On the other hand, they had been able to take advantage of the enfeeblement and the increasingly lax attitude that prevailed in Spain. The latter had advanced their own positioning and economic benefits. A good example of that was their indirect participation in international trade through smuggling.

The reassertion of power brought by the Bourbons took place at the expense of the American elites. Henceforward, the "criollos" (creoles) were excluded from obtaining positions within the American administration, which were reserved for Peninsular Spaniards. But at the same time, the firm centralizing hand with which the metropolis began to act, curtailed most of the benefits that American elites had enjoyed from Spanish inertia.

Several commercial monopolies, established on behalf of Spanish companies, proved highly detrimental to the economic interests of the local oligarchies. Meanwhile the local elites were not given the option to participate as investors. Moreover, the social standing of the so called "castas" (mixed race groups) was improved at the expense of the creoles. The Bourbons, as with the Portuguese, also expelled the Jesuits from their American territories, but given that a good number of them were creoles, such action added to their sense of grievance.

As it happened, the measures taken by the Bourbons to increase their power ended up by weakening it, and in turn, generated a negative reaction among the American elites. As a result, the latter began to develop a sense of American identity differentiated from Spain. This promoted a convergence of interests among the aggravated elites, the expelled Jesuits who ended up being instrumental in promoting a distinct creole identity, and a group of active "revolutionaries". The most notorious of such revolutionaries was the Venezuelan, Francisco de Miranda, who for decades conspired against Spain from Europe and the United States.

To openly alienate the Hispanic American elites was not the best of ideas. Indeed, the same ideas of the Enlightenment which guided the actions of Bourbon reformers, were filling the heads of many of the creoles through the example of the American Revolution and the impending French Revolution.

Napoleon and the Two Different Routes of Iberian America

As Brazilian elites were closing ranks behind the Portuguese Crown, Hispanic American ones were diverging from Madrid. Events in Europe, sometime later, were to reaffirm these tendencies. In 1808, the Portuguese monarch fled from Lisbon as the invading Napoleonic troops were approaching his capital. Upon moving the Crown to Rio de Janeiro, Brazil was transformed into the epicentre of the Portuguese Empire. Needless to say, that this movement dramatically strengthened the popularity and reach of the monarchy in Brazil, especially because since the monarch's arrival, substantial institutional advancements took place there.

In 1821 King John VI returned to Portugal after 13 years in Brazil. Those 13 years were decisive enough to give a new sense of unity to the vast Brazilian territory, under the undisputable legitimacy of the Crown. Moreover, they were instrumental in greatly isolating Brazil from the wars of independence that were taking place in the surrounding Spanish American territories. At the same time, they provided the necessary institutional strength to crush the bid for independence and republicanism that took place in Pernambuco in 1817. Without the royal presence in Brazil during those decisive years, which helped in consolidating the centralization process initiated by Pombal decades earlier, such an immense landmass could not only have fractured but also taken the route of republicanism.

The invasion of Spain by Napoleon's forces, generated totally opposite results in Hispanic America. For a second time, since Pombal and the Bourbons, similar processes produced completely different outcomes. Upon invading Spain, Napoleon summoned the feuding Spanish royal family to France and forced King Ferdinand VII to abdicate. A new Bonaparte dynasty, under the reign of his brother Joseph, was to replace the Bourbons. Meanwhile the deposed Spanish King was imprisoned in France. The majority of Spaniards did not recognize the usurper and uprisings took place throughout the country.

As a result, "juntas" (provisional governments) that defended the rights of the deposed King, sprang up in various cities. Traditional Spanish political theories on the contractual nature of the monarchy, asserted that upon the absence of the monarch, the suzerainty went back to the people. Such "juntas", as expressions of popular suzerainty, could exercise power until the return of the true King. Eventually the different provisional governments converged under the authority of one: The Supreme Junta, established in the city of Seville.

In 1808, creoles in Hispanic America, following the example of Spain, tried to establish "juntas" in different capitals of the region. For

Spanish authorities in the Americas, though, that was a totally different proposition. The fact that the creoles could assumed provisional sovereignty in absence of Ferdinand VII, even if it was to preserve his rights, was unacceptable. This led to widespread repression in the region, including the execution and imprisonment of some of its leaders. For creoles, this was a brutal reminder of their lower status in the eyes of Peninsular Spaniards, which widened the gap even more between both.

In 1810, the Supreme Junta fled Seville as the French army approached, taking refuge in the city of Cadiz. Situated in an island, and under the protection of the British Navy, the city of Cadiz became a symbolic spot of Spanish suzerainty in a country at that moment totally controlled by the French. Precariously surviving under a land siege by the enemy, the Junta decided to reconstitute itself into a Regency Council. The difference being that while the Junta implied popular suzerainty, the Regency did not. The latter was a simple prolongation of the authority of the monarchy.

For most American creoles, the Regency Council was not acceptable. To begin with, it did not make much sense to submit to a powerless spot which could fall under French control at any moment. Moreover, the window of opportunity for directly assuming popular suzerainty was highly attractive. For some, it represented a leap forward in advancing the autonomy of the American provinces. For others, such autonomy was the natural first step in the direction of independence.

Starting with Caracas, which was the first to receive the news coming from Cadiz, many of the provincial capitals of the Americas began establishing juntas to protect the rights of the absent King. This time, nonetheless, creoles took good care in neutralizing the Spanish authorities. Certain provincial cities, though, decided to remain loyal to the authority of Cadiz. Such was the case, among others, of Coro, Maracaibo, Montevideo, Cordoba, La Paz and Asuncion. This generated the first acts of war, as capitals such as Caracas or Buenos Aires sent military expeditions to reduce the dissenting cities to their authority.

Inevitably the road to independence had been opened. One way or another the tide would, from now on, forcefully move in that direction, ever more unstoppable. Within this process Mexico followed a different path, as its independence movement was not led by the creole elites. Much to the contrary, it was a popular movement propelled by the peasantry and resisted by the creoles in conjunction with the local Spanish authorities.

The severity of what lay ahead varied from one place to another. In some of the future countries there was relatively little bloodshed, while in others it was dramatically high. Venezuela, which lost a quarter of its population due to the war, topped the list of the victims. These conflicts were fought both as irregular and conventional warfare, being at the same time wars of liberation and civil wars. Sometimes, war took place between American armies or American guerrilla forces against Spanish conventional armies. Other times, it was essentially a confrontation between Americans.

There were many Spanish American leading war figures, of which the most important were Simon Bolivar from Venezuela, Jose de San Martin from Argentina, Bernardo O'Higgins from Chile, Antonio Jose de Sucre also from Venezuela and Miguel Hidalgo and Jose Maria Morelos from Mexico. There was also a clear precursor and ideologue of Hispanic American Independence: the Venezuelan Francisco de Miranda.

At the top of the group was Simon Bolivar. He fought 472 battles of which 79 were important, liberated six nations and during his campaigns rode on horseback 123,000 kilometres, 10 times more than Anibal, three times more than Napoleon and twice as much as Alexander the Great. Referring to Bolivar, British historian John Lynch wrote:

> "He was a revolutionary who freed six countries, an intellectual who argued the problems of national liberation, a general who fought a war of unremitting violence (…) As a soldier Bolivar displayed not only great implacability but also immense powers of endurance; he was there at the beginning of the war of independence, and fifteen years later, in 1824, when the last viceroy surrendered, he was still in command".[4]

[4]History Today (1983). Simon Bolivar and the Spanish Revolutions. Volume 33, Issue 7 July. http://historytoday.com/john-lynch/simon-bolivar-and-spanish-revolutions. Accessed 22/10/2015.

Spanish American Wars of Independence

Even though warfare took place all around Spanish America, there were three main theatres of operations: two in South America and one in Mexico. Of the former, one initiated in Venezuela and followed a descendant trajectory that reached Upper Peru (current Bolivia), while the second one began in Rio de la Plata (current Argentina) and followed an ascendant trajectory up to Peru.

The descendant trajectory was led by Bolivar, who between 1811 and 1821 fought in the Captaincy General of Venezuela and the Viceroyalty of New Granada, liberating New Granada in 1819 and Venezuela in 1821. This was a hard fought and bloody conflict, which included a combination of civil war and conventional war. The latter implied confronting an army of Spanish veterans of the Peninsular War against Napoleon, led by one of the best generals of such conflicts. The most important military exploit of that process was Bolivar's crossing of the Andes Mountains with his army in 1819. Bolivar's feat has been compared to Anibal's crossing of the European Alps.

Once the task of liberating Venezuela and New Granada was accomplished, Bolivar followed south and, with the help of his second in command Antonio Jose de Sucre, liberated the Presidency of Quito and the Province of Guayaquil in 1822. Venezuela, New Granada, Quito and Guayaquil were integrated by Bolivar into a single Republic: Colombia (present day Venezuela, Panama, Colombia and Ecuador).

The ascendant trajectory was carried out by Jose de San Martin. The Vice Royalty of Rio de la Plata (present day Argentina) easily fell in the hands of the pro–independence revolutionaries. Nonetheless, some of its provinces remained in the hands of the royalists. One of them was Upper Peru, in the Andes range, against which three unsuccessful military expeditions were sent. In 1817, San Martin was put in charge of the Army of the Andes, but instead of advancing on Upper Peru, he decided to cross the Andes into the Captaincy General of Chile. A feat comparable in daring to that of Bolivar a couple of years later. With the help of Bernardo O'Higgins, San Martin could defeat the Spaniards.

The assault on the Viceroyalty of Peru ensued. With the help of Admiral Cochrane, a retired British navy officer who distinguished himself in the fight against Napoleon and who commanded the Chilean naval forces, San Martin moved his army to Peru. Establishing a base at the north of its capital

Lima, he entered discussions with the colonial authorities. He proposed to establish an independent constitutional monarchy with a Spanish prince of royal blood on the throne.

Before concluding the negotiations, the Spanish viceroy and his army decided to abandon Lima and move into the impregnable Andes highlands. This allowed San Martin to enter the city in 1821. However, being in control of Lima meant little if an undefeated Spanish army was still on the loose. Between negotiations about taking that city and the inability to follow the Spanish army in the highlands, San Martin's campaign remained bogged down for two years.

In 1822, San Martin and Bolivar met in Guayaquil. Their projects were not easy to reconcile as Bolivar was a staunch republican and San Martin believed, as mentioned, in the need of establishing an independent constitutional monarchy under a European prince. After discussing the alternatives, San Martin decided to retire from Peru, opening the way for Bolivar to follow the campaign against the Spaniards. This implied the demise of monarchy as an option for the new states of Hispanic South America. With his usual energy, Bolivar began to organize the ascension of the Andes Mountains with his army, to confront the royalists. In 1824, relying on the invaluable support of his deputy Antonio Jose de Sucre, Bolivar had defeated the Spaniards and liberated Peru.

Referring to his liberation of Peru, Robert Harvey states:

> "Bolivar's achievement in Peru had been as staggering as any in his career of a year, from holding a strip on the country's north coast while himself nearly moribund, he and Sucre had taken on and defeated an army of 18,000 men and secured a country the size of nearly all of western Europe to add to the vastness of Colombia…The investment of personal energy, the distances covered and the four army expeditions across supposedly impassable mountain ranges -west to east across the Andes, back the other way, down to central Andes to Quito, and up again to Cerro de Pasco- had qualified him for superhuman status…His stamina and military achievement put him at the forefront of the global heroes of history". [5]

[5] Harvey, R (2011). *Romantic Revolutionary: Simón Bolívar and the Struggle for independence in Latin America,* pp. 318–319. London: Constable.

Nonetheless, the issue of Upper Peru remained. By a combination of warfare and defections within the Spanish ranks, Upper Peru was freed in 1825. Sucre, who had commanded the campaign, convened a Congress of Upper Peruvians which had to decide whether to be part of the Independent Provinces of Rio de la Plata, part of Peru or an independent State. The Congress opted to become a sovereign State and named it Bolivia in honour of Bolivar. Sucre was appointed President of the country.

In 1825, Simon Bolivar was the most powerful man in South America. At that point, he was both President of Peru and Colombia, while his deputy was President of Bolivia. Not even the Emperor of Brazil could have matched the combination of resources at his disposition, particularly the military ones.

Along with these two theatres of operations in South America, there was a third one in Mexico (Viceroyalty of New Spain). The uprising against the Spaniards began in 1810 when the creole priest Miguel Hidalgo revolted. His proposal contained three objectives: the abolition of the Indian tribute, the return of Indian lands and death to the Spaniards. An explosive reaction of the peasantry followed, making this revolution a totally different proposition from the ones in South America. While South America's were creole led, Mexico's uprising had a clearly popular character. As such, both Spaniards and creoles were equally targeted.

Due to indecisiveness, confrontations at the top of his ranks and anarchy among his followers, Hidalgo was militarily crushed, captured and executed within a year. However, resistance followed under the leadership of Jose Maria Morelos, a much more able military commander and adroit politician. Land redistribution and full political integration of Indians and mixed blood mestizos, became his aim. Under his stewardship independence was nominally declared in 1813. A year later, though, he was also captured and executed.

Actions followed for several years, but of less intensity and under less military leadership by the rebels. If revolution came from below, independence would come from above. Agustin de Iturbide, a creole that commanded the Spanish military forces in Mexico, opted for independence. Events in Spain, where a military coup imposed a Liberal Constitution upon King Ferdinand VII (back to the throne since 1814), convinced Iturbide about the need for Mexico to follow its own course. To such end, he contacted and convinced the rebel leader Vicente Guerrero to forge an alliance against the Spanish government.

Together Iturbide and Guerrero issued in 1821 the so–called Iguala Plan, according to which Mexico would become an independent monarchy with either King Ferdinand VII or one of his brothers as Emperor. In a few months' the Plan was accepted not only by a majority of the leading Mexican forces but also by neighbouring Spanish jurisdictions: The Captaincy General of the Yucatan and the Kingdom of Guatemala (today Mexico's states of Yucatan and Chiapas plus current Guatemala, Honduras, El Salvador, Nicaragua and Costa Rica).

Neither the Liberal government in Spain nor Ferdinand VII, accepted the independence or the offered Crown. Their repudiation created a void which was filled by Iturbide in 1822 when his troops proclaimed him Emperor under the name of Agustin I. Devoid of legitimacy, though, he could not convey a royal aura. Creole aristocracy could not trust the son of a merchant, while the army regarded him as a simple political schemer. His was, thus, a short–lived reign followed by a Republic declared in 1823. Yucatan and Chiapas remained part of the new Mexican Republic, while Guatemala, Honduras, El Salvador, Nicaragua and Costa Rica seceded.

As it happened, an independent Crown in the Americas was offered to the Spanish reigning Bourbons both by San Martin in Peru and by the proponents of the Iguala Plan in Mexico and neighbouring Central America. In both cases it was not accepted. Otherwise, the Bourbon dynasty could have reigned, independently from the Spanish government and Spanish institutions, over the two richest and more cultivated territories of Spain's former American possessions. That was a mistake that the Braganza dynasty of Portugal did not commit.

Brazilian Stability and Hispanic American Turmoil

In 1821, King John VI returned to Portugal and his son, Crown Prince Pedro, remained as Regent in Brazil. According to Robert Harvey:

> "The truth was that Brazil had been effectively independent for fourteen years–indeed it has become the dominant partner in the Portuguese Empire–and was not prepared to be reabsorbed without a struggle.

> On leaving Rio de Janeiro the King had advised his son, 'If Brazil should decide on separation, let it be under your leadership, since you are bound to respect me, rather than under one of these adventurers'. In secret communications from Lisbon Joao now urged Pedro to resist re–assimilation into Portugal foreseeing that it would lead inevitably to such radical revolutions as was being experienced throughout Spanish America".[6]

When the Lisbon Parliament decided to return Brazil to the colonial status it had before 1808, cancelling its political equality with Portugal and its freedom of trade, Prince Pedro championed the sense of outrage that emerged in Brazil. Moreover, when recalled to Portugal by the Lisbon government, he flatly refused to obey. In 1822, on the banks of the River Ipiranga, near Sao Paulo, he loudly rejected going back, proclaiming the separation from Portugal. This was the famous "Shout of Ipiranga", which sealed the independence of Brazil. Soon after, he was crowned Emperor Pedro I of Brazil.

In sum, while Brazil's Hispanic American cousins where involved in a long, bloody and wearing fight against the Spaniards, Brazil simply got away with a shout. The Brazilians, as indicated, literally woke up to find themselves an Independent Empire. But more significantly, the legitimacy embodied by the Crown allowed Brazil to follow a much more benign historical course than that followed by Spanish America.

Brazil's legitimacy manifested itself on three levels. First, it was instrumental in maintaining Brazil as a single state. Second, it became a safety net against internal confrontations as it offered the possibility of arbitrating the plurality of interests and political visions within the country. Third, it allowed the new country to enjoy a high degree of international recognition and respect.

Much to the contrary, Spanish America was submitted to deficient legitimacy on those three counts. That deficiency translated into the following results: a fracture into numerous independent countries as the order that held them together was dissolved; a process of generalized civil wars as domestic differences could not find instances of conciliation;

---

[6]Harvey, R (2000). *Liberators: South America's Savage Wars of Freedom 1810–1830, pp. 478–479.* London: Robinson.

a severe international weakness as their status as second–class international actors made them prey to stronger states.

Brazilian intellectual Darcy Ribeiro talks of Brazil in plural, referring to the five different countries that coexist within one.[7] That Brazil could remain as a single entity, amid its wide variables, is clearly attributable to the fact that the historical glue that had held it together for 300 years, remained virtually intact after independence. Brazil, the size of the rest of South America together, could assimilate its racial and cultural differences. It also assimilated the diverse patterns of behaviour deriving from its multiplicity of latitudes and climates. Consequently, it could preserve a unitary sense of nationality.

As we shall see, the arbitration and conciliation of differences between the provinces and their vested interests were to be of utmost importance for the preservation of Brazil's sense of nationality. Nonetheless, centralization of power was also fundamental. According to Alan K. Manchester: "The creation of the mechanism of a sovereign state in Brazil…produced a centralized national bureaucracy which looked to Rio de Janeiro as the source of authority".[8] This process had begun when the Portuguese court migrated to Brazil, giving rise to an impressive growth in the civil and military bureaucracy. This implied not only the creation of institutional structures, but of strong centralized structures.

The sudden beheading of the established order in Hispanic America, on the contrary, led to institutional chaos. The inexistence of a substitute to the Spanish Crown, able to enjoy widespread recognition, generated orphanhood and disaggregation. It was difficult, even in the best of circumstances, for the American offspring of Spain to remain together as a single entity. Its gigantic extension, many times larger than Brazil, and its numerous administrative divisions generated a natural centrifugal pressure. Still, had old administrative jurisdictions remained intact, just three or four independent states might have emerged from the dissolution of the Spanish Empire. Instead, more than a dozen did.

This proliferation of countries was largely attributable to the Bourbon reforms of the late 18th century. These not only created new jurisdictions, but

---

[7] Ribeiro, o*p. cit.*

[8] Quoted by Claudio Véliz, *op. cit.*, p. 114.

fractured old ones by scrambling their components in different ways. As a result, attachment to old institutional structures was greatly weakened. Upper Peru is a good example. Having historically belonged to the Viceroyalty of Peru, it was ascribed by the Bourbons to the newly created Viceroyalty of Rio de la Plata. As a result, Upper Peruvians felt no loyalty to Rio de la Plata and had cut its traditional links with the Viceroyalty of Peru.

Simon Bolivar was acutely aware of the fact that a plethora of weak states was no match for threats which could have come from different sources: the newly formed Holy Alliance of conservative monarchies in Europe; the emerging power of the United States; or the predatory impulses of some European countries. Divided, the new Spanish American countries were easy prey. That is why Bolivar fought for the creation of strong states and their integration within wider institutional structures.

Referring to Bolivar, John Lynch wrote:

> "His ambition was to unite…the Spanish American peoples. He created the great state of Colombia, comprising Venezuela, New Granada and Ecuador. He then sought to unite this with Peru and Bolivia in a Federation of the Andes. And he dreamed of the 'great day of America' when its peoples would come together in a league of nations. Unity would ensure peace and well–being. And unity would earn greater respect for other nations…In Bolivar's view foreign indifference towards Latin American independence was a consequence of the proliferation of tiny sovereignties, squabbling among themselves".[9]

In Bolivar's words, "Fatherland is America", which explains why he insistently tried to shape an Iberian American confederation of nations. According to Marie Arana:

> "He had always made it clear that the continent could not function as a single, integrated country; the landmass was too sprawling, the population too diverse. To complicate matters, Spain had never encouraged camaraderie among its colonies–travel and commerce had been forbidden and punished by death- and so for three hundred years the colonies had answered to Madrid as spokes to a hub, with no contact whatsoever

[9]History Today, *op.cit.*

among them. They did not know one another well enough to be fellow citizens. But Bolivar saw the Spanish-speaking nations of America as potential brothers in a grand fraternity, bound by common law and protected by a single military…Although each nation would remain a separate entity, there would be but one army, one code of racial conduct, one face against the world".[10]

Bolivar died though, a disillusioned man, with his dreams of unity shattered by the centrifugal impulses of myopic political leaders who only thought of building what he called "mini–governments". Hence, Spanish America ended up being a constellation of weak republics. With a cynical tone, Argentinian statesman and literary figure, Domingo Faustino Sarmiento, wrote that in Central America every village was transformed into a Republic.

At a national level, on the other hand, the legitimacy of the Brazilian monarchy was instrumental in guaranteeing internal peace. Needless to say, Brazil was not isolated from the problems the rest of the region faced. However, the Crown could carry on, while it survived, with what was labelled as the "politics of conciliation". Conciliation ensured that problems could be contained within the broad framework of constitutional order. No other institution could have attained such level of respect and recognition from provinces, factions and vested interests, thus guaranteeing the arbitration of its differences.

Conversely, civil wars plagued Spanish America as conflicting societal visions within their republics could not be reconciled. While Conservatives wanted to cling to the remainders of the old order, Liberals wanted to get rid of it, and while Federalists wanted to devolve political and economic power to the provinces, Centralists wanted to concentrate it in the capitals. The Brazilian Emperor could arbitrate such confrontations, but the President of the Republic had no power to do so in Spanish American countries. Indeed, as it happened, Presidents were always part of the conflict and their job, the prey to be conquered. Therefore, important differences could only be resolved on the battlefield.

---

[10]Arana, M (2013). *Bolívar: American Liberator,* p.353. New York: Simon & Schuster Paperbacks.

Internationally, Brazil as a monarchy was a simple extension of the European monarchies. As such, it not only benefited from the friendship and support of this select group, but was also excluded from the group's predatory instincts. Moreover, its insertion within the monarchical system and the strength derived from it, represented for Brazil a guarantee vis–à–vis the United States hegemonic and imperialistic impulses. Washington knew very well that Rio de Janeiro was in a different league from the rest of the Latin American capitals, being entitled to deferential treatment.

While this happened in Brazil, Spanish America had become a victim of the predatory impulses of both the United States and European countries, as Bolivar had feared. According to historian Marcello Carmagnani, Hispanic American republics enjoyed a second class status as international actors. Their sovereignty was only partially recognized given that they were considered more governments *de facto* than *de jure*. This treatment gave way to the myth of the political inferiority of such states, which was to prolong itself in the European mind until the beginning of the 20th century.[11]

The only protection against European incursions in the region came from the United States' Monroe Doctrine. However, in practical terms, this only meant that there could only be one predator with the exclusion of all the others. As a result, the United States appropriated half of Mexico, divided Colombia to take control from the Panama Canal Zone which was to be governed by US laws, and after 1903, invaded the Caribbean Basin countries 34 times, occupying some of them for extensive periods.

Still, as soon as there was a pause in the application of the Monroe Doctrine, because of the US Civil War, France occupied Mexico and imposed a tributary monarchy there, while Spain reoccupied the Dominican Republic. Moreover, even with the Monroe Doctrine in place, the United Kingdom could get hold of part of Venezuelan and Guatemalan territories.

Latin American Convergence

Hence, the Brazilian Crown role during those formative years was highly positive. Even so, preserving slavery at a time when most of the world had

[11] Carmagnani, M (2004). *El Otro Occidente: América Latina desde la Invasión Europea hasta la Globalización*. México: El Colegio de México/Fondo de Cultura Económica.

abolished it, including Spanish America, was undoubtedly a black spot for the institution. As it happened, the fate of the monarchy was to be tied to the fate of slavery. When the Empire supressed it, in 1888, the coffee elites of Sao Paulo, the most powerful of the country, saw no remaining reason for keeping the monarchy alive.

In 1889, Sao Paulo oligarchs promoted a coup. A group of generals, won over by the cause of republicanism through the teachings of the Positivist movement, were eager to comply. It was a bloodless takeover that did not generate active opposition from within the Brazilian ruling classes. Vested interests had become too powerful to keep seeking conciliation from the top.

A Federalist Republic, which suited the interest of the province of Sao Paulo well, was put in place. Nonetheless, it also worked well for Minas Gerais–the second most powerful province of the nation. While Sao Paulo was a big coffee producer, Minas Gerais was the largest cattle and milk producer. A coalition of these two big federal states ended up running the country for a few decades. Not surprisingly, the coalition was labelled as the coffee and milk alliance. As a result, there was a clear transition into a more oligarchic form of politics. Not only because the coffee elites of Sao Paulo joined forces with the cattle barons of Minas Gerais, but because the nationwide older parties prevailing during the Empire lost all their influence. Under the new political structure, power was devolved to the regional oligarchies.

Once again, Brazilians fell asleep one night with one political form of government and woke up to find themselves with a different one. While Spanish American countries had bloodied themselves to attain liberty or by subsequent internal conflicts, Brazilians passively evolved from one stage to the next. However, in 1893, a millenarian rebellion led by a Catholic visionary took place at Canudos, in the north–eastern state of Bahia. Even if the revolt was directed against the secular Republic, it was the frustrated reaction against their fate by the dispossessed peasantry of a declining sugar province.

As Brazil turned into a Republic, the country became more politically attuned with the rest of Latin American nations, with whom it shared similar challenges. Moreover, Brazil fell into a curious form of synchronicity with many of them, alternating between democratic and military governments.

But even if coups d'états were to become a familiar feature within Brazil, they would always have their own national characteristics. Indeed, "counting the cannons", which meant bending to whichever side could show greater military strength, would become the natural way of settling differences within their armed forces. Hence, Brazilian coups were to be bloodless. Brazilians showed themselves to be a pragmatic lot.

Don Quixote of La Mancha by Miguel de Cervantes, the greatest Spanish novel of all time and a founding work of modern western literature, offers the opportunity of an analogy. As it is well–known, the novel's main characters are Don Quixote, a knight pursuing windmills, and Sancho Panza, his down to earth and pragmatic squire. While Quixote is always involved in grandiose quests, Sancho Panza aims at satisfying more practical needs. In a certain way, Portugal embodies a Sancho attitude, while Spain the attitude of Quixote. The same analogy applies to Spanish America, always in grandiose quests, whereas Brazil displays more practical behaviour.

All told, despite their differences in origin and governance in post–colonial times, nowadays Brazil and Spanish America share a strong sense of common destiny and solidarity. Their opposite souls, which could be an element of divergence, currently tend to complement each other in a constructive way, thus enriching the match. Their common Iberian and Latin past, their many similar political and economic experiences some of which will be discussed later, and their status as neighbours, have converged into what today is a shared regional identity.

To solidify such a shared identity, both have created and intermingled a web of economic and political organizations. Among them, MERCOSUR, the Latin American Association of Integration, the Group of Rio and UNASUR, to name a few. In 2017, Brazil and Hispanic America are a thriving community of 577 million inhabitants. Even a common tongue — the "portuñol" — is beginning to emerge from the frequent mixed use of cousin languages: Portuguese and Spanish.

CHAPTER 4

SPANISH AMERICA: ONE OR MANY?

As we have seen Brazil and Spanish America have commonalities, and differences. But what about Spanish America's specific traits? Are there sufficient common denominators to use the singular when referring to Spanish America? What unites the region? What differences exist among their countries? Exploring Hispanic America's homogeneity and heterogeneity, provides us with a route map.

Few other regions in the world, if any, can show so many common elements: same language, same religion, a shared history and same social values. Sharing a language implies possessing the most powerful instrument for the transmission of a cultural identity. Sharing a religion represents not only an attachment to common spiritual values, but the same cultural manifestations of that faith expressed through its numerous festivities and arts. Sharing a history means a partnership through different eras: beyond the ocean; when confronted to a new world and while attaining independence and nation building. Sharing social values translates into a commonality of visions about the roles of the individual, family, and society; with the family representing the fundamental building block of society.

Whereas in Europe or Asia, culture expresses itself within national boundaries — explaining why there have been so many wars — cultural traits in Hispanic America express themselves within regional boundaries. Many of these elements are also present within an Iberian American context that would include Brazil.

Of these many elements, three are particularly relevant: The Hispanic heritage shared by all; the language that they all use and the similar experiences lived in the last 500 or so years.

The Glue that Holds the Group Together

Spanish heritage is the glue that holds the group together, despite the existence of two other pivotal identity elements–the indigenous and the Afro–American ones. Of the three, though, the Hispanic has not only been the dominant identity factor that has set the tone through history, but it is the only element shared by all with equal relevance. In fact, both Afro–American and indigenous identities are very important in some countries, but negligible in others. Moreover, they cannot be encapsulated in clear cut identities given the diversity of their origins.

All Hispanic American countries share the Spanish defining mark. Moreover, at a time when Spain is affected by the centrifugal forces of its different identities, Spanish America emerges as a bulkhead of Hispanicism. This has two basic explanations. On the one hand, the aforesaid divergent forces never reached the Americas. Not only because Catalonians, the most outward pushing force, did not participate in the American colonization process, but because such enterprise was clearly under Castilian stewardship. And Castile, one must remember, was the epicentre of Hispanicism.

Catalonians and Basques reject Spain, because they have strong identity alternatives. Hispanic Americans do not. They may have an acculturated identity, but that is different from saying that they have an alternative one. If they were to eliminate their Spanish common linkage, if it were at all possible, they would become strangers to one another.

What would Colombians and Argentinians, Chileans and Cubans, Dominicans and Uruguayans have in common if the Spanish identity element was subtracted? Not much. There would be no common language, no common religion, no common social values and no natural bridges of understanding. As such, Hispanicism comprises many of the other elements already noted.

Curiously enough, though, everything in Hispanic America emphasizes the breaking–off with Spain. Nothing like Brazil's perception of its Portuguese past exists in Spanish America. Nationality in the region is identified with the independence wars against Spain and with the deeds of those who fought against it. Moreover, during the second part of the 1980s and during the 1990s Spain attempted rapprochement with Latin America, and not for the better in terms of positive emotional bonds.

Spain's rapprochement attitude requires some explanation. Except for Cuba and Puerto Rico, which remained as Spanish colonies until 1898, all closeness between Spain and Hispanic America ceased after 1824–when the Spaniards lost their last battle in the region. On the one hand, through large part of their independent history Hispanic American countries showed no interest in creating bonds with Madrid, because anti–Spanish feelings took long to subside. On the other hand, during the greater part of the 19th and 20th centuries, Spain's problematic domestic agenda constrained its positioning in Hispanic America.

Civil wars; military putsches or putsch attempts; change of reigning dynasties; establishment and fall of a republican system; a war with the United States; a protracted colonial war in Morocco; violent protests in Catalonia; the downfall of the monarchy; crisis of the ensued republican system; a new and devastating civil war; plus, isolation, poverty and national introspection: these were some of Spain's historical features during the century and a half after 1824. Hence, Spain was in no position to try to be influential in Hispanic America. Except for Spain's migrations to the region, former motherland and ex–colonies drifted apart during that long period. This situation persisted until a few decades ago.

After its entry into the European Economic Community in 1986, Spain felt that the large Spanish–speaking population of the other side of the Atlantic was susceptible to increasing its leverage vis–á–vis its European partners. Claiming a special knowledge over that part of the world, Spaniards set themselves to become privileged interlocutors with Hispanic America and natural intermediaries between them and Europe.

During the 1990s, Spain's quest to re–establish a link with the Americas was compounded with its economic discovery of Latin America. Under the ideological command of neoliberal policies, low priced privatization of valuable state–owned assets took place in the region during that decade. Spanish companies set out to invest and were the ones that benefited the most from such process. Their smaller size had kept Spanish companies marginalized from the European scene, which is precisely why they turned their eyes towards Latin America. However, after a few years of extraordinary capitalization of their regional investments, which represented nothing but a massive transfer of wealth on their behalf, the Spanish corporations could return to the European stage but this time around as major players.

The high standing position upon which Spain relaunched its interaction with Hispanic America, brought back its old memories from the region. And those memories could only be those of their last close relationship: the one preceding Spanish American independence. How else could Spain contextualize the interaction with people of whom it had no direct knowledge since its time as a colonial metropolis?

As if these elements were not enough to propitiate a certain degree of haughtiness on the part of Spain, it also happened that the migration patterns that had existed for a long time were reversed. Instead of Spaniards being the ones who migrated to Latin America in search of better economic opportunities or escaping from political persecution, the opposite materialized. The brown faces from Hispanic America were the ones that arrived in droves into Spain. Not surprisingly, racism entered the equation as well. The term "Sudaca", which refers to all Spanish Americans, emerged as an epithet full of pejorative meanings.

Spain insists on its privileged understanding of Hispanic America based on historical and linguistic considerations. The history that Spain remembers, though, might better be forgotten, as it relates to bygone imperial times. The common language, on the other hand, only serves for Spain's wrongly believing that the decoding of Hispanic America's cultural clues can be obviated. Other countries not burdened by a neo–colonial baggage, and more concerned in decoding a culture that they don't pretend to understand, have proven to be better interpreters of the region.

Spanish American old memories in relation to Spain have also been awoken. Especially because this complex rapprochement coincided in time with the celebration of the 500 years of Columbus' arrival to the New World. The destruction of ancient pre–Columbian civilizations by the Spaniards have thus come into fresh light. All in all, this mutual rediscovery has created many practical ties, some of which are undoubtedly beneficial for Spanish America. What this rediscovery has not been able to do, though, is to promote positive feelings vis-a-vis each other.

Hence, the common Spanish denominator that the nations of the region share, and that represents the glue that held them together, transcends contemporary Spain. So long as this communal heritage constitutes the integrative link that holds the region together, every other consideration is superseded and becomes superfluous.

A fundamental part of that heritage is the Spanish language. Certainly, it is the language of Cervantes, one of the treasures of the world. But there is more to that, as the language spoken in the Americas is not the same of the Spaniards of today. Spanish in the Americas remained anchored to many archaic words and uses, as some of the idiomatic changes introduced in Spain in the 17th and 18th centuries never took root, or did so slightly, in America. Moreover, it is an acculturated language, as it received local influences that never reached Spain. That doesn't mean, though, that it is not a cultured language. Moreover, it is the same language spoken from Mexico to Patagonia. As such, it is an immensely powerful instrument of homogeneity within Hispanic America.

When Hispanic America separated from Spain there was the obvious risk that the language could be corrupted and fragmented. That is what had happened many centuries ago with Latin. When the Roman Empire collapsed, its offspring gave free reign to their ways of speaking it. If unchecked, these factors could have led to an idiomatic anarchy, where every country followed its own way. Trying to avoid that risk Venezuelan philologist and humanist Andres Bello published in 1847 its monumental grammar "for the use of Americans".

The result of such endeavour was a set of common grammatical rules for all Spanish American countries. Without renouncing to the unity of the language, a renovation process took place, adapting it to the uses of the Americas. Slang, expressions or particularisms may vary from one country to another, but nonetheless a precise set of idiomatic norms prevails. Bello's initiative was strengthened by the subsequent contribution in the same direction of Colombian philologist Rufino Jose Cuervo. So, instead of building barriers amongst themselves, using corrupted versions of Spanish, Hispanic Americans are united by this powerful homogenising mechanism.

More than Five centuries of Shared Experiences

The experiences shared during more than 500 years, are another fundamental commonality. Some of these experiences have been referred to in the previous two chapters. In particular, how Spanish America underwent similar processes during the conquest period, in colonial times and during the independence uprising.

Referring to the independence uprising Carlos Fuentes wrote:

> "The distances within the American continent are gigantic…Even today in the jet era it takes 16 hours to fly from Mexico City to Buenos Aires. It took several months in 1800. That is why it is so surprising that in the single year of 1810 the independence uprisings manifested themselves with such speed and synchronicity, from Mexico in the Viceroyalty of New Spain to Buenos Aires in the Viceroyalty of the Silver River. In April, Caracas deposed its Captain General. In May, Buenos Aires expelled the Viceroy. On the 15th of September, Hidalgo raised against the Spanish regime in Mexico. And on the 18th of the same month and year, in the far away city of Santiago de Chile, the independent movement emerged. Such simultaneity is amazing given the lack of communications and immensity of distances. The commonality of language and purposes that united the different patriotic movements, again from Mexico to Argentina, revealed the existence of strong spiritual and intellectual ties between the Spanish colonies of America".[1]

These ties reappeared when armies and military leaders left their places of origin to fight in neighbouring countries. All of this creates common historical memories and strong links. Heroes like Simon Bolivar, Jose de San Martin, Antonio Jose de Sucre or Francisco Morazan, to

[1] Fuentes, *op. cit.*, p. 245.

mention a few, are each shared and revered as their founding fathers by several Hispanic American nations. Few other regions of the world could claim as much. But there is much more: after independence, the same processes repeated in cyclical waves in most of such countries.

From Dreamers to "Caudillos"

Most of the region experienced a brief period of Liberal regimes immediately after independence. Among them were those of Ramon Freire and Francisco Antonio Pinto in Chile; Francisco de Paula Santander in Colombia; Vicente Guerrero in Mexico or Bernardo Rivadavia in Argentina. They had exceedingly ambitious views of liberty, rejected the Spanish past and looked for emulation to the United States or Europe beyond the Pyrenees (which separates the Iberian Peninsula from the rest of the continent). In Claudio Veliz' words:

> "They…found it hard to resist the temptation of proclaiming themselves staunch liberals, federalists, opponents of absolutism in all its forms, republicans to a man, defenders of the laws of nature, and, at any rate, zealous upholders of decentralization at all costs".[2]

Liberals addressed the problems that emerged by the sudden beheading of the established order in these distant and underpopulated regions, as if they were part of Europe and inhabited by well–read liberal Europeans. Not surprisingly, they generated anarchy everywhere. Bolivar had admonished about what could happen if this direction was followed: "Absolute liberty invariably lapses into absolute power…Abstract theories create the pernicious idea of unlimited freedom".[3]

And the result, indeed, was a backlash. After a period of much disorder came a wave of authoritarian regimes of a Conservative nature. "Caudillos" — i.e., strong men who advanced their interests by an able combination of military and political skills — controlled the region for a

[2] Veliz, *op. cit.*, p. 147.

[3] Lynch, J (2006). *Simón Bolívar: A Life,* p.122. New Haven: Yale University Press.

generation. Among them were Antonio Lopez de Santa Anna in Mexico, Juan Manuel de Rosas in Argentina, Fructuoso Rivera in Uruguay, Jose Antonio Paez in Venezuela or Juan Jose Flores and Gabriel Garcia Moreno in Ecuador.

According to Arturo Uslar Pietri:

> "When Latin America found itself abandoned to its own devices, it looked abroad trying to adopt foreign institutions such as a French-style Republic or an American style-one or a British-style Parliament… which ended up in failure. It then produced the only original political creation of Latin America–the caudillo".[4]

Latin American "caudillos" would not be limited to this period, reappearing on other occasions and circumstances. What characterized them at that point in time, however, was the simultaneity and spontaneity with which they emerged when everything else seemed to have failed. And for lack of better options, they would look back to the past for answers, wearing conservative gears.

The Liberals believed in the sovereignty of the people and by extension in periodic elections and representative institutions. They also believed in the freedoms of speech, thought, association and religion, and in individual rights to property and personal security. They were outward looking and firm believers in free trade. Following the example of the United States, they tended to be federalists, even though in Argentina they began by being centralists. The Conservatives, on the other hand, wanted to preserve the institutions and norms that had survived after the fall of the Spanish Empire. That implied, among other things, preserving the wealth and social influence of the Church and the special legal privileges of the clergy and the army. They aimed to preserve, as well, the social legal restrictions imposed upon the "castas" (people of mixed origin). Theirs was a hierarchical and inward–looking society. Contrary to the Liberals, they tended to be centralists, aiming at holding on tight to the reins of power.

Under the banners of Conservatism vs. Liberalism or Centralism vs. Federalism, several civil wars would flare up all throughout Hispanic

---

[4] Pietri, AU (1982). *Fachas, Fechas y Fichas,* p.191. Caracas: Editorial Ateneo de Caracas.

America. At times, especially in South America's southern cone, these civil wars transformed themselves into inter State wars, as similar factions from two different countries allied themselves against the opposite factions. Colombia (the name retained by the old New Granada when the Republic of the same name created by Bolivar collapsed), Mexico, Argentina, Venezuela, Chile, Peru or the Central American countries would all experience civil wars.

Liberals and Positivists

In the second half of the century, though, Liberalism had gained ground again all around the region. Political and military successes were also helped by the European rising demand for minerals and foodstuffs that manifested from 1860s onwards. As free traders, the wind blew at their backs. Figures such as Bartolome Mitre and Domingo Faustino Sarmiento in Argentina; Benito Juarez and Sebastian Lerdo de Tejada in Mexico; Tomas Cipriano Mosquera in Colombia; Jose Galvez Egusquiza in Peru; the Monagas brothers in Venezuela, were representative of this second wave of Liberals.

Again, their agenda would be put in place. Supporting the politicians was an active Liberal intelligentsia. Their reaction against conservatism included a virulent repudiation of Spain and everything Spanish. This would come in parallel with the glorification of contemporary French, British and North American values. Almost by definition this second–generation of liberals were ardent supporters of *laissez–faire* economics.

But in the 1880s and 1890s, Liberalism lost ground and was supplanted by Positivism. For many reasons, and in several countries, this simply looked as an evolution from one regime to the other. While the two movements coincided in their admiration for the United States, Britain and France and aimed at following their steps, Positivism was more attentive to societal results than to political means. While Liberalism advocated individual rights, Positivism believed that order and progress within society prevailed over such rights. To pave the way for genuine liberal democracy, material conditions needed to be created. Hence, strong governments and even dictatorships were acceptable if they were instrumental for the creation of such conditions. An ordered peace was thus a necessity.

Probably the best example of such philosophy of government was provided by Mexico. Through the long dictatorship of Porfirio Diaz, the country managed to solve many of its longstanding problems, setting the road to modernity. From 1876 to 1910, Mexico made more economic progress than at any other time since independence. The economy grew an average of eight per cent a year as railways, new technologies in mining and agriculture, and industrial developments in textiles, light industrial goods and processing of mineral ores, modernized the economy.

This long period of peace, economic progress, political stability and consolidation of the central power, could have indeed paved the way for the emergence of a constitutional democracy after the passing of the "caudillo". However, conflicting visions about the future within the regime; accumulated political discontent; profound social, economic and racial inequalities; and social complexities brought up by modernization; swept away the so called "Porfiriato". As Porfirio Diaz departed for a French exile, the country drifted into an anarchical and bloody revolution.

Progress, according to Positivists, required scientifically demonstrable propositions and was at odds with superstitions and the backward pushing traditions or religious beliefs. This implied, on the one hand, a rejection of the Spanish heritage even greater than that of the Liberals. On the other hand, the presence of an acculturated and crossbred population was a great societal burden. All expressions of "primitive" cultural manifestations, or in other words of popular culture, also had to be abandoned.

A dichotomy civilization vs. barbarism was put in place, with the latter being identified with the inherited historical burden that did not allow the population to attain progress. Hence, it was necessary not only to import ideas and technologies from the United States or modern Europe, but also people. "Whitening" the society, by fostering the immigration of industrious Europeans, became a priority. Latin American positivism and Social Darwinism were thus closely linked.

All throughout Latin America, Positivism prevailed and many important supporters of Liberalisms decided to engrossed its ranks. That was clearly the case of the Argentinian, Domingo Faustino Sarmiento. Moreover, Positivist ideas had given the intellectual justification for the Brazilian army to topple the monarchical regime. Henceforward, the movement became prevalent in Brazil as well, as shown by the fact that the new Republican flag would carry the device "order and progress", which were the catchwords of Positivism. As noted, from then on, Brazil and the Spanish American countries tended to follow a similar path. Creole oligarchies were thus running the show everywhere.

Ariel

The end of the century brought with it the entrance of a new member of the Spanish American family: Cuba. The new 20th century brought another one–Panama. While Cuba had remained firmly under control of Spain until 1898, Panama seceded from Colombia in 1903. There should have been a third entrant to the group of independent republics of Spanish origin: Puerto Rico. Unfortunately, its access to statehood did not materialize. The common denominator in all three cases was the United States. Or more precisely, the US' imperial policies.

Both Cuba and Puerto Rico were taken from its Spanish metropolis in 1898, because of the war between Spain and the United States. Both former Spanish possessions (together with The Philippines and Guam), fell under US control. While Cuba became nominally independent, in practice it was to remain an American Protectorate for years to come. The 1901 Platt Amendment gave Washington the right to militarily intervene in the island–nation at its convenience, which indeed it did. Puerto Rico, on the other hand, was to maintain colonial status in relation to the United States. The Foraker Act of 1900 gave the island the right to elect a Lower House (Delegates House), but the Upper House and the Governor were to be appointed by Washington. In 1914, the Delegates House unanimously voted for independence but this decision was rejected by the US Congress as unconstitutional, as it contradicted the Foraker Act.

Panama was a northern province of Colombia, neighbouring the Central American nations. Thanks to the critical intervention of American gunboats it breached away from Colombia in 1903. Washington had envisaged for many years the construction of a canal across the Isthmus and, as negotiations with Colombia didn't attain results, Washington decided to push for the secession of Panama. Henceforth, the country was to become a de facto protectorate of the United States. In the so–called Canal Zone, though, the American legal system was imposed.

Not surprisingly, these events resulted in a generalized anti US sentiment within Spanish America. Previous admiration for such a country, of which both Liberals and Positivists had been so laudatory, was replaced by a pan–Hispanic movement. The catalyst for this volte face was a book entitled *Ariel*, published in 1900 by the Uruguayan political essayist Jose Enrique Rodo.

Ariel was to become immensely influential throughout the Hispanic American world for decades, articulating the fears and cultural anxieties derived from the US juggernaut. From this moment on, the United States would be considered a threat, and not the model to be emulated. And, as the years passed and US actions became bolder, regional resentment increased.

Enfranchising the Middle Classes

With the new century, as well, new parties representing the middle and working classes began to emerge around the region. For the first time since independence, white oligarchies were not confronting each other but defending their accrued political privileges. Their main political challenge came from middle class parties which demanded greater liberal reforms. Among them, wider and cleaner suffrage systems, respect for civil rights, an end to privileges and monopolies for the upper classes.

The first triumph of a middle class party happened in Uruguay in 1903, when the Colorado Party led by Jose Batlle y Ordoñez won the election. Subsequently, the electoral base and employment by the state were widened, while social legislation was introduced. In 1911, Batlle y Ordoñez was elected for a second time.

Creole oligarchy in Argentina had responded to middle class pressure by liberalizing the electoral law in 1916. This allowed the Radical Party, which represented the new constituencies, to win the election that same year. Hipolito Yrigoyen became the new President, reproducing some of the policies already in place in Uruguay. This expanded the political and social participation of the Argentinian electorate.

Chile was a tougher case. A military coup was required in 1925 for the middle classes to begin advancing their interests through the rewriting of the Constitution in more inclusive terms. Arturo Alessandri's presidency led to the opening of the floodgates. It took Brazil until 1930 to dislodge the coffee and milk oligarchic coalition that had emerged from the downfall of the monarchy. As in Chile, a military rebellion was needed in Brazil for such a purpose.

Venezuela took even longer and required a coup d'état. In 1945, the middle class party Accion Democratica, supported by the young officialdom of the Army, arrived in power under the provisional presidency of Romulo Betancourt. A few months later the well–known writer Romulo Gallegos of the same party won the elections. Similar events happened through the region.

During the 1940s, every Latin American country, save Paraguay, El Salvador, Honduras and the Dominican Republic, was operating under inclusive democratic regimes. Reform–oriented governments extended the franchise, legalized unions, expanded public education, implemented social security programs, and provided health care.

Enfranchising the middle classes and breaking the monopolistic power of the traditional elites was not, an easy task. It not only took decades, but was frequently subjected to drawbacks. At times, it could unleash the forces of chaos. That was the case in Mexico when upper class politician Francisco Madero began mobilizing the middle classes to dislodge the "caudillo" Porfirio Diaz. Unwittingly, he opened a Pandora's Box that led to the cataclysm of the Mexican Revolution.

Even though the armed phase of the Revolution ended in 1920, Mexico continued to encounter high levels of political unrest. These included a bloody confrontation between the state and the supporters of the Church and the assassination of the undisputed leader of the country, President elect Alvaro Obregon. To channel the disruptive energy of the Revolution through institutionalized mechanisms, former President and new political boss Plutarco Elias Calles founded, the National Revolutionary Party (later renamed Institutional Revolutionary Party) in 1929. This party, whose longevity in power was to become proverbial, co–opted and gave voice to the different sectors of society.

Hispanic American countries were thus submitted to parallel or similar historical processes. The Mexican Revolution was undoubtedly a very particular phenomenon as would be the Cuban Revolution a few decades later. In general terms, though, Hispanic American countries, and Brazil, after the downfall of its Empire, followed certain regular patterns. This would become particularly true once the dynamics of the Cold War came into play, and would remain after the collapse of the Soviet Union under a different set of circumstances.

Cold War and the National Security Doctrine

During the 1950s, and with the encouragement of the United States who distrusted the uncontrolled nature of democracy and the uncertainty of ballot boxes, the region followed the route of military dictatorship. Washington found, indeed, that it greatly preferred anti–Communist authoritarian regimes to the possibility of the Soviets penetrating the region through the openness allowed by democratic regimes.

Anastasio Somoza in Nicaragua, Efrain Rios Montt in Guatemala, Fulgencio Batista in Cuba, Rafael Leonidas Trujillo in Dominican Republic, Marcos Perez Jimenez in Venezuela, Gustavo Rojas Pinilla in Colombia, Manuel Odria in Peru or Alfredo Stroessner in Paraguay, were among the members of the International of the Sword. A sort of unofficial military lodge that supported each other's governments and presented a common front against the resurgence of democracy. Needless to say, that a concurrent fraternity of dislodged democrats, fighting against the military regimes in power, also emerged.

Many of these democrats would attain power the following decade. But in some instances, only for short periods, as military dictatorships, again under the blessing of Washington, would reappear. During the 1960s, 1970s and 1980s, they prevailed almost everywhere: Argentina (Juan Carlos Ongania, Roberto Levingston, Alejandro Lanusse, Jorge Videla, Roberto Viola, etc.); Brazil (Humberto Castelo, Artur Da Costa e Silva, Emilio Garrastazu Medici, Ernesto Geisel and Joao Figueiredo); Chile (Augusto Pinochet); Bolivia (Rene Barrientos, Alfredo Ovando, Hugo Banzer, Celso Torrelio, Guido Vildoso, etc.); Ecuador (Ramon Castro Jijon, Guillermo Rodriguez Lara, Alfredo Poveda, etc.); Uruguay (Civic–Military Junta); Peru (Francisco Morales Bermudez); Nicaragua (Anastasio Somoza Jr.); Paraguay (Alfredo Stroessner); Panama (Manuel Noriega); Honduras (Oswaldo Lopez Arellano, Juan Alberto Melgar Castro, Policarpio Paz Garcia, etc.); El Salvador (Revolutionary Government Junta); Guatemala (Efrain Rios Montt, Oscar Humberto Mejia). And so on.

The great majority of those regimes would have an extreme right political orientation and follow the National Security Doctrine. Very exceptionally some of them would be moderates with even three progressive governments in their ranks. The latter were the cases of Juan Velazco Alvarado in Peru, Omar Torrijos in Panama and Juan Jose Torres in Bolivia, during the 1970s.

The National Security Doctrine, followed by the majority, was responsible for the disappearance, torturing and murdering of hundreds of thousands of left wing citizens. According to historian and Columbia University Provost John Henry Coatsworth, the number of victims therein derived in Latin America, far surpassed that of the Soviet Union and the Eastern Bloc during the period 1960 to 1990.[5] Victims included leftists' union and peasant leaders, priests and nuns, students and teachers, intellectuals and suspected guerrillas.

Latin American army officers began to see themselves as the only sector of society capable of guaranteeing "national survival" against the existential threat of communism. Any decision taken by them under the realm of national security was not to be questioned. Those decisions were to be considered vital not only for the survival of society but also of Western and Christian values. Under such an assumption, the military broke up the structure of civil societies completely.

Latin American military personnel trained in the United States or at the School of the Americas at Fort Gulick, in the Panama Canal Zone, learned counterinsurgency or "special war" techniques. Moreover, they were also indoctrinated about the new role that they were called to play in defence of their countries and the "free world". Such a role aimed at confronting the internal enemies that could conquer societies from within. In Chile's President Augusto Pinochet's words:

> "Contemporary reality shows that Marxism is not only a doctrine intrinsically perverse. It is also a permanent form of aggression following the designs of the Soviet empire...This modern form of aggression

---

[5] Coatsworth, JH (Date?). The Cold War in Central America, 1975–1991. https://www.scribd.com/doc/109666536/The-Cold-War-in-Central-America-1975-1991-John-H-Coastsworth-Ch-10. Accessed 10/12/2016.

> generates a non-conventional war, were the foreign invasion of the territory is supplanted by the attempt of controlling the State from the inside".[6]

Given that this "camouflaged" internal aggressor could be anywhere, destroying the institutions behind which he could hide became a legitimate target within this non–conventional war. As Joseph Comblin put it:

> "The National Security Doctrine supplanted politics by a state of permanent war and general mobilization. For weak and unstable countries, as those of the developing world, such doctrine created havoc, as it destroyed the nation building process undertaken patiently for decades".[7]

Moreover, as in the case of the International of the Sword of the 1950s, these military regimes collaborated closely among themselves. Operation Condor, whose key members were the governments of Argentina, Chile, Uruguay, Paraguay, Bolivia and Brazil (with Ecuador and Peru joining later in peripheral roles), acted as a structured grouping whose aim was to eliminate common enemies. With governments acting as bands of thugs, the assassination or imprisonment of their own citizens, when found in any other of these countries, became common. Former heads of state, dissenting generals or left wing personalities, enjoying political asylum in any of such nations, were repeatedly targeted. Under such a state of paranoid delusion, all kinds of excesses became possible.

At a point, Mexico, Venezuela, Colombia and Costa Rica were the only countries of the region free from military regimes and, as such, safe havens for the exiled and the persecuted. This was, no doubt, one of the ghastliest periods in the history of Latin America. But, as in the case of exiled democrats during the 1950s, a new brotherhood of democrats would emerge from these trying times.

The increasingly unmanageable debt crisis of the end of the 1970s and beginning of the 1980s, became the major inducement for the Latin American military regimes abandonment of power. The debt crisis was

---

[6] Comblin, J (1977). *Le Pouvoir Militaire en Amerique Latine: L'idéologie de la Sécurité Nationale,* p.35. París: Jean-Pierre Delarge Editeur.
[7] ibid., p. 166.

like a hot potato in their hands, of which they wanted to get rid of. So much so that even amid Ronald Reagan's administration clear preference for military regimes, democracies began to flourish everywhere. By the mid–1980s most of the military regimes had devolved power to civilians by calling elections. The most resilient were the military regimes of Panama, Paraguay and Chile. Chile's regime, which had been the only one able to attain economic success, was the last to go. But in 1990 even Pinochet had to say goodbye.

So strong was this trend that, in 1991, the members of the Organization of American States (OAS), gathered in Santiago de Chile, committed to counter attempts to overthrow democratic governments in the Americas. Moreover, in 1992 OAS member states amended the Organization Charter to authorize that, upon a vote of two thirds of its members in the General Assembly, any government which had seized power by force could be suspended from the group.

The debt crisis hit Latin America very hard. According to Daniel Yergin and Joseph Stanislaw between 1975 and 1982 regional debt increased from US$45.2 billion to US$333 billion.[8] This increase had much to do with the snowball effect derived from interest rates over 22%. But while interest rates and the amount of the debt were speeding up, commodity prices were rapidly falling. Such an unexpected downturn in the price of natural resources gravely affected the capacity of Latin American governments to meet their debts. While the sources of currency income were dropping, external debt was spiralling out of control. By early 1980s both Argentina and Brazil had defaulted on their debts. For the army still in power it was time to go. In the case of Argentina, the disastrous Malvinas/Falklands War made the situation even more untenable.

From the Washington Consensus to the Tide to the Left

This period of extreme weakness combined with the appearance of a new economic paradigm: the neoliberal model. Just when Latin American governments were faced with the necessity of renegotiating their debts,

---

[8]Yergin D & Stanislaw, J (1998). *The Commanding Heights*, p.234. New York: Simon & Schuster.

and acquiring new loans to pay the old ones, they were confronted with this ideological juggernaut. With its negotiating strength reduced to its minimum, the region was faced with the premise of the Washington Consensus and the directives of its executive arm, the International Monetary Fund (IMF). With the IMF acting as a sort of international bankruptcy receiver, indebted countries renegotiating their debts had no other option than to accept its terms.

As a result, emerging democracies around the region had to align themselves with the Washington Consensus agenda, which resulted from the convergence of positions of a group of institutions based in Washington, chiefly the US Treasury Department, the World Bank and the IMF. Such an agenda included structural reforms such as privatization of public assets, trade liberalization, economic deregulation, fiscal discipline, fiscal reform, etc. These reforms imposed a huge burden on the citizenry, resulting in drastic austerity policies, increase in prices of goods and services, and contractions on jobs and social benefits.

These were not the most auspicious of circumstances for fresh and still shaky democracies. However, populations which had suffered, in some cases for decades, the hardships of authoritarian regimes, were willing to accept such costs in exchange for newly acquired political freedoms. Not surprisingly, then, the first social uprising against such structural adjustment policies came from Venezuela in 1989. Having been one of the few democracies of the region enjoying an oil export bonanza, until a few years earlier, this country was particularly ill prepared for the costs herein involved.

And, while after a few years the macroeconomic conditions ameliorated in several countries, economic growth was anaemic and social costs were enormous. In Steven Levitsky and Kenneth M. Roberts words:

> "By the late 1990s, however, the neoliberal consensus had begun to unravel. Although the free market model succeeded in controlling inflation, in much of the region it was plagued by anaemic growth, periodic financial crisis, and deepening social and economic inequalities".[9]

---

[9] Levitsky, S & Roberts, KM (2011). *The Resurgence of the Latin American Left,* p.3. Baltimore: The Johns Hopkins University Press.

Moreover, according to Greg Grandin:

> "...during the era of free market fundamentalism, the average per capita income stagnated at 0%. By the late seventies, 11% of Latin Americans could be considered as poverty-stricken...By 1996, the number of indigents rose to a third of its total population. That is, 165 million people. And by 2005, 221 million people lived below the poverty line, an increase of 20 million in just a decade".[10]

Not surprisingly, then, constituencies around the region began looking for left wing alternatives. The wave began in 1998 when Hugo Chavez, a former army officer who had led a failed military uprising six years earlier, was elected President of Venezuela. He was followed in rapid succession by Socialist Ricardo Lagos in Chile and Worker's Party leader Luiz Ignacio Lula da Silva in Brazil, both in 2002.

In 2003, it was the turn of left wing Peronist Nestor Kirchner, while in 2004 Alberto Tabare Vasquez from the Leftist Broad Front won in Uruguay. In 2005 Evo Morales of the Movement towards Socialism was elected as the first indigenous President of Bolivia. The year 2006 witness the triumph of Daniel Ortega from the Sandinista National Front in Nicaragua, left wing economist Rafael Correa in Ecuador, Socialist leader Michelle Bachelet in Chile and left wing politician Manuel Zelaya in Honduras.

Left wing Peronist Cristina Fernandez de Kirchner was elected President of Argentina in 2007. As the end of the decade approached, left wing Catholic Bishop Fernando Lugo was elected in Paraguay and Mauricio Funes from the Farabundo Marti National Liberation Front was elected in El Salvador. In 2010 Jose Mujica from the Leftist Broad Front was elected in Uruguay and in 2011 Worker's Party candidate Dilma Rousseff was elected in Brazil. In 2013 Hugo Chavez successor Nicolas Maduro was elected in Venezuela. At the same time, re–elections took place in Venezuela in 2000, 2006 and 2012; in Brazil in 2010 and 2014;

---

[10] Grandin, G (2006). *Empire's Workshop: Latin America, the United States, and the Rise of the New Imperialism*, p.198. New York: Metropolitan Books.

in Argentina in 2011; in Bolivia in 2009 and 2014; in Ecuador in 2009; Chile in 2014, Uruguay 2015 and in Nicaragua in 2011 and 2016.

Since the election in Argentina in 2015 of the centre–right candidate Mauricio Macri, a reversal process seems to be taking shape. With Mexico, Colombia and Peru having remained in the right hand side of the net, Macri's success, Dilma Rousseff impeachment and Lula Da Silva's judicial problems could turn the match around.

Spanish American political history, which since 1898 was followed by Brazil, moves in tides. Apart from the passing from oligarchic regimes to middle class controlled ones, which was more a tendency than a tidal, the region shows a synchronicity unknown to other parts of the world. The same kind of synchronicity is also present at the economic level, as we shall examine in Chapter 9.

Geography and Ethnicity

But beyond their commonalities, Hispanic Americans also show differences. Two of them turn out to be of particular relevance. The first are those which derive from the variety of latitudes, topography and climate. They determine a whole range of character traits. The second one emerges from the diverse racial mixtures or from the lack of them.

Hispanic America is a huge and varied region. Its countries coexist within different geographical contexts. This in turn translates into dissimilar attitudinal characteristics. From the permanent summer of the tropical nations to the four seasons of the austral ones; from the altitude of the mountainous areas with its lower temperatures to the sea level; from coastal areas to distant inland places where a physical sense of isolation prevails; from tropical jungle environments to deserts; Spanish America is indeed a complex geographical proposition where nature influences character.

Not surprisingly then, the introverted demeanour of Chileans or the extroverted nature of Venezuelans, the melancholic attitude of Bolivians or the joyful expressivity of Dominicans, the guarded attitude of Paraguayans or the open one of Cubans. And so on. Given the fact that few places on earth exhibit such geographical diversity, it must be assumed that Spanish Americans are also diverse.

But even within the same countries, variations in geography can translate into different patterns of behaviour. People from the coast would normally exhibit a more open nature than those coming from the high plateaus. Not surprisingly, for instance, people from the coasts in Venezuela and Colombia have more similarities between themselves than with their fellow citizens of the high plateaus.

But together with geography we also find ethnicity and by extension cultural identity. As the three original human components of Hispanic America brought with them different cultural traits, it is logical to assume that their mixture or lack of it produced different outcomes.

To begin with, the indigenous and black elements of society that mixed with the Spanish one, were highly heterogeneous in nature. Indeed, indigenous populations were extremely miscellaneous. In today's Mexico, we find 66 different indigenous people who speak between 72 and more than 100 languages. In Peru, there are 55 indigenous people and 40 different languages. In Guatemala, 23 different Indian languages are currently in use, whereas in Bolivia there are 36. Even in Venezuela, where the indigenous population only represents 2.2 per cent of the total, there are 44 different indigenous groups. Hence, when mixed with Spaniards, each combination produced particular cultural traits.

Something similar can be said about black ethnicity within the miscegenation process. Slaves came from a wide range of West African regions and tribes. Each with a distinct identity. Moreover, given the fact that their current cultures took shape in the Americas, by way of oral transmitted recollections, they tend to be profoundly heterogeneous in nature.

African traditions in Cuba are thus different from those in Venezuela or Colombia. Moreover, in Cuba itself we find different African religions, among them the Palo, the Santeria or the Abakua. Each of them with its own specificity. Dominican Republic, on the other hand, exhibits 21 religious divisions. And so on. There are of course basic elements to them all, as it is the case of an animistic sphere where spirits play a fundamental role. But beyond those common elements, every one of them follows different routes. Hence, here as well, particular combinations with Spaniards produced particular brands of cultural identity.

Consequently, while the Spanish ethnicity plays a centripetal role, the Indian and African ones play a centrifugal one. In gross brushstrokes, the

Indian personality tends to be reserved and suspicious with an introspective demeanour and a tangential approach to others. Nonetheless, numerous differences exist within this very general approach. A Mexican and a Peruvian Indian will be very different. That being the case, a Mexican or a Peruvian "mestizo" will only be linked through their common Spanish heritage.

Something similar could be said of the African American personality. Broadly, it tends to be spontaneous, extroverted and expressive, with a joyfulness for rhythm and a certain degree of haughtiness. But from this point onwards differences emerge from one place to the other. Thus, a Cuban or a Colombian of pure African descent will not share the same cultural identity. Their cultural commonalities pass by the Spanish link.

Three Hispanic Americas

But in addition to these centrifugal cultural forces in play, we find that Hispanic America is divided into three basic areas according to their ethnicity. There is a Spanish America of strong indigenous roots which, running down from Mexico and Guatemala, extends along the length of the basin of the Andean Pacific, penetrating Bolivia and Paraguay. African roots can also be found in this area but playing a minor role.

There is also a Hispanic America of deep African roots that starts in the Spanish–speaking islands of the Caribbean and extends towards Panama, Venezuela, the Colombian coasts and the Mexican state of Veracruz. Indigenous populations are also present there, but to a lesser extent. Needless to say, that white populations are present both in this area and in the previous one, varying in numbers according to the countries.

Nonetheless, there is a mostly white area located in the Southern Cone of South America and in the Central American country of Costa Rica. Indigenous and African roots are negligible there. More importantly is the presence in Argentina and Uruguay of a huge percentage of people with Italian roots, competing with the Spanish heritage predominance.

Each of these three areas has a cohesive cultural stance. Even if important differences exist inside each of them, very particularly in the first two, they are culturally closer among themselves than in relation to the others. Hence Venezuelans, coastal Colombians, Cubans, Panamanians or

Dominicans will have larger affinities within their area than with Bolivians or Peruvians where the indigenous presence is very important, or with mostly whites Uruguayans or Argentinians. Argentinians and Uruguayans, on the other hand, will share many things in common while finding greater distance in relation to Caribbean or High Plateau Andean nations.

The countries of those areas give different connotations to the phenomenon of miscegenation and to their non–European roots. Some look at it favourably and give proper recognition to its ethnic diversity, while others see it with pejorative eyes. This requires some background.

During the 19th century, the controlling white elites shared a highly negative view about the so called "castas". These included, as previously mentioned, mixed blood populations and pure Indian or African ones. Such perceptions began to change for the first time with the success of the Mexican Revolution and the militant activity of Jose de Vasconcelos, the Minister of Culture. Vasconcelos was responsible for bringing miscegenation at the forefront of Mexican values. It was then, as Carlos Fuentes said, that the country learnt to face the totality of its past, being able to deal with its inherited contradictions. Moreover, the struggles of Mexico's revolutionary Emiliano Zapata to win back the Indian peasantry's ancestral communal lands, gave impetus to the vindication of Indian rights all around the region.

In the first decades of the 20th century the so called "indigenista" movement took roots in Peru, thanks to the action of intellectuals such as Manuel Gonzalez Prada, Juan Carlos Mariategui and Victor Raul Haya de la Torre. Such movement regarded the Indian culture as the source of true national values. Haya de la Torre was as well a gifted politician who founded the most influential party of 20th century Peru: APRA. In the beginning, the party fought for a continent wide "Indo–America" alliance against US imperialism. This generated, as in the case of Zapata's fights, a validation of the indigenous populations in Spanish America.

Around the same period a similar validation process took place in Cuba. This time in relation to the African–American population. Well known novelist and musicologist Alejo Carpentier began asserting the importance of African roots in Caribbean culture, while the poet Nicolas Guillen gave rise to a "black" poetic movement in the Caribbean. Famous writers such as the Venezuelan Romulo Gallegos or the Ecuadorian Adalberto Ortiz also wrote about Negro themes.

Currently, much of the Spanish American countries recognize miscegenation as a fundamental force of their national identities. Moreover, Indian and African identities are also given their proper value, with several constitutions around the region placing indigenous languages at the same standing as Spanish. Guatemala, for instance, has 24 official languages of which Spanish is just one. Bolivia recognizes 37 official languages, one of which is Spanish. Even Venezuela, with a relatively tiny Indian population, has 39 indigenous languages sharing with Spanish the status of official ones. Moreover, a whole chapter of Venezuela's Constitution is dedicated to the rights of indigenous peoples.

While the above is the case for the majority, Argentina still holds a Eurocentric vision in which "whiteness" remains a fundamental value. Two considerations are of relevance here. The first concerns the ambitious immigration process that took place at the end of the 19th century and beginning of the 20th changing the face of the nation. According to Carlos Fuentes, in 1869 Argentina had a population of two million inhabitants, but between 1880 and 1905, three million European immigrants arrived in the country.[11] Indian and Negro roots, which were never fundamental, were flooded into numeric irrelevance as a result.

The second consideration is that Argentina underwent something like the US' "Conquest of the West", which in this case was called the "Conquest of the Desert". This took shape under the stewardship of General Julio Argentino Roca, twice President of the country. In the 1870s, he launched a military campaign with the aim of establishing dominance over the Patagonia region, at the time inhabited by indigenous populations. In the process, Argentinian troops killed or displaced thousands of Indians. Such displacement created the conditions for the arrival of European settlers, who developed the land for agriculture and turned it into a breadbasket. Thanks to those lands, Argentina became an agricultural powerhouse. This "Conquest", though, has been labelled as genocide by some revisionist historians.

[11] Fuentes, *op. cit*, p. 309.

Argentina's narrative in this matter is not very dissimilar to that of the United States. Indeed, it places value in the entrepreneurial qualities that built the country and not, as the majority in the region does, in the historical debt towards the excluded populations. In that sense, there is a gap between the prevailing perceptions of both sides.

As can be seen, Hispanic America has convergent and divergent elements between its different components. As such it cannot be considered as a homogeneous region. Nonetheless, it can claim to be a community within a unitary vision of the multiple. A region where Simon Bolivar's notion of "America as the fatherland" or Jose Marti's concept of "Our America", are very strong. The solidarity shown between its members is rarely seen in other parts of the world. Even the Argentinians, at times the region's most reluctant members, have felt such solidarity in moments of need. That was the case during the Malvinas/Falklands War or when confronting some of its economic crises.

Not surprisingly, when seen from abroad it is the vision of the whole that comes into view. That explains why in the United States all peoples fall under the general category of Hispanics or Latinos, while in Spain they all become Sudacas. Such a sense of community projects itself outside statehood boundaries, and includes the millions of Latinos that currently live in the United States. They are very much part of the same people as shown by their continuous efforts to preserve their cultural heritage. That includes of course Puerto Rico and Puerto Ricans, who were never able to attain an independent nationality but who are a natural component of Hispanic America.

CHAPTER 5

WHERE DO LATIN AMERICANS BELONG?

In his seminal book *The Clash of Civilizations and the Remaking of World Order*, Samuel P. Huntington makes a distinction between a "Latin American Civilization" and Western Civilization. The Western being circumscribed, according to him, to Europe, English speaking North America and some countries of English settlement such as Australia and New Zealand. In his words:

> "Latin America, however, has a distinct identity which differentiates it from the West. Although an offspring of European civilization, Latin America has evolved along very different path from Europe and North America...The West, then, includes Europe, North America, plus other European settler countries such as Australia and New Zealand".[1]

Behind the courtesy of granting Latin Americans their own civilization, lie ancestral prejudices. American political scientist Howard J. Wiarda explains such prejudices as follows:

> "These attitudes of condescending superiority have deep roots. They derive, in part, from historical prejudices held by Protestant and

[1]Huntington, SP (1996). *The Clash of Civilizations and the Remaking of World Order*, p.46. New York: Simon & Schuster.

> Anglo–axon civilization towards the essence of a Catholic, Latin and even inquisitorial culture. In part, they also derive from the belief, widely held in the United States, that Latin America and its leaders have low marks for talent and accomplishment”.[2]

The Black Legend

As explained by Wiarda those prejudices transcend Latin America and attain the Iberian world and, in particular, Spain. A quote by Kenneth Clark in another seminal book, *Civilisation*, gives us a sense of its extent. When explaining why Spain had been excluded from his tale of Western civilization he says:

> “…but when one asks what Spain has done to enlarge the human mind and pull mankind a few steps up the hill, the answer is less clear. *Don Quixote*, the Great Saints, the Jesuits in South America? Otherwise she has simply remained Spain”.[3]

To say that about a country that has produced Trajan, Hadrian and Seneca; Greco, Velasquez and Goya; Miro, Gris, Dali and Picasso; Quevedo, Lope de Vega and Calderon de la Barca; Perez Galdos and Garcia Lorca; Unamuno and Ortega y Gasset; Suarez, Victoria and de las Casas; Vives, Moratin, Jovellanos or Feijoo; Ramon y Cajal and Marañon, Albeniz, Falla, Granados and Rodrigo, implies ignorance or outrageous bias. These are universally known names, to which many others could be added, of those who have advanced the course of civilization in a very substantial way.

Clark's prejudices respond to an old tradition that goes back to the 16th century when the “Black Legend” against Spain began taking shape. According to it, inquisition, intolerance and counter reform were the three main traits of the country. It is a vision linked to the mighty opposition of

[2]Hardy, AT (2002). *The Age of Villages: The Small Village vs. the Global Village*, pp. 421–422. Bogotá: Villegas Editores

[3]Clark, K (1969). *Civilisation*, p. xvii. New York: Harper & Row Publishers.

Spain's Charles V against religious reforms in Germany, England and other parts of Europe. Or of his son Phillip II's feud with England's Elizabeth II or his bloody crushing of dissenters in the present day Netherlands.

The strong preconceptions associated to this tradition, which were fed as well by the description of the cruelties performed by the Spaniards in the New World, survive to our day. This not only attains Spain but, by extension, its offspring in the Americas. Needless to say, that there was much more than a grain of truth in the Black Legend. However, the blunt denial of everything that Spain has done for the cause of civilization, as exemplified by Kenneth Clark's position, defies all standards of objectivity.

All that aside, however, Huntington touched a sore point of debate which Latin American themselves have not been able to resolve: Are they part of Western Civilization or not?

Even well–known Mexican intellectual Leopoldo Zea speaks of two Americas: The Iberian and the Western. Although he recognizes that both derive from Europe, he does not equate them. In his words:

> "The two Americas, the Iberian and the Western one, have their origin in European culture (…) While one put its faith in what it was, the other did it in what it hoped to be. Two different ways of being in these two Americas -the Iberian and the Anglo–Saxon or Western".[4]

By extension, the above assertion assumes that the Iberian Peninsula is not part of Western Civilization. An assertion believed by many for whom Spain, and to a lesser extent Portugal, do not fully belong to the West. More than a century ago Anatole France coined a phrase that has gone a long way: "Europe begins behind the Pyrenees". In other words, the Iberian Peninsula would not be considered properly European.

Arguments in that direction insist that two movements which were responsible for some of the essential features of Western thought — the Renaissance and the 18th century Enlightenment — scarcely reached them. Not surprisingly, this line of thought has firmly permeated Latin American intellectuals, generating important doubts as to the real belonging of their civilizational roots.

---

[4]Zea, L., pp. 18, 19.

The thesis about the Renaissance and the Enlightenment not reaching the Iberian Peninsula, is certainly truer with respect to Spain than to Portugal. Portugal experienced a distinct form of Renaissance, separated from those experienced by other European countries, where reinforcing influences prevailed. Portugal had an autonomous Renaissance which, even if poorly connected to that of the Italian, the French or the English, was sustained by its Age of Discovery. Indeed, at a time when Portugal was reaching India and East Asia, its perception of the world was widened and so were its pockets. This resulted in its own arts, humanities and science flourishing.

Something similar can be said about the arrival of Enlightenment to Portugal. Such movement is identified with the overbearing figure of the Marquis de Pombal, who imposed it upon the country, but in his very particular terms. Enlightenment in Portugal consisted primarily in useful tools for enhancing autocracy, diminishing the power of nobility and the clergy, intensifying book censorship, supressing criticism and consolidating personal control. It was certainly not the Enlightenment of Voltaire and the French Encyclopaedists, even though it brought wide modernizing reforms both to the country and to Brazil. As a result, it can be argued that Portugal experienced both Renaissance and Enlightenment, but it did so on its own terms.

The case of Spain was different. Referring to the Renaissance issue, Mark Williams says:

> "Humanism and other aspects of the Renaissance made some tentative inroads into the Spain of Carlos V. Erasmus of Rotterdam, the leading humanist, actually served as a royal counsellor until he became identified with heresy. Humanist scholars were later exiled and their works appeared on the first *Index* of prohibited books. After opening briefly, the window onto Renaissance Europe was closing. Under Carlos's successor it would be slammed shut".[5]

Spain, though, could have evolved in a very different direction. Al–Andalus, as the Iberian Peninsula was called under the Moors, had been a beacon of light amid the obscurantism of Medieval Europe. Beauty,

[5]Williams, *op. cit.*, p. 109.

scientific knowledge and reason flourished there. Moreover, its libraries were not only among the largest in the world, but had preserved the texts of European classical antiquity. The fusion between Arab and Jew scientific, philosophical and financial advancements, plus the ancient texts therein preserved, could have been the main source of the European Renaissance.

It would have been difficult for Portugal to benefit from it, as its liberation from the Moors came too early. Spain, though, defeated the last Moor bastion when Renaissance was flourishing in other parts of Europe. Referring to that bastion, Granada, Elmer Bendiner said: "In its latter days the city had been made glorious by refuge artists, poets, architects, teachers, engineers, musicians".[6] Had Spain retained and absorbed what Al–Andalus had to offer, it could have become a fundamental focal point of the ongoing European revolution.

Moreover, the Spaniards could have opened their minds to the rich civilizations of the New World that they encountered. This would have allowed them to incorporate into their cultural heap all the important knowledge that these civilizations possessed. Especially so in areas such as astronomy and mathematics. The synergy resulting from the combination and incorporation of gigantic and diversified sources of knowledge, as those represented by the Arabs, the Jews and the New World's civilizations, would have had a game changing effect over the history of Spain.

However, after Ferdinand and Isabella defeated the Moors, the Spaniards chose to reject and eliminate everything that did not conform to their narrow vision of the world. Spain, indeed, sacrificed at the altar of religious fundamentalism all the sparks of knowledge, beauty, reason and science that they encountered. In doing so, they not only erased their opportunity of leading the Renaissance movement, but placed themselves on the opposite shore of this movement.

As for Enlightenment in Spain, Williams expresses the following:

> "Standing squarely in opposition to 'enlightened' progress was the Catholic Church and its dreaded Inquisition, living symbol of how far out of step Spain remained…Yet Enlightenment did make some inroads in Spain. However, the intellectual ferment, affected only a tiny minority.

---

[6]Bendiner, E (1995). *The Rise and Fall of Paradise: When Arabs and Jews Built a Kingdom in Spain*, p. 239. New York: Barnes & Noble Books.

> Devotion to the Catholic religion remained the strongest force in Spain, especially among superstitious commoners".[7]

Indeed, figures such as Jovellanos, Feijoo or Floridablanca, during Charles III's reign, tried to the best of their ample abilities to project European modernity upon Spain. Nonetheless, opposition from the Church and the common people ended up being overwhelming. Hence, their reforms and initiatives skim the surface of the country without penetrating it. In any case, upon Charles III's death such modernizing efforts died as well.

On the Fringes of the Fringe

Arturo Uslar Pietri confronted this conundrum about the Iberian world identity, and essentially about that of Spain, following the arguments of Carlos Fuentes. According to such reasoning the Iberian Peninsula remained "eccentric" (far from the centre) in relation to the nucleuses of Western Civilization, as symbolized by countries such as France or England. This not only has a cultural meaning but a geographic one as well, as Portugal and Spain represent the most extreme points of the European landmass. Hence, these countries have many things in common with Russia, another "eccentric" nation who neither had a Renaissance Italian style or an Enlightenment French style.[8]

That being the case we find that the starting point of Latin American cultural heritage is a fringe model, as both Spain and Portugal were "eccentric" countries. But then, upon arrival to the Americas, Iberians did not conform a settler's society as the English did in North America, Australia or New Zealand. Much to the contrary, they mixed with indigenous and African elements given rise to an acculturated society. In other words, Latin America represents a sort of fringe version of the Iberian fringe model itself. Not surprisingly then, Latin Americans harbour so many doubts in relation to their own identity.

---

[7] Williams, *op. cit.*, pp. 145–46.

[8] Pietri, AU (1981). *Fantasmas de dos mundos*. Barcelona: Seix Barral.

These "existential" doubts are substantially greater in relation to Spanish Americans than to Brazilians. This has several explanations. To begin with, as seen, Portugal was a more open society. While Spain tried systematically to impose its own narrow views upon others, Portugal enlarged its mindset because of its contact with different societies. But more importantly, for Spanish Americans independence meant not only the beheading of the established order but also a breach with its own past. For Brazilians, it just represented a new step within an evolutionary process in which the past was never questioned.

In the antechamber of the office of the Brazilian Minister of Foreign Affairs hangs a portrait of John VI, the Portuguese King who moved the court to Rio de Janeiro. It would be unthinkable that a portrait of Spain's Ferdinand VII would be hung on any official place of Hispanic America. Similarly, the date of the foundation of the Brazilian Navy is 1808, that is, 14 years before the independence of the country. The reason being that such was the year in which the Portuguese Navy moved to Brazil. Thus, when tracing the history of the Brazilian Navy, it is necessary to go back in time several centuries and follow the tale of the Portuguese one. Examples like these are common in Brazil and unimaginable in Spanish America.

In other words, Brazil is at peace with its past, which certainly is not the case of Hispanic America. In relation to Brazilians, Leopoldo Zea says:

> "They were not confronted, as the leaders of mental emancipation in Spanish America were, with the obstacle of their past. They did not see in their Portuguese inheritance what Hispanic Americans saw in their Spanish one. They never felt the need, as the Hispanic Americans did, to cut, to breach, with their colonial past. Much to the contrary they saw in the past a good instrument for assimilating and incorporating new options for a desirable future".[9]

In other words, they not only had no quarrel with their past but saw it as a useful guidance for building the future.

---

[9]Zea, L. *op. cit.*, p. 203.

Not surprisingly then, upon independence Eclecticism would become the prevailing social philosophy in Brazil. This school of thought aims at conciliating the extremes, searching for the middle ground. Again, in Zea's words:

> "Eclecticism as a doctrine of conciliation served perfectly well to the equally conciliatory spirit of Brazilians. Without leaps into the dark, they took all they could from their colonial past and tried to adapt it into the new forms of political, social and economic organization that the country required".[10]

With the fall of the Brazilian Empire another school of thought would replace Eclecticism. Indeed, Positivism was in vogue in the Western World and took its rightful place in Brazil as well. Nonetheless, while in Spanish America this new philosophy acquired radical tones, as we shall see, in Brazil it was just seen as a useful instrument for dealing more appropriately with the new emerging social and political situation. As in the case of Eclecticism, this knew philosophy aimed at serving reality without disturbing order.

Soul–Searching

Spanish Americans were on very different ground. In Uslar Pietri's words:

> "If something could characterize Hispanic Americans is this soul–searching attitude of continuously asking themselves: Who am I? Where do I belong? This doubt, this sort of ontological anguish, has conditioned their position in the world...Spanish Americans are continuously testing the floor where they stand, questioning it, rediscovering it". [11]

Nobody has expressed better this Hispanic American sense of identity anguish, than Literature Nobel Laureate Octavio Paz. In his book *The*

---

[10]*Ibid.*, p. 207.

[11]Pietri, AU (1982). *Fachas, Fechas y FiChas,* pp. 181–182. Caracas: Editorial Ateneo de Caracas.

Labyrinth of Solitude he describes how the Mexican, lost in the labyrinth of its confused identity, is condemned to solitude. In his words:

> "The Mexican defines himself in terms of rupture and denial. And, at the same time, as expression of a willingness to overcome this sense of exile. In sum as a vivid manifestation of solitude, both historical and personal".[12]

After attaining independence, three main interpretations of the colonial past and its meaning emerged in Spanish America. The first was that of the Conservatives. They wanted everything to remain as it had been before insurgence, with the only difference that the foreign overlords were gone. The second was represented by the Liberals, and by extension to them by the Positivists. For the Liberals–Positivists it was necessary to erase the colonial past and all traces of Spain. The third, was provided by a group of Venezuelan thinkers, and followed, later, by other distinguished Hispanic American figures. This aimed at moulding a future with the inherited social and human clay.

Conservatives were not on the best of standings. Their formula of everything remaining equal proved to be unsustainable after they had remained in power for a couple of decades. Like in the case of old age dementia, when people go back to a childhood surrounded by familiar faces and places that don't exist anymore, theirs was an unattainable quest. With raw force trying to fill the void of lost monarchical legitimacy, it was impossible to artificially sustain in the long term a crumbled model.

From the mid-19th century onwards, and except for Chile which could create a durable Conservative structure, regimes ascribed to this line of thought were out of the game. In Mexico, though, they tried to provide the missing link: monarchical legitimacy. Through the experiment of a royal blooded foreigner as Emperor, Mexican conservatives managed to obtain a few additional years of respite before leaving the scene permanently.

The idea of erasing the colonial past and with it old traces of Hispanicism, had a larger longevity. It began with a first wave of Liberals, immediately after independence. However, in a few years, theirs would become a losing

---

[12] Paz, O (1992). *The Labyrinth of Solitude*, p. 36. México: Fondo de Cultura Económica.

proposition, as Conservatives took control of the political stage until around the 1850s. At this point, a second wave of Liberals attained power, and remained there until superseded by the Positivists around the 1880s.

Positivists not only kept alive the idea of erasing the colonial past and all traces of Spain, but were even more radical than the Liberals in this purpose. As a result, many of the old Liberals simply changed hats and transformed themselves into Positivists. Famous names like Domingo Faustino Sarmiento, Juan Bautista Alberdi, Esteban Echeverria or Jose Victorino Lastarria, were among them. This power ideology or philosophy, as it was both, remained in place until the 20th century was well advanced. In some countries like Mexico it disappeared together with the "Porfiriato" in 1911, while in others like Venezuela its representatives preserved their influence until 1937.

The third approach, which began in Venezuela, accepted as a given fact the Hispanic American baggage: its colonial past, its mixed blood and its acculturation. But while the Conservatives wanted everything to remain as it had been, this line of thought aimed at building a new society. A new society where the answers would not be copied from abroad, but created in accordance to surrounding realities. Simon Bolivar, man of action and ideas, and his two teachers Simon Rodriguez and Andres Bello, the three of them Venezuelans, were the first to define this route. In the short term, unfortunately, theirs was a losing proposition. Sandwiched between Conservatives and Liberals, and their extreme views, there was no room for this option. Later in time, nonetheless, this third way would prove to be the most successful one. Names like Jose Marti, Jose Enrique Rodo or Jose de Vasconcelos would follow this direction.

With Conservatives having little to propose, and hence proving to be short–lived, the big debate in the long run would be between the other two approaches. On the one hand, those asserting to discard their Spanish heritage and import political and societal models from "modern" Europe and North America. On the other, those aiming at institutional and societal building within a clear Hispanic American specificity.

The Big Debate

The first of these two propositions felt ashamed of the Hispanic roots and of all which had been bestowed by way of Spanish societal and cultural heritage. Such heritage was seen, indeed, as a heavyweight, susceptible of jeopardizing Latin America's viability as an organized, educated and well–structured society. Hence, divesting from this unsolicited burden and importing models from more appropriated places became the only option.

According to Argentinian Esteban Echeverria:

> "We are independent but we are not free; the arms of Spain no longer oppress us, but her traditions weigh us down...The social emancipation of Latin America can only be achieved by repudiating the heritage bequeathed by Spain and by embracing the liberal heritage of France and Britain".[13]

As seen in Chapter 1, this attitude proved fundamental in accepting the term Latin America, notwithstanding its imperialist origin.

Later, under the Positivists, this line of thinking would evolve in the direction of searching for massive European immigration, as a way of "cleaning" the stigma of mixed–blood populations. Opening the floodgates of white blood would complement the importing of institutions and models. In Domingo Faustino Sarmiento's words:

> "We need to mix with the population of more advanced countries than ours, so that they transmit to us their arts, their industries, their activity and their attitude towards work".[14]

Argentinian Jose Ingenieros was even blunter when expressing:

> "There are clear elements which allow us to rejoice with the advent of an Argentinian white race that will allow us to erase the inferiority stigma with which Europeans associate South America".[15]

In another line of his work Ingenieros wrote:

> "In the new Argentina...millions of whites will read about the tales of an extinguished indigenous race or about the mixed–blooded gauchos, which retarded the formation of a white race".[16]

---

[13] Veliz, C p. 16.

[14] Zea, *op. cit.*, p. 149.

[15] *Ibid.*, p. 324.

[16] *Ibid.*

It must be added, though, that Mexican Positivism never subscribed the massive immigration thesis, just aiming at creating through education the "yanquees of the south".

Referring to this line of thought, Leopoldo Zea says:

> "The Spanish American discovered, while analysing himself, that he was full of contradictions. Feeling incapable of realizing a synthesis between these contradictory traits, he opted for the easiest solution: amputation. He chose one of the traits of his character and tried to definitively cut with the other (...) This way the Spanish American attempted the almost impossible task of amputating his past".[17]

To be able to build a future the Spanish American renounced his past. In the end, he had no past, his present had not yet been realized and all his hopes were pending on a future that might never materialize. Hence, while the Conservatives had tried to cling to a past that no longer existed, the Liberal–Positivists were hanging on to a future that might never come to be.

The other approach seemed much more realistic. It began with Simon Bolivar's attempt to build new republics. In John Lynch's words:

> "Laws, remarked Montesquieu, should be suited to the people for whom they are made. Rousseau maintained even more explicitly that constitutions must take account of national character. Bolivar was no less insistent: constitutions must conform to the environment, character, history and resources of the people. 'This is the code we must consult, not the code of Washington'. Bolivar still thought something corresponding to Spanish American reality, not a North American imitation".[18]

Bolivar emphasized the need to give a factual framework to Spanish American institutions and societies, rooting them in their own realities. Referring to Bolivar's efforts, Carlos Fuentes says:

> "How to govern ourselves after winning independence. It can be said that the Liberator exhausted his soul trying to find an answer to that

[17] *Ibid.*, pp. 56–57.

[18] Lynch, D (2007). *Simón Bolívar: A Life,* p. 120. Conneticut: Yale University Press.

> question...Bolivar tried to avoid the extremes that would overwhelm Spanish America all along the nineteenth century and part of the twentieth. Tyranny or anarchy? 'Do not aim at what is impossible to attain, because in our quest for liberty we may fall into tyranny. Absolute liberty always leads to absolute power and among these two extremes is social liberty'. In order to find this equilibrium, Bolivar proposed a 'clever despotism', a strong executive power able to impose juridical equality there where racial inequality prevailed. Bolivar warned against an 'aristocracy of rank, employment and fortune' that while 'referring to liberty and guarantee' it would just be for themselves and not for the people. They want freedom in order to elevate themselves but not for levelling with members of lower classes'...He is a disciple of Montesquieu in his insistence that institutions have to be adapted to culture".[19]

Two other relevant Venezuelans, which happened to be Bolivar's teachers in his youth, also followed this direction. Their names were Simon Rodriguez and Andres Bello. According to the first of them, Spanish America was in no way inferior to Europe or the United States and should avoid imitating models that did not correspond to its own realities. These were different from those of other regions, thus making of imported institutions imperfect instruments to solve very specific problems. Spanish America had the obligation of being "original", which implied creatively designing institutions that fitted its own circumstances. But that implied beginning by knowing and understanding what those circumstances were. For him, as in the case of Bolivar, education was the fundamental tool to overcome the inherited limitations.

Andres Bello, the greatest humanist of the Spanish–speaking world during the first half of the 19th century, talks about the "cultural autonomy of Spanish America", inviting the new generations to learn to think independently. From Europe, they should only imitate their capacity to study and learn from its own realities. He cautions against the dangers of intellectual obsequiousness in relation to Europe, which would only lead to their lack of respect for Hispanic America. He finds merit in the region's past which, notwithstanding excesses and mistakes, allows for

[19]Fuentes, C p. 272.

the search of a synthesis. He insists that Spanish Americans are in full capacity to make important contributions in natural sciences, in politics, in literature, and in other fields, all of which would be dependant from their drinking on their own sources and experimenting on their own realities.

As previously mentioned, these ideas would not be listened to during the greater part of the 19th century. Notwithstanding the eminence of their proposers, this was a time of extremes. Approaching the end of the century, though, the great figure of Jose Marti, Cuba's founding father, added his name to this list. He cautioned that it was not with a decree copied from Hamilton, or with a phrase of Sieyes, that the problems of the region would be solved. He talked about the absurdity of wanting to erase the Indian or the Negro, as if that was possible.

> "A government has to be born from a country. The spirit of a government has to be that of its country. The way of governing has to be in tune with the nature of the country. A government is only an instrument of equilibrium of the natural elements of a country".[20]

For him, the strength of Hispanic America had to come from its realities, and those realities were inevitably linked to the past.

As mentioned in the previous chapter, Uruguayan intellectual Jose Enrique Rodo published an immensely influential book entitled *Ariel* in 1900. From that moment onwards, the reign of Positivists in Latin America was subjected to a powerful intellectual counterbalance. Rodo vindicates Latin American culture and identity, while attacking the United States. He castigated those in the region (namely the Positivists), who blindly subscribed to the utilitarian gospel of the United States, while ignoring the spiritual richness of their own identity. In his own words:

> "I don't see the glory, or for the matter the purpose, of denaturalizing the character of a people — its natural genius — in order to impose upon them an affinity with an alien model, to which they are willing to

---

[20]Zea, *op. cit.*, p. 454.

sacrifice the originality of its own spirit, naively believing that such affinity can be attained through imitation".[21]

A couple of decades later another important voice would be included within this line of thinking: Jose de Vasconcelos. He was the architect of the Cultural Revolution that took shape within the triumphant Mexican Revolution. He also attacked those in the region who were ashamed of their own cultural roots. How laughable it must be for Europeans and North Americans, he reasoned, this spectacle of shameless imitating their own models. His book *The Cosmic Race* also attained immense influence around Latin America.

At this point in time, Positivism was within its last gasps throughout the region. The empowering of an autonomous culture, in tune with the past, was spreading rapidly. Vasconcelos saw in the Latin American capacity to assimilate different races and cultures — by melting them — the best way to attain lineage in history. His own concept of "race", which is the opposite of racism, is based on the values of miscegenation and acculturation. Spanish America, according to his reasoning, had given birth to a "cosmic race" because it had produced a synthesis race.

But even if the long march of Liberals and Positivist was about to end, the ravages that they had caused in the cultural life of the region remained. A strong modernist movement, taking hold in Latin America at the time, expressed well all the confusion caused by these two movements. Referring to such confusion, Edwin Williamson expressed:

> "But for Latin Americans the disorientation was more profound: their Iberian heritage had been largely discredited by liberal intellectuals and the pre–Columbian cultures were too remote to be meaningful. In terms of high culture, Latin America seemed to exist in a void — cut off from a serviceable past yet threatened by a future outside its control. For this reason its reception of the techniques and themes of modernism — which tended to emphasize rupture, discontinuity and alienation — could not be purely imitative: these were soon transformed into original explorations of a unique situation — a state of isolation in time present,

[21] *Ibid.*, p. 426.

> from where there were no clear avenues back to the past nor forwards into the future. Indeed the great theme of the Latin American artist of the twentieth century was to be the condition of orphanhood, and the resultant search for ways out of what the Mexican poet Octavio Paz famously called 'the labyrinth of solitude'".[22]

At the end of the day the only thing that remains tangible is that no other people on earth seem to have written so many pages about their own identity. As Arturo Uslar Pietri says:

> "Why keep asking who we are? That is a question that Africans, Asians or North Americans do not pose to themselves — at least not with the degree of anguish that we do. They all seem to be much more secure about their belonging…At least, I may say, this existential doubt seems to be a proof of originality".[23]

The Main Question

But after so many words written here as well about the subject of identity, the main question remains unanswered: Are Latin Americans part of Western Civilization? A brief background is in order before providing an answer. Such a civilization was the result of the interweaving between the Classical tradition — meaning Greek and Roman — and the Judeo–Christian world. Other elements (like Renaissance and Enlightenment, by instance) were also added, but these remained the central ones.

There were several instances in which the emergence of such a civilization could have been aborted or, once in existence, could have simply disappeared. The first came with the invasion of Greece by the Persians. In Tom Holland's words:

> "As subjects of a foreign king, the Athenians would never have had the opportunity to develop their unique democratic culture. Much that made Greek civilisation distinctive would have been aborted. The legacy

[22] Williamson, E, p. 515.

[23] Pietri (1982), *op. cit.*, p. 182.

inherited by Rome and passed on to modern Europe would have been immeasurably impoverished. Not only would the West have lost its first struggle for independence and survival, but it is unlikely, had the Greeks succumbed to Xerxe's invasion, that there would ever have been such an entity as 'the West' at all".[24]

But the Roman part of the story could have been aborted as well if instead of a "Carthago delenda est", there would have been a "Rome delenda est". That is, if instead of Rome prevailing upon Carthage in the Punic Wars, the opposite had happened, as it closely did. Meaning a similar destruction but in the opposite direction. In such case there would have never been a Classical tradition.

The Jews might have never returned from their imprisonment in Babylon, in the same way in which Christianity might have never become what it did, if Saint Paul had not converted into this new religion. Nor would Christianity and the Roman Empire have got together, if Emperor Constantine had not prevailed in the struggles and civil war that took place within the so called Roman Tetrarchy.

Tons of so–called "contrafactual history" could be written in relation to this subject, where other "plausible worlds" could have emerged.[25] In the end, though, a very particular mixture of traditions and knowledge, which were able to survive against all odds, became the essence of Western Civilization.

What are the entitlements of Latin Americans in relation to such heritage? Arturo Uslar Pietri provides the answer:

"Colonization was a process of incorporation unto the Western values. Family, home, urbanization, social relation, the situation of women and children, came to us by way of the Church and the Law of the Indies, directly from Roman law by wfay of the Castilian Statutory Code of the 'Siete Partidas'. The concept of law, of the State, of crime and punishment,

[24]Holland, T (2005). *Persian Fire: The First World Empire and the Battle for the West*, p.xvii. London: Little, Brown.

[25]In relation to "contrafactual history" see Hawthorn, G (1993). *Plausible Worlds: Possibility and Understanding in History and Social Sciences.* Cambridge: Cambridge University Press.

of property, came to us in a straight line that originated in the Justinian Code. We do not have any other legal base, nor do we have any other conception of the human being and its dignity. During five centuries we have been submitted to Western culture, which is not only ours but also the only one we have. We certainly belong to it, but in our own way. We have a Latin American way of being Westerners".[26]

But, what can it mean a Latin American way of being Westerners? To begin with it must be remembered that Latin America is an acculturated society, which by extension should entail that it has an acculturated identity. However, even if powerful influences moved in every direction within this process of acculturation, not all of its three original components contributed in equal measure to the final product. Within this mix, the Indigenous and Negro cultural heritage had to submit to the cultural predominance of the Iberians. The latter remained the undisputed guiding force within the mix, determining language, religion, law, family values and architectural traditions. In other words, a Roman–Christian heritage.

Latin America's culture is Roman Catholic, Latin, Scholastic and Thomist. Meaning, a group of the fundamental traits of Western Civilization. Even accepting the deficiencies of Spain and Portugal as full members of such civilization, and adding to it the acculturation process that took place in the New World, Latin Americans are still Westerners. Indeed, Iberian Americans have retained sufficient elements within their culture to be considered part of the Western World.

Samuel P. Huntington implies in his *Clash of Civilizations and the Remaking of the World Order* that the fact of not having subscribed to the Reform of the Church, that is, not being Protestants, distances Latin America form Western Civilization. That is precisely the meaning of his saying that Latin America is becoming more Westernised because of the penetration in the region of the evangelical churches. If the aforementioned was the case, what then of the French, or the Italians, or the Austrians or the southern Germans, or the Wallon Belgians, or the French or Italian Swiss, all of which are Catholics? Are they less Western than the British, or the Swedes, or the Danish or the northern Germans? Prejudices apart, religion cannot be an element of distinction.

---

[26]Pietri (1995), *op. cit.*, p. 278.

The Latin American Periphery

Latin Americans, however, are on the periphery of Western Civilization, as explained earlier. They are an acculturated society with a clearly dominant Roman–Christian set of values which coexist, sometimes peacefully, sometimes wistfully, and even belligerently, with the values of its other cultural identities.

As such, even if they are within the perimeter of Western civilization, their location lies very close to the walls that encapsulate this world. Their neighbourhood borders the exit gates of such civilization. In the past, Liberals and Positivists felt ashamed of this "poor" zip code and aspired to imitate ritzier downtown neighbours. Fortunately, such snobbism is a matter of the past.

Perhaps the most notable feature of Latin Americans is their open mindset. This comes from their condition of being inhabitants on the fringe, able to move with total ease inside the perimeters of Western Civilization, while at the same time being able to cross outside and observe their walls with a critical and even surprised perspective. Few other Westerners, if any, enjoy such a flexible condition. A very intriguing one indeed.

As a result, Latin Americans excel in lateral thinking — not surprisingly magical realism is a regional brand. Creativeness, imagination and improvisation come easily to them, given the variety of its roots and influences and the necessity to continuously search for a synthesis within themselves. Method and discipline, tough, don't come so naturally.

Not surprisingly, literature, the movie industry, the entertainment industry or software, are among the areas where Latin Americans are internationally recognized. A good example of this is the Venezuelan Youth Orchestra System, known as El Sistema. This is an unconventional cultural program, which over the last four decades, has taught three million children to play classical music. Exported to at least 25 other countries, it has become a world recognized feature. You don't get to do such a thing without enormous input of eclecticism, opportunism and improvisation, which does not preclude of course a very important degree of organization.

CHAPTER 6

LATIN AMERICA AND UNITED STATES: A DICHOTOMY

Latin America, a peripheral Western region, shares the same hemisphere with the United States, a country that epitomizes the Western World. While Latin America is still on a quest for its economic development, amid periodical social and political turmoil, the United States has become not only the hegemonic power of the continent, but of the world.

Both began as overseas colonies of European countries. Both were amply endowed with natural resources. Both achieved their independence during the Age of Revolutions in the late 18th or beginning of the 19th centuries. In the case of United States and Spanish America, revolutionary wars were needed to consolidate separation from their respective colonists. But at this point the similarities ended.

Why was one so successful while the other got mired in so many problems and limitations? Even if this great dichotomy took shape after independence, the reasons behind it were forged during their respective colonial periods. We have, thus, to dissect their colonial pasts to understand why the United States could follow a straight line towards economic prosperity, political stability and hegemonic preponderance — with the single important obstacle of a bloody civil war — while Latin America was hindered by endless problems.

Nuances

Two important nuances must be addressed, though, before delving into the subject. The first, has to do with the differences between North and South in colonial United States. The second, relates to the differences between Spanish and Portuguese America. While North and South followed divergent societal and economic paths since colonial times, Spanish and Portuguese Americas showed distinctions between them. The extremes emerge when the Yankee North is compared to Hispanic America, but when the South of Anglo–Saxon North America or Portuguese America are included in the picture, distinctions cease to be so clear cut. Consequently, a few clarifications are required.

North and South shared the view that the British role in America was limited to empire–wide public goods, such as security and international trade. They also gave paramount importance to its property rights, religious freedom and political entitlements through colonial assemblies. Still, they had important differences in other areas.

In the Yankee sphere, religious puritanism produced a homogenized society. Such a social structure was characterized by its austerity; its capacity for hard manual labour amid harsh soil and severe climate; its conviction that material success and divine favor were linked; its contempt for pleasure and luxury; its discipline; and its preference for activities such as trade and craftsmanship.

In the South, a landowner's society that mirrored English gentry prevailed. Slavery; contempt for direct manual labour; high sense of personal honour and love for a stylish life: these were some of its main traits. The Anglo–Saxon South and Iberian America were not so far apart, at least in relation to these characteristics.

Nonetheless, when comparing colonial United States with colonial Latin America, reference must be made essentially to the Yankee North. The reason being that the independent United States ended up being shaped by the North. Indeed, in 1861 two visions of society were immersed in a protracted conflict. Four years and 600,000 deaths later, only one vision remained: that of the industrialized North, whose values had taken shape during colonial times. These came to be the values that defined the nation.

As Felipe Fernandez–Armesto puts it:

> "There were lots of civil wars in the nineteenth century; what made the United States's special was that it happened in an industrializing context. It was unlike those of Latin America, more like the contemporary civil wars of Germany, Italy, and Japan. In all these conflicts of the 1860s, a common pattern prevailed. Industrializing regions imposed on unindustrializing neighbors and created centralized political systems, fuelled and furthered by the resources that industrialization made possible…In all these conflicts, old–fashioned agrarian societies — like Confederacy with its planters and slaves — succumbed to the industrializing giants: Prussia in Germany's wars of unity, Piedmont in Italy's Risorgimento, Chosu and Satsuma in Japan's Meiji Restoration, and the Union in the American Civil War".[1]

In the cases of Spanish and Portuguese Americas, as previously seen, the latter tended to be less extreme and more pragmatic than Spanish America. Moreover, while in Brazil the conditions were created for the colony to become a unitary state after its independence, the opposite happened in Hispanic America, which would fracture into numerous countries after its liberation. At the same time, while in Brazil the prevailing circumstances helped create the basis for the country to become an independent monarchy, Spanish America evolved into the republican system. These elements contributed to Brazil having a more moderate and stable political evolution after independence.

Even so, having taken these differences into account, Spanish America and Brazil had many elements in common. They included highly centralizing metropolises; limited trade options; overwhelming religious surveillance and censorship; rigidly stratified societies; seigneurial societies where manual work was tantamount to loss of social status. It must be added, though, that in most of these matters Spanish America presented a more extreme situation than colonial Brazil.

Notwithstanding the advantage derived from Brazil's post–independence political stability, the country was unable to have a distinct economic

[1] Fernandez–Armesto, F *Op. Cit.,* Chapter 5, Loc 1551.

evolution from the rest of Latin America. It remained, indeed, as a primary products exporter, being subjected to foreign dependence and market volatility. Moreover, once a republic, Brazil mimicked the political instability that plagued the rest of region. The elements in common with Spanish America seemed, thus, to have been sufficiently significant to hinder the possibilities of capitalizing in its post–independence political stability. That being the situation, there is no obvious reason for presenting Brazil as an exception within Latin America.

Among the differences that marked the colonial histories of the United States and Latin America — and that defined inverted evolutions once independence was attained — were the following: centralization vs. political autonomy; imperial mercantile regulations vs. development of intercolonial trade; religious impositions vs. religious openness; stratified societies vs. homogenised societies; seigneurial societies vs. work oriented societies. Let us review those differences.

Rules and Self–Rule

The first of those differences is centralization vs. political autonomy. Centralization was pervasive in the Iberian case, with Spanish America having experienced it for a longer period and with more intensity. Nonetheless, after 1755 Portuguese centralization surpassed that of Spain. Endless rules, norms and regulations, within a bureaucratic and legalistic environment, defined relations with the metropolis. By 1635, 400,000 decrees for the colonies had been issued by the Spanish Crown, which was the equivalent to 2,500 annually since Columbus arrived in the Americas.[2] The only line of defense against such centralizing impetus was distance, which allowed a certain degree of practical but not juridical autonomy.

Within that context even the smallest of decisions had to be deferred to Spain. Ecclesiastical matters were no exception, with royal approval being required at every level. Juan Garcia Icazbalceta remarks:

> "Without the authorization of the King no church, monastery or hospital could be founded, nor could bishoprics or parishes be

[2] Veliz, C p. 43.

established. No priest could cross to America without a specific royal permit".[3]

Even judicial power remained in the hands of the Spanish State. Only at the lowest level, represented by the town councils, could creoles exert direct participation.

In contrast with the above, English colonies in North America enjoyed wide political autonomy. Colonial assemblies, working with a British Governor whose salary they paid, held broad authority over local public goods, property rights, religious freedom and contract enforcement. Over the 100 years that preceded The Seven Years War — held between 1756 and 1763–Britain accepted local political freedom in exchange for the colonists accepting British control over the Empire. During that time, Great Britain gradually gave these assemblies wide autonomy and freedom, which they use to underpin essential political, personal, religious and economic rights.

At the end of such period the colonists were in a very strong position. According to Robert Harvey:

> "Already the thirteen colonies, far from behaving as subordinate to British rule, considered themselves on an equal footing with the mother country. They had their own parliaments and political systems. They elected their own officials. They were English-speaking freemen — much freer, indeed, that many of their peers in Britain, where the upper and middle classes remained dominant, though comparatively small and exclusive. They provided their own defence forces and police".[4]

Problems began when Britain won The Seven Years War with France. On the one hand, London had a large debt to pay because of the conflict. On the other hand, it acquired a huge empire in the Americas, and the 13 colonies became much less important within its new broader picture. Britain began pressuring the future United States to finance a portion of the debt. Simultaneously,

---

[3] *Ibid.*, p. 40.

[4] Harvey, R (2001). *A Few Bloody Noses: The American War of Independence,* p. 43. London: John Murray.

it could now exercise a more centralized power, not only because it was aiming at empire–wide policies, but because once the threat of France had been removed, the colonies were much more firmly under its control.

As a result, a downward spiral of action and reaction took shape with London tightening the screws and the colonies increasing their defiance. Without the threat of the French, the colonists as well felt less need of British protection and were willing to act more boldly. In Robert Harvey's words:

> "But the 'French and Indian War' had eliminated the common enemy that made the Americans most reliant on British protection. For the first time in their history they had no need for a military strong ally… What became known afterwards as the Seven Years War had completely transformed the American perception of themselves as a people incapable of defending their own territory without British assistance".[5]

London's willingness to suspend colonial legislature turned out to be a bridge too far to cross. Suspension of all the acts of the New York Assembly and the disbanding of the Massachusetts Assembly, became a direct affront to everything that the colonials held as inalienable liberties. Especially so because British heritage emphasized a group of fundamental rights, among which political representation was a towering one. Thus, war became inevitable.

Bullion and Manufacturing

The second difference is imperial mercantile regulations vs. development of intercolonial trade. Trade regulations imposed by Madrid and Lisbon worked against the development of intercolonial trade and the creation of a network of ports across the region. Their only interest was transporting the colonies' bullion and agricultural products to the metropolis. To such an end they created the fleet system, which governed transatlantic trade.

Several consequences followed. First, instead of promoting a wide network of ports across thousands of miles of coast line, Spain allowed

---

[5] *Ibid.*, pp. 43–44.

just three ports in the Americas to trade directly with the metropolis. As a result, for example, products from Buenos Aires, had to travel 1,000 miles overland to the habilitated port in Peru instead of using Buenos Aires a natural port. In the case of Portugal, until 1766 it just allowed the ports of Rio de Janeiro and Salvador de Bahia in Brazil. Second, direct trade between the colonies was forbidden as everything had to pass through the metropolis.

Had this not been the case, those colonies, and very particularly the Spanish ones, could have developed very differently, including: dynamic trade relations among them; economically active coastal areas and a stronger system of economic specialization. Considering only fiscal considerations, the Iberian mercantile system heavily constrained the economic development of its colonies. Industry within them was totally discouraged.

According to Douglass C. North, William Summerhill and Barry R. Weingast:

> "The wide range of endowments across Spanish America should have led to the same type of dense economic development along many South American coasts as observed on the east coast of North America. Yet the Spanish mercantile system explicitly prohibited this…The crown had its motives, however. Spanish regulations worked to keep the bullion flowing to Spain, but did not promote the economic development of the New World".[6]

British North America not only promoted the creation of numerous ports, but allowed each to compete for trade. That permitted a dense economic expansion within the colonies, while providing them with invaluable commercial experience. Moreover, because of a system of economic specialization, shipyards, sawmills, flour mills, lumber yards or tanneries emerged in the New England colonies, while textiles, shipbuilding, beer production or iron works appeared in the Middle colonies. In other words, industrialization was sown. Meanwhile, Southern colonies

[6] North, DC, Summerhill, W and BR Weingast (2000). Order, Disorder and Economic Change: Latin America vs. North America. In *Governing for Prosperity.* BB de Mesquita and HL Root (eds.), p. 23. New Haven: Yale University Press.

specialized in raw materials that included tobacco, indigo, furs, rice, corn or vegetables.

As a result, when independence arrived, the 13 colonies were not only economically integrated within a complementary trading system, but the expansion of its manufacturing base was on a strong footing. The British system, contrary to the Iberian one, allowed maximizing the economic development of the colonies while making them interdependent.

Modernizing Christianity or Christianizing Modernity

The third difference was religious impositions vs. religious openness. According to Leopoldo Zea:

> "There was a struggle between those wanting to modernize Christianism and those wanting to Christianise modernity... Spain and Portugal (opting for the latter) resigned themselves to be the past and dragged with them their American colonies".[7]

Inquisition was brought to the Iberian colonies but, as converted Jews and Moors were not allowed to travel to the Americas (especially in the Spanish case), guarding their behaviour was not one of the Inquisition's main roles. Preventing religious or moral deviations and intellectual inquisitiveness were more in line.

As Michael Baigent and Richard Leigh state:

> "Because the domains of the Spanish monarchs comprised a species of theocracy with Church and State working in tandem, the Spanish Inquisition was as much an adjunct of the Crown as it was of the Church. It functioned as an instrument not only of ecclesiastical orthodoxy, but of royal policy as well".[8]

In other words, its role transcended that of an instrument of Catholic orthodoxy to become a sort of secret police.

---

[7] Zea, L., p. 33.

[8] Baigent R and R Leigh (2000). *The Inquisition,* p. 63. London: Penguin Books.

The Inquisition also became an instrument for profit. Again, in the words of Baigent and Leigh:

> "For the most part, Inquisition in Mexico busied itself in amassing wealth, in managing and profiting from the goods and properties it confiscated. Not infrequently, it would trump up charges against individuals for the sole purpose of obtaining their goods and property — which would never be returned, even if the accused were exonerated".[9]

In the latter part of the 18th century, the Inquisition derived new impetus from the persecution of "free–thinkers". Freemasons, followers of the Enlightenment ideas, putative or real revolutionaries, and all other perceived adversaries of the regime, became the Inquisition's targets. At this phase, the "secret police" role became fundamental.

In the Anglo–Saxon North competition for attracting colonists also meant that there was a broad spectrum of different religious denominations to choose from. In fact, the start of English colonization arose from the search of religious freedom. According to Andre Maurois:

> "Spain did not allow its religious heterodox to go to the colonies as it feared that they could contaminate them. England, more realistically, thought that the heterodox was the perfect exportation product".[10]

In 1620, the Mayflower arrived in Massachusetts with its charge of pilgrims who were to found Plymouth. In 1691, they merged with the puritans of Massachusetts Bay colony, who had arrived in 1629 and had founded Boston. There began a whole process of colonization based in the search of religious freedom and the freedom to search religious options.

At times, religious intolerance could become too oppressive in certain colonies, leading some of its inhabitants to found new colonies. Such was the case of Roger Williams, who felt that Boston's leader John Winthrop had become too close minded and decided to found, with some followers

---

[9] *Ibid.*, p. 87.

[10] Maurois, A (1972). *Historia de los Estados Unidos,* p.33. Barcelona: Círculo de Lectores.

the colony of Rhode Island. That was also the case of Thomas Hooker and his followers, who, unhappy with the developments in Massachusetts decided to create the colony of Connecticut.

Virginia was thus Anglican, Maryland was Catholic, Pennsylvania was Quaker, Massachusetts was Calvinist, Georgia was Baptist, Rhode Island and Connecticut were liberal Calvinists, and so on. In other words, colonists wanting to make a new life for themselves and their families could choose from a whole array of religious alternatives.

Pyramids, Protestants and Hidalgos

The fourth difference was stratified societies vs. homogenised societies. Iberian America represented the former and the future United States the latter. In the case of Spanish America, this was compounded by a high degree of urbanization, which was also important in Brazil but not to the same extent. The opposite happened in the North American colonies where, in 1770, only 3.8 per cent of its population lived in cities, of which just five had more than 8,000 inhabitants.[11] Conversely in 1800, Mexico City had 137,000 inhabitants; Habana 80,000; Lima 64,000; Buenos Aires 55,000; Caracas 42,000, Santiago de Chile 31,000 and Bogota 30,000.[12] Urbanization was a relevant consideration as cities were much more stratified places than rural societies.

Iberian American societies were like pyramids composed of several levels. At their base were the African slaves followed an echelon higher by the Indians. Further up were the several variables of racial mix, each of which was duly stratified. The mixture of Indian and Negro was beneath that of African and white, which in turn was topped by that of Indian and white. Further up, were the "criollos" in Hispanic America or "mazombos" in Brazil, who were whites of Spanish or Portuguese descent born in the Americas. Finally, at the top, were the Peninsular: Spanish or Portuguese. Every member of this pyramid had its role in society. Except for the Peninsular, each was circumscribed to lesser or higher limitations.

[11] *Ibid.*

[12] Carmagnani, M., pp. 99–100.

Urban environments made these distinctions much more visible, imposing a rigid code that had to be followed.

North American colonies, with the exception of the Southern ones, conformed to much more egalitarian societies. As the Indian population was kept at bay, living in separate spheres, white settlers only diverged in their respective economic status. Protestants were a highly homogenised lot with Calvinists representing the extreme: austere, industrious and disciplined. More particularly, America meant for the great majority of colonists the promise of a new life, away from the class system that prevailed in the Old World. Moreover, in an essentially rural environment in which manual labour prevailed, there was not much room for social distinctions.

The fifth difference was seigneurial societies vs. work oriented societies. According to Carlos Fuentes:

> "Conquerors wanted to be 'hidalgos', gentry. Being a 'hidalgo' meant not having to work, but making others work for you. It meant obtaining glory in war so that you could be rewarded with lands and workforce. Land as war recompense became one of the basis of economic power in Spanish America just as it had been in Medieval Spain".[13]

Gentry enjoys life and takes care of expanding riches by making land productive through the workforce at its disposal. In Iberian America, Indian and Negro hands made such workforce.

At the end, a vicious circle in which nobody wanted to work conformed the basis of the productive process. Conquerors and their descendants felt entitled, as gentry, to have someone else working for them. The Indian and the African slave were forced to work against their will for the benefit of their overlord or owner. Hence, the work ethic developed in colonial Iberian America was extremely fragile to say the least.

In the Anglo–Saxon colonies of the North, with the exception of the Southern ones, which replicated much of the aforementioned patterns, work was a fundamental part of the social tissue. As an essentially Protestant society, and further to its submission to God, the only thing that

[13] Fuentes, C., p. 139.

really moved the internal fibres of the settlers was work and, by extension, the acquisition of wealth.

But why aim for wealth amid an austerity that denied all enjoyment to life? Here, predestination entered onto the scene: according to Calvinists, Lutherans or Baptists mankind is born with salvation or damnation adhered to its beings. And if nothing can be done to change what has already been preordained, material success can be interpreted as a sign of divine favour and hence of eternal salvation. This explains the anxiety in the search of material success.

Moreover, manual work, contrary to the Iberian notion of "hidalguía" or the French one of "derogance", did not imply the loss of social status in the Anglo–Saxon North. Much to the contrary, hard work in all its forms was an expression of social discipline and industriousness. Prevailing against hardships, through personal effort, was a sign of good citizenship and hence of social recognition.

Once independence was attained on both sides of the hemisphere, the previous five considerations led to specific consequences. These showed in the following areas: identity; political institutions; economic development; individualism and freedom of expression; democratic space and work ethic and the pursuit of wealth.

Identity and Institutions

Identity evolved in different directions in the United States, Spanish America and Brazil. According to Samuel P. Huntington:

> "The main culture of the United States was and remains that of the colonists of the seventeenth and eighteenth centuries who founded the American society. The nuclear elements of such society can be defined in different ways, but they include Christian religion, Protestant values and morals, a work ethic, the English language, British traditions on law, justice and the limitation of government's power, as well as an artistic, literary, philosophic and musical European legacy. Through such culture the colonists developed, in the seventeenth and eighteenth centuries, the American creed with its principles of liberty, equality, individualism, human rights, representative government and private property...Given

not only its origin but also its continuity in time it can be said that the United States remains a colonial society".[14]

The United States was, thus, able to transit into independent life preserving its colonial inheritance and the values derived therein. They became a route map into the future and provided the country with a strong sense of national identity. The only big subject left unresolved within such "American creed" was slavery. It would take a cruel civil war to solve this issue.

Spanish America encountered a very different situation. As seen in the previous chapter, independence brought with it a long and consuming identity crisis that disrupted societal evolution and led to numerous internal conflicts. The colonial inheritance remains up to the present day a relevant topic, not in the positive and reassuring way in which it does in the United States, but as a highly contentious subject.

Brazil, given its natural evolution into an independent empire, without a traumatic break with the past, was on a middle ground situation in relation to the previous two cases. It did not undergo the identity crisis of its Spanish American cousins, but neither was it enriched by inherited convictions and values, as the United States was. Brazil's experience represented a pragmatic accommodation with a past, from which it derived no pride or foundational values. No wonder, the country's most visible trait is an acute pragmatism devoid of inspirational principles.

Political institutions evolved in different directions. During the 18th and the first half of the 19th centuries the United States could create a stable political democracy. It was a natural evolution from the wide political autonomy and self–government experiences, which it had enjoyed during its colonial past. A whole array of institutional and legal traditions emanated from England, had been represented in such colonial rights.

With such a strong background, the United States could forge its own institutional structures with ease and conviction. The Constitution, replacing the articles of Confederation and enriched by the debates derived from the Federalist Papers, represented the first written foundational covenant

[14] Huntington, SP (2004). *¿Quiénes Somos? Los Desafíos de la Identidad Nacional Estadounidense,* p. 65. Barcelona: Paidós.

of a new nation. It was a well–specified system of political and economic rights that provided a credible commitment for the future, and a stable basis upon which to keep building a society.

Spanish American nations, by contrast, imploded in a costly and bloody spiral of confusion, warfare and "caudillismo". With the beheading of a highly centralized colonial political structure, and totally inexperienced in self–government, such countries lost their compass. The situation was compounded by the huge human, economic and material losses resulting from the independence wars. Disorder prevailed for decades, revealing a complete absence of institutional arrangements capable of guaranteeing cooperation among rival visions and conflicting groups.

Brazil, contrary to the Hispanic American nations, was spared such traumas, as its centralized political structure could continue under the independent empire. As the monarchical institutions were the natural continuation of the colonial ones, no loss of direction was experienced. Under such circumstances rival groups and interests could be conciliated at the top, avoiding open confrontation.

Nonetheless, when the Brazilian Empire was toppled and the country entered its republican phase, the absence of institutions capable of reconciling divergent views and interests became evident. Under such circumstances, democracy was submitted to the same constraints experienced by the Hispanic American nations. The military, as in the rest of the region, became the only institution able to impose order when conflicts became unmanageable. That implied the military takeover of government, which began to happen with a certain regularity.

Economy and Individualism

Economic development took very different routes. In colonial times, the United States had been able to become economically integrated, while establishing the baseline for its industrialization process. This allowed entry into independent life on very firm economic ground. Consequently, the country could participate in the early stages of the Industrial Revolution. From then on, expansion came in a very natural way.

In contrast, both Spanish America and Brazil got trapped in an export system based on primary products. According to Felipe Fernandez–Armesto:

> "Latin American countries tended to remain economically dependent on monocultures or on a few primary products, while the United States experienced an industrial revolution. From an economic point of view, the early nineteenth century was probably a bad time to gain independence. Free trade, which was a shibboleth of the independent revolutionaries through the Americas, favoured industrializing economies that produced cheap goods and condemned the Latin American states, which emerged as fully free-market players in that era for the first time, to underdevelopment; they could not catch up with the industrial revolutions of Europe and North America and so became locked into a role as producers of primary products for other people's industrialization".[15]

The prohibition faced by Spanish and Portuguese colonies to trade among themselves, closed the door for economic specialization and hence for industrialization (industrialization, on any account, had been discouraged by the metropolis). Lacking trade experience, Iberian American countries were not able to upgrade their export base once independence was attained. Therefore, their only option was to replace their old Iberian metropolis for a new one: Britain.

Freedom of expression also diverged. In colonial Protestant America, every citizen was his or her own priest, while in Iberian America, the Inquisition and the Church safeguarded the proper way of thinking. The result was obvious. While the former became an incubator for freedom of expression, which in turn strengthened the democratic spirit, the overbearing presence of the Catholic Church worked in the opposite direction.

In Lawrence E. Harrison's words:

> "In his 1835 book for the ages *Democracy in America*, Alexis de Tocqueville argues that you can't have democracy without democrats. He explains the successful US experiment as importantly the consequence

[15] Fernandez–Armesto, *op. cit.*, Chapter 5, Loc 1538.

of a 'form of Christianity which I cannot better describe than...a democratic and republican religion. This contributed powerfully to the establishment of a republic and a democracy...from the beginning, politics and religion contracted an alliance which has never been dissolved'".[16]

Constrained during three centuries in their liberty of expressing their thoughts, repressed whenever personal opinions contradicted religious dogma, Iberian Americans did not develop the habit of expressing their minds openly and freely. This would become, in independent times, an open invitation for authoritarian regimes. Moreover, as the quest for inquisitive knowledge was always kept at bay, there would be a manifest deficit in scientific curiosity.

Spaces for Democracy, Spaces for Work and Wealth

Democratic spaces became totally different as well. The social homogenization prevailing in the 13 colonies became an excellent space for the development of democracy. As if entering independence with the accrued experience of self–government was not enough, the United States also enjoyed the benefits of an egalitarian society devoid of a class system. Obviously, the fact that the Indians were not integrated into white society while slavery was still in place, greatly helped. Dissolution of slavery would certainly change the rules of the game and create new challenges. Nonetheless, during the first vital decades of democratic consolidation, the country was freed from the complexities of acute social inequality.

Much to the contrary, Iberian America was plagued by inequalities which by comparison dwarfed the European class system. According to Felipe Fernandez–Armesto:

"In much of Latin America, even the northern model of racially selected democracy, which excluded blacks and corralled Indians in reservations, was impracticable. Miscegenation had already created too many racial classifications (...) Latin America was deficient, on the whole, not in formal constitutional provisions for voting, or in democratic rhetoric, but

[16] Harrison, LE (2013). *Jews, Confucians and Protestants: Cultural Capital and the End of Multiculturalism,* p. 127. Plymouth: Rowman & Littlefield Publisher, Inc. .

> in the actual spaces where shared identities could be forged among people of different classes".[17]

Moreover, except for Brazil, slavery had been supressed earlier than in the United States. The possibility of placing the vote in the hands of the so–called "castas" — Africans, Indians or mixed raced groups — was one of the reasons that made democracy so difficult to digest for Latin America's dominant white society. So, the decisive formative years of democracy were immersed in this high voltage conundrum.

Work ethic and the pursuit of wealth greatly differed as well in the United States and Latin America. Profound differences prevailed in both cases, resulting from the cultural patterns conformed in colonial times. The contrast between the predestination approach, common to different Protestant denominations, and the Iberian "hidalgo" mentality was simply too gigantic even to compare. This was compounded as well by the Catholic religion approach to poverty and wealth. According to Catholics, suffering in this life is a way of obtaining eternal reward in the next, which by extension promotes resignation in the poor. Wealth, on the other hand, is always under moral suspicion.

And, as if the Puritan cultural background had not been enough to create an insurmountable gap between the United States and Latin America, Social Darwinism would later emerge on the scene. In the final years of the 19th century a marriage of convenience between puritanism and Social Darwinism took place in the United States. Predestination was, thus, merged with Herbert Spencer's ideas, according to which society was to be seen as a sort of biological organism where only the fittest survived.

Marianne Debouzy explains the nature of this amalgam well:

> "The two doctrines, puritanism and Darwinism, got together in order to provide justification to wealth, which was thus presented as a combination of Divine favour and natural selection".[18]

Not surprisingly, this double compulsivity towards work and wealth began producing, in those years, self-made men such as Rockefeller, Carnegie, Morgan, Crocker, Frick or Mellon.

---

[17] Fernandez–Armesto. *op. cit.*, Chapter 5, Loc 1492.

[18] Debouzy, M (1972). *Le capitalisme "sauvage" aux Etats-Unis, 1860–1900,* p. 144. París: Éditions du Seuil.

CHAPTER 7

LATIN AMERICA AND THE UNITED STATES: A HISTORY IN SEVEN CHAPTERS

Since their inception into independent life, the United States and Latin America were bound to follow very different routes. Culture imposed itself with opposite results. One had the wind at its back, speeding its movements. The other had the wind at its face, slowing and hindering them. Not surprisingly the relationship between the two was to become profoundly unequal.

The history of this relationship can be told in seven well defined chapters: Anticipation; Monroe Doctrine; Manifest Destiny; Empire; Good Neighborhood; Cold War; and Trade and Security. Let us explore into each of them.

The first chapter is Anticipation. The future Latin American countries were still mere colonies, when two of the founding fathers of the United States were already looking at them as prey. According to Brian Loveman:

> "Thomas Jefferson worried (in 1786) that Spain might be too weak to hold onto to its colonies 'till our population was sufficiently advanced to gain it from them piece by piece' (...) Six years later Alexander Hamilton advised: 'Beside eventual security against invasions, we ought

> certainly to look to the possession of the Floridas and Louisiana, and we ought to squint at South America'".[1]

These assertions undoubtedly required much foresight as at that point in time the Iberian empires in the Americas showed, at least on the surface, great strength. Not only were their universities one or two centuries older than those of the United States, but their cities were much larger and magnificent. In 1790 New York had 33,000 inhabitants, Philadelphia 28,000 and Boston 18,000. Meanwhile in 1800 Mexico City had 137,000 people. Fortunes in Hispanic or Portuguese America were also much larger than those in the North. It was difficult to foresee that the correlation of power between these two spheres would be reversed in the way it did. Eventually political, economic and cultural reasons, such as those explained in the previous chapter, would be the cause for that process. But in the 1780s this was far from obvious.

It would only be after the Hispanic American wars of independence that all the flaws of the Spanish Empire would become evident. That in addition, of course, to the immense destruction brought about by the conflicts themselves. In Felipe Fernandez–Armesto's words: "The independence wars were, in short, the making of the United States and the ruin of much of the rest of the Americas".[2] To that he adds that, in every department, the countries of Latin America receded in stature while the United States towered.

The Monroe Doctrine

The second chapter was the Monroe Doctrine. The United States foremost declaration regarding the Western Hemisphere is represented by this doctrine, which was issued in 1823. It responded to the threat of reconquest of the former Spanish colonies by a coalition of European monarchies integrated in the so–called Holy Alliance.

---

[1] Loveman, B (2006). US Foreign Policy towards Latin America in the 19th Century. Oxford Research Encyclopaedia of Latin American History, July 2016, http://oxfordindex.oup.com/view/10.1093/acrefore/9780199366439.013.41. Accessed 23/03/2017.

[2] Fernandez-Armesto. *op. cit.*, Loc 1449.4.

In this context James Monroe, fifth President of the country, delivered a message to Congress stating:

> "The American continents by the free and independent condition which they have assumed and maintain, are henceforth not to be considered as subjects of future colonization by any European powers..."

To which he added:

> "We could not view any interposition for the purpose of oppressing them (the Spanish Americans), or controlling in any other manner their destiny, by any European power in any other light than as a manifestation of an unfriendly disposition to the United States".

Later, he warned the Holy Alliance in the following terms:

> "It is impossible that the allied powers should extend their political system to any portion of either continent without endangering our peace and happiness; nor can anyone believe that our southern brethren, if left to themselves, would adopt it of their own accord. It is equally impossible, therefore, that we should behold such interposition in any form with indifference".[3]

The American President, thus, was clearly stating that any attempts to reconquer the recently independent Spanish American states, or to impose upon them a monarchical form of government against their will, were inadmissible. These "prohibitions" would clearly be violated during the American Civil War. Taking advantage of the United States' turmoil, France invaded Mexico and imposed a monarchy upon the country. At the same time Spain invaded and occupied Santo Domingo. After the Civil War, the United States had enough muscle to make them accept the Monroe Doctrine. But that was more than four decades later. In 1823, though, the doctrine was impossible to enforce.

---

[3] Monroe, J (1823). http://avalon.law.yale.edu/19th_century/monroe.asp. Accessed 19/02/2017.

According to Henry Kissinger:

> "The Monroe Doctrine proclaimed in 1823, made a moat of the ocean which separated the United States from Europe. Up to that time, the cardinal rule of American foreign policy had been that the United States would not become entangled in European struggles for power. The Monroe Doctrine went the next step by declaring that Europe must not become entangled in American affairs...Daringly, it warned the European powers that the new nation would go to war to uphold the inviolability of the Western Hemisphere (...) America was at one and the same time turning its back on Europe, and freeing its hands to expand in the Western Hemisphere".[4]

Again, as previously noted, the United States was anticipating what it aimed to become and, under those circumstances, was clearly delimitating a sphere of influence. Furthermore, the motto of the doctrine "America for the Americans", had in the mind of John Quincy Adams, Monroe's Secretary of State and architect of this initiative, a precise meaning. As he had stated in 1811: "The whole continent of North America appears to be destined by Divine Providence to be peopled by one nation...".[5]

It was of course too early in time for the materialization of such ambitions. Nonetheless, the doctrine was laying the ground so that in the future the aspirations of Jefferson, Hamilton and Adams, would not be jeopardized by any foreign power. There were far reaching designs involved. The Monroe Doctrine, as expression of a sphere of influence, was thus to endure in time.

Around the same year in which the Monroe Doctrine was issued, the diplomatic recognition of the new Iberian American states began. This had been delayed awaiting the ratification by Madrid of a pivotal agreement for the United States: the Adams–de Onis Treaty. In accordance with this treaty, Spain ceded East Florida to the United States and accepted the claims of the latter in relation to West Florida. In 1822, once the ratification had taken place, the recognition process began. By 1825 Washington had diplomatic relations with Colombia, Mexico, Chile the United Provinces of Rio de la Plata and the Brazilian Empire. Others would follow.

[4] Kissinger, H (1994). *Diplomacy,* pp. 35–36. New York: Simon & Schuster.

[5] Bemis, SF (1959). *John Quincy Adams and the Foundations of American Foreign Policy,* p. 182. New York: Knopf.

Manifest Destiny

The third chapter of this saga was the Manifest Destiny. American journalist John O'Sullivan coined the term in the late 1830s. Nonetheless its most quoted version dates to 1845, when he wrote about the

> "right of our manifest destiny to overspread and to possess the whole continent which Providence has given us for the development of the great experiment of liberty and federated self-government entrusted to us". [6]

But which were the geographical boundaries of this manifest destiny? O'Sullivan spoke about the "whole continent". But going back in time to previous expressions, Adams had referred to North America, Jefferson had implied that the whole Spanish American Empire was within grasp, and Hamilton had mentioned South America. Finally, the term ended up including Mexico and the Caribbean Basin. Debates on annexing all of Mexico, Cuba and Panama would take place in the United States during the 1840s and 1850s.

An expansionist process began in the 1840s. Part of it materialized during what was labelled as the Manifest Destiny era, when half of Mexico came into US hands, and Nicaragua almost did as well. In Henry Kissinger's terms: "Until the turn of the twentieth century American foreign policy was basically quite simple: to fulfil the country's manifest destiny, and to remain free of entanglements overseas".[7] The rest of the Caribbean Basin, including the Isthmus, would fall under this expansionist spiral during the subsequent era: The Empire one. This began with the war over Cuba against Spain in 1898.

The annexation of half of Mexico's territory began with Texas. Very unwisely Mexico had open its deserted lands in Texas to colonization by US citizens. As mentioned by Niall Ferguson:

> "From 1821 until 1834 Stephen Austin established and ran his colony with the consent of the Mexican authorities, which were in fact more generous than the United States towards would-be-settlers...As late as 1832 his 'standing motto' was still 'Fidelity to Mexico'. Two years before, a decree

[6] Loveman, *op. cit.*

[7] Kissinger, *op. cit.*, p. 34.

> had prohibited Americans from settling in Texas. But although this prompted the settlers to summon their own convictions, they resolved merely to send Austin to petition the government in Mexico City. Only in 1835, after Austin had spent the better part of a year and a half in jail, and after harassment by Mexican troops, did the settlers take arms".[8]

By a combination of courage, endurance and tremendous good luck, the American settlers ended up defeating the Mexican troops under the command of President Antonio Lopez de Santa Anna. In 1836 they declared independence, and began lobbying for the incorporation of Texas into the United States. Even if there was reluctance in Washington, as this implied including into the Union another state where slavery was allowed, there was no reluctance in profiting from the opportunity of grabbing territory from Mexico. In 1845 President James K. Polk seized the chance to declare war on Mexico based on a claim by American citizens (at this point in time they were Texas citizens), that Mexico owned them 6.5 million dollars. In General Ulysses S. Grant words, this was "one of the most unjust wars ever waged by a stronger against a weaker nation".[9]

By force of arms and through the Treaty of Guadalupe Hidalgo of 1848, which followed the three years war, the United States had taken from Mexico, California, Colorado, Utah, Nevada, New Mexico and Arizona. Texas itself had been incorporated into the Union in 1845. Mexico had lost half of the country while the US had substantially augmented its territory.

In 1855, in a different episode, the Tennessean William Walker raised an army and launched an invasion on Nicaragua. Upon winning over the surprised local troops, he declared himself President of the country. Immediately recognized by the United States he became its "de facto" proconsul for a few years, before being deposed. He hinted annexation of the country by the United States, but having re–established slavery in Nicaragua, this became a tricky subject. The geopolitical importance of Nicaragua derived from the fact that together with the Central American Isthmus, which was part of Colombia, it constituted the best option for a transoceanic canal.

---

[8] Ferguson, N (2004). *Colossus: The Rise and Fall of the American Empire*, p. 39. London: Allen Lane.

[9] Ibid., p. 39.

From a Latin American perspective, the only breeze of fresh air during this Manifest Destiny era, would had come from President Grover Cleveland. Elected in 1885 as the first Democrat President since the Civil War, he formally rejected further American expansionism. Moreover, he forced Britain to stop its land grabbing of Venezuela's territory and to submit to international arbitration on the matter. Unfortunately, his Secretary of State, Richard Olney, added his own addendum to the Monroe Doctrine (the Onley Corollary), in terms that no American authority had dared to do before. Indeed, the corollary expressed: "Today the United States is practically sovereign on this continent and its fiat is law upon the subjects to which it confines its interposition".[10]

Onley's addendum, together with Alfred Thayer Mahan publication in 1890 of the immensely influential book *The Influence of Sea Power on History, 1660–1783*, laid the ground for the emergence of the next era. In his book Mahan articulated the idea that a powerful American navy, having as its bastion the Western Hemisphere over which the United States exercised "practical sovereignty", had to project its power around the world.

Empire

The fourth chapter, Empire, arrived in 1898 with the war against Spain. That year the American battleship Maine exploded in Havana harbour. Spain not only denied responsibility of the explosion, but did its best to rescue survivors. It was, though, the perfect occasion to declare war on Spain and to annex its remaining colonies, as many in both US political parties were demanding. President William McKinley complied and, after a swift victory over Spain, the latter was forced to relinquish them to the United States. Through the Treaty of Paris of that same year, Cuba and Puerto Rico in the Caribbean and the Philippines and Guam in the Pacific, became the bounty of the winner.

Military occupation of Cuba and Puerto Rico followed. In 1902 a protectorate regime was imposed upon Cuba under the Platt Amendment to Cuba's new Constitution. Within its clauses was the right to militarily intervene in Cuba when necessary. This "right" was to be exercised on

---

[10] Loveman, *op. cit.*

several occasions, beginning in 1906 when a provisional government was established under an American Governor–General.

Puerto Rico, on the contrary, was to remain a colony. The Foraker Act of 1900 gave its citizens the right to elect a Lower House (Delegates House), but the Upper House and the Governor were to be appointed directly by Washington. As previously mentioned, in 1914 the Delegates House unanimously voted for independence. This decision, though, was rejected by US Congress as unconstitutional, on the basis that it contradicted the Foraker Act.

In 1903, under President Theodore Roosevelt, a US sponsored and supported insurrection separated the Isthmus of Panama from Colombia. An American protectorate regime over this new country was subsequently established. At the same time, and according to the Hay–Bunau–Varilla Treaty of same year, Panama ceded in perpetuity to the United States the control over the Canal Zone that crossed the country. This culminated a long held American dream.

In 1905 the President issued the "Roosevelt Corollary" to the Monroe Doctrine, according to which:

> "In the Western Hemisphere, the adherence of the United States to the Monroe Doctrine may force the United States, however reluctantly, in flagrant cases of wrongdoing or impotence, to exercise an international police power".[11]

This corollary explicitly justified not only unilateral intervention and military occupation, but also the imposition of protectorate regimes upon those countries which, according to US judgement, had behaved in an improper manner.

President Woodrow Wilson went even further. According to Niall Ferguson:

> "The implicit Wilson Corollary was that only certain types of government would be tolerated by the United States in Latin America… Against unacceptable regimes the United States reserved the right to use force".[12]

[11] Roosevelt, T (1905). https://www.ourdocuments.gov/doc.php?flash=true&doc=56&page=transcript. Accessed 25/04/2017.

[12] Ferguson, *op. cit.*, p. 53.

The determination of which regimes were to be "tolerated" fell unilaterally on the United States. Not surprisingly, during the Empire era, US troops invaded countries from the Caribbean Basin on 34 occasions. In the process, they occupied Mexico, Honduras, Guatemala and Costa Rica for short periods and remained in Cuba, Nicaragua, Panama and the Dominican Republic for longer stays.

Moreover, one of the two main reasons why the American Congress denied adherence to the League of Nations, after World War I, was because it constrained the US' unilateral imposition of its will in Latin America. According to Henry Kissinger:

> "The League was believed to be incompatible with the Monroe Doctrine because collective security entitled, indeed required, the League to involve itself in disputes *within* the Western Hemisphere".[13]

During this period, the United States was confronted with an experience as frustrating as the one it would undergo decades later in the wars of Vietnam and Iraq. Indeed, for six years it fought an exhausting war against Nicaragua's Cesar Augusto Sandino, who resisted an American invasion during the 1920s and the 1930s.

In the process, it must be said, the Americans learned much about warfare. According to Greg Grandin:

> "Starting in the late 1920s, Nicaragua offered the marines their most effective proving ground, becoming, according to a *New York Times* reporter who accompanied the expedition, the 'first practical laboratory for the development of post-war aviation in coordination with ground troops'...in a war that allowed them to practice what would become standard elements in twentieth century air warfare".[14]

Again, in Greg Grandin's words:

> "By the late 1920s, then, the United States had apprenticed itself as a fledgling empire in Latin America, investing capital, establishing control

[13] Kissinger, *op. cit.,* p. 372.

[14] Grandin, *op. cit.*, p. 22.

over crucial raw materials and transit routes, gaining military experience, and rehearsing many of the ideas that to this day justify American power in the world".[15]

The Good Neighborhood

And then, suddenly, this phase was over. Indeed in 1933 the seventh chapter of this saga, the Good Neighborhood, was set in motion by the election of Franklyn Delano Roosevelt. In his inaugural address, he stated:

> "I would dedicate this nation to the policy of the good neighbor — the neighbor who resolutely respects himself and, because he does so, respects the rights of others — the neighbor who respects his obligations and respects the sanctity of his agreements in and with a world of neighbors… We now realize as we have never realized before our interdependence on each other; that we cannot merely take but we must give as well".[16]

Shortly after his inauguration he withdrew occupation forces from the Caribbean, abrogated the Platt Amendment to the Cuban Constitution and abandoned a series of treaties which provided Washington with special privileges in several Caribbean and Central American countries. Puerto Rico alone was to remain as a sad exception to this process.

Moreover, Roosevelt officially established a policy of absolute non–intervention in Latin American affairs. Facts supported this policy when Washington accepted the emergence of several progressive governments around the region. In addition, the United States tolerated manifestations of economic independence by several countries, including the nationalization of American oil companies' holdings in Mexico, the world's largest exporter.

The US government sided, for the first time ever, with Latin American nations in their labour disputes with abusive American corporations. At the same time, it backed infrastructure loans to the region. In a 1933 address to the Pan–American Union, which gathered all the countries of the hemisphere, Roosevelt expressed that the institution "must be a

---

[15] Ibid., p. 23.

[16] Roosevelt, FD, in Grandin, *op. cit.*, p. 34.

structure built on confidence, cemented by a sympathy which recognizes only equality and fraternity".[17]

What reasons motivated this behaviour, which not only had no precedents but was not to be repeated after Roosevelt? Certainly, important political and economic considerations made advisable a change of orientation from Washington. However, it is remarkable that, subjected to multiple challenges, Roosevelt opted for openness and not for a further tightening of the screws.

The following factors required a change in the course of relations with Latin America. First, the need to find solutions to the economic depression that was affecting the United States. Second, the recognition that within cost–benefit considerations, the use of force was not an efficient tool, as proved by the wearing down war with Nicaragua's Augusto Sandino. Third, the acceptance of the fact that the wind of change in Latin America, as exemplified by the Mexican Revolution, was a force to be reckoned with. One that could not be managed by way of confrontation.

But, in addition, was it the fact that Roosevelt was committed to the dissolution of the British Empire, which he considered utterly out of touch with the modern world. By necessity he had to preach using his actions as an example. How could he impose upon Churchill the need to undo the British Empire, when the United States was acting as an imperial power within its own hemisphere?

Sadly for Latin America the Good Neighborhood policy was to be the exception and not the rule. How different Latin American history would have been otherwise. For two years after Roosevelt's death, his successor Harry Truman, persevered with this policy towards Latin America.

Then, in 1947, Truman radically changed course. Hence, the beginning of the eighth chapter of this story: Cold War. According to Greg Grandin:

> "One reason for this turnaround was, of course, the Cold War. Washington found that it greatly preferred anti–Communist dictatorship to the possibility that democratic openness might allow the Soviets to gain a foothold on the continent".[18]

---

[17] Ibid., p. 28.
[18] Ibid., p. 41.

The Cold War

Latin America's traditional oligarchies, the Catholic Church and the military, took note of this change of heart in Washington, and launched a continental counteroffensive against progressive governments. One after another, the democratic regimes of Latin America began to be toppled with the benediction, and sometimes with the sponsorship, of Washington. Since its inception in 1947, the CIA began establishing close contacts with military officers and right–wing leaders around the region.

The first full scale destabilization operation carried out in Latin America by the CIA took place in 1954, under the presidency of Dwight D. Eisenhower. It targeted Guatemalan democratic President Jacobo Arbenz. As historians recognize today, he was just trying to implement a New Deal–style program of reform over his country's backward plantation economy. In the process, he unwittingly expropriated without full compensation the uncultivated lands of the United Fruit Company. No stone was left unturned until he was forced to leave the presidency.

A similar full scale operation was organized against Cuba's Fidel Castro a few years later. This not only included an economic, commercial and financial embargo but an invasion. The 1961 Bay of Pigs invasion, planned under Eisenhower but executed under his successor, was a total failure. Therefore, President John F. Kennedy tried to drown the influence of Castro within the region by other means. He promoted New Deal–style democracies that could win the support of their own populations, while his Alliance for Progress poured billions of dollars into developmental aid. At the same time, his so–called Peace Corp aimed at winning hearts and minds.

Through this strategy, Kennedy hoped to build a containing wall around Cuba. Had this been his only course of action, he would certainly have been remembered fondly within the region. Unfortunately, there was a darker side to his policies as well.

Kennedy committed his administration to strengthening the counter-insurgency capacities of the region's governments. Latin American military personnel began to be trained in counterinsurgency, or "special war" techniques, while indoctrinated about the new role that they were called to play in the defence of their countries and the "free world". At the same time, CIA advisors helped in modernizing the internal security apparatus around the region. It was the beginning of a nefarious trend.

However, during Kennedy's time rationality still prevailed, and only after his death all kinds of excesses began to take place. Referring to the fact that during the Cold War period the US was confronted with a country of the hemisphere that was a military and political ally of its chief adversary, Jorge I. Dominguez says:

> "In its subsequent conduct of the key aspects of its policy towards Latin America, the US government often behaved as if it were under the spell of ideological demons. Moreover, from the mid–1960s to the end of the Cold War in Europe, this ideologically–driven US policy often exhibited non–logical characteristics".[19]

These "ideological demons" guided President Lyndon B. Johnson's totally "non–logical" military invasion of the Dominican Republic in 1965, the first in more than three decades. Two years earlier, a democratically elected President, Juan Bosh, had assumed power. Although administrative probity and political freedom had characterized his government, he was toppled because Washington considered him too soft on Communism. An entirely corrupt military junta took his place until 1965, when a group of young officers rebelled. Their announcement that they would return Juan Bosh to the presidency, generated a counter coup instigated by Washington. As the latter failed, Johnson sent 23,000 soldiers to take control of the country.

In Jorge I. Dominguez' words:

> "It turned out that there was no 'second Cuba' in the making. The Soviet Union was wholly uninvolved and Cuba was involved only trivially... The United States deployed massive force to ward off a threat that did not exist".[20]

---

[19] Dominguez, JI (1999). US-Latin American Relations during the Cold War and its Aftermath. In *The United States and Latin America: The New Agenda,* V Bulmer-Thomas and J Dunkerley (eds.), p. 33. Cambridge, Mass.: Harvard University Press.
[20] Ibid., p. 42.

During Johnson's period, the short–lived democracy promotion and development aid of Kennedy's time, faded away. Founding and support for counterinsurgent activities, on the contrary, were wholly sustained.

Richard M. Nixon's administration presided over a cycle of military coups that had begun under Johnson. According to Greg Grandin:

> "Nixon's praise of Latin American dictators, therefore, was not just personal opinion but conveyed the essence of the Nixon Doctrine, which charged the security forces in each country with keeping their own house in order — not unlike Kennedy's promotion of counterinsurgency but stripped of its ennobling rhetoric about development and democracy".[21]

The toppling of Chile's Socialist President Salvador Allende in 1973, after a relentless campaign by the CIA to make his government unworkable, was the most notable feature of this period. Allende had indeed expropriated the assets of some American corporations, nonetheless his links to Moscow were almost inexistent. Nixon had instructed the CIA to "make the economy scream", and indeed it did. Augusto Pinochet's bloody coup, in which Allende lost his life, followed. Subsequently, a systematic and violent repression took place. It was a time when the National Security Doctrine policy, referred to in chapter four, covered the region.

President Gerald Ford followed in Nixon's footsteps during his short period in The White House. These policies continued four years after the end of his mandate, upon Ronald Reagan's arrival in The White House. Within the region, the Reagan administration prioritized Central America.

Again, in Grandin's words:

> "Reagan came down hard on Central America, in effect letting his administration's most committed militarists set and execute policy. In El Salvador, over the course of a decade, they provided more than a million dollars a day to fund the lethal counterinsurgency campaign. In Nicaragua, they patronized the Contras, a brutal insurgency led by discredited remnants of the deposed dictator's National Guard designed to roll back

[21] Grandin, *op. cit.*, p. 588.

> the Sandinista revolution. In Guatemala, they pressed to re-establish military aid to an army that was in the middle of committing genocide, defending the country's born–again president even as he was presiding over the worst slaughter in twentieth–century Latin America. All told, US allies in Central America during Reagan's two terms killed over 300,000 people, tortured hundreds of thousands, and drove millions into exile".[22]

During Reagan's time in office the Falklands/Malvinas War took place. The military regime in Argentina, convinced that its closeness to Washington and its active role in the Cold War agenda entitled them to a parity status with Great Britain in the eyes of the United States, launched an invasion on the islands. They believed that Washington would accept the "fait accompli". A product of British imperialism land grabbing, this British colonial territory had been claimed by Argentina since its inception to independence.

The US' unconditional support for London, and the help that it provided for the expedition to retake the islands, generated great malaise in Latin America. Washington was not only forgetting its treaty obligation towards the region, in the case of a foreign incursion, but did not even feel the need to opt for neutrality (although at the beginning of the crisis it staged an arbitration pantomime). Not surprisingly, when the US invoked the same treaty obligations many years later, on the occasion of the twin towers attack, the majority of Latin American countries did not feel bound by it.

Between the Nixon–Ford and Reagan administrations came Jimmy Carter. The "Good Neighbour" policy of Franklyn D. Roosevelt had represented a parenthesis, between two particularly harsh chapters. In the same manner, Carter's presidency represented a refreshing interlude between two especially tough periods in the Cold War chapter. He introduced a much–needed wedge during a period characterized by repression and excesses of all sorts.

Carter aimed at confronting Communism through the counterweight of ethical values. Human Rights became the essence of such strategy. He also tried to prioritise interdependence, while relaxing the ideological

---

[22] Ibid., p. 71.

demons. As a result, military regimes that had committed all kinds of human rights violations, under Washington's green light, found themselves in the accused bench. At the same time, he actively promoted social and land reform policies, particularly in Central America where the gap between the haves and the have nots was enormous.

The ideological and political confrontation with Havana was also greatly reduced. The United States and Cuba opened Representation Offices in each other's capitals. Simultaneously, and going against 87 percent of America's public opinion as expressed in the polls, Carter signed in 1977 the Torrijos–Carter treaties. These agreements not only derogated the draconian terms of the 1903 Treaty with Panama, but committed both countries to a gradual transfer of suzerainty over the Canal Zone. The year 2000 was established as the moment when total suzerainty would pass to Panamanian hands.

During his time in office he also visited several Latin American countries, bringing with him expressions of respect and goodwill. Carter, as Roosevelt before him, duly valued Latin America. Unfortunately, both their administrations represented the exception to the rule.

Trade and Security

Suddenly, at the end of the 1980s, the Cold War ended. George H. W. Bush became the first President under the next chapter of this saga: Trade and Security. During this period, which would follow its course until the end of Barack Obama's presidency, relations with the region were essentially focused on those two considerations.

Trade was represented by Bush's Enterprise for the Americas Initiative. Launched in 1990, it aimed to establish a free trade zone stretching across the whole Western hemisphere. It also included a loan program and a multilateral investment fund to be administered by the Inter–American Development Bank, as well as a debt relief program for Latin American and Caribbean countries.

According to its original formulation, the main objective of the Initiative was to promote market reforms in this hemisphere. The driving force of those reforms, even if not formally mentioned in the document, was the Washington Consensus. To be eligible for the Enterprise of the

Americas programs, countries had to adopt the International Monetary Fund and the World Bank promoted structural reforms. These reforms, which responded to the Washington Consensus' agenda, included economic deregulation and opening with respect to both trade and investment.

The first of the elements of the Initiative was the Free Trade Area of the Americas (FTAA), which aimed at negotiating multiple trade agreements with the nations of the Western Hemisphere. The North American Free Trade Agreement (NAFTA), which included the United States, Canada and Mexico, was number one in line.

Elements two and three of the Initiative were of much lesser importance as the sums therein involved were practically meaningless. For instance, the debt relief program for Latin America and the Caribbean proposed an elimination of between 10 to 15 percent of the 12,000 million dollars that their countries owed the United States government. Given that the total debt of those regions to commercial banks, multilateral financial institutions and other creditors amounted to 425,000 million dollars, the proposed debt relief made no difference whatsoever.

Together with the aforementioned initiative, The White House formulated a "war on drugs" strategy in 1989. Different from his successors who would emphasise external supply, Bush aimed at eradicating drug use by primarily focusing on internal demand. Not surprisingly, the war on drugs would soon put him in conflict with the strongman of Panama, Rafael Noriega.

A favourite ally of the CIA during the Cold War period, Noriega believed that his services to Washington within that context, shielded his dark businesses with drug lords. And probably it would have, had it not been for the fact that the Cold War was reaching its end. According to the Wall Street Journal:

"The US knew Noriega was a drug trafficker for years but didn't act against him because he was helpful in the Cold War said Michael Shifter, president of the Washington–based Inter–American Dialogue. When the Cold War ended, and the drug issue became more salient, Washington ousted him".[23]

[23] de Córdoba, J (2017). Former Panamanian Dictator Dies at 83 (31 May 2017). The Wall Street Journal.

At the end of 1989, President Bush ordered the military invasion of Panama to overthrow a government accused of drug trafficking. The new chapter that put an end to the grisly Cold War period, was thus to begin with another military invasion. It was the first in more than 20 years.

Bill Clinton closely continued with the duality of trade promotion and the war on drugs. Regarding the former it concluded the negotiations on NAFTA, imposing additional conditions on Mexico as requested by Congress. At the beginning of 1994 the agreement entered in force, with the Clinton administration taking charge of its initial implementation. This White House was also very much in tune with the Washington Consensus, which guided its economic rapprochement to Latin America.

The war on drugs, on its part, was extended beyond drugs itself, assuming a broader security character. With Colombia being the main drug producing and export centre of the Americas, and with the guerrillas of that country involved in the drug business, the two issues became intertwined. In 1998 and 1999, Clinton and Colombia's President Andres Pastrana, conceived the Plan Colombia. Its goal was twofold: combating drug cartels and the left–wing insurgency, aiming at ending cocaine trafficking and production and the Colombian armed conflict.

Colombian security forces, which received aid and training from the US, were involved in supporting human right abuses by right–wing paramilitary forces. Moreover, the security forces would eventually be directly involved in the killing of many innocents with the aim of presenting them as guerrilla members. This resulted from one of ugliest aspects of the plan: awarding monetary compensation for the dead bodies of guerrilla fighters. The American supported aerial fumigation to eradicate cocaine, also became highly controversial. This activity not only destroyed legal crops but had adverse health effects on the peasants. Plan Colombia, initiated during Clinton's years, would end up being a localized and smaller scale reminder of the abuses committed under the Cold War chapter.

The George W. Bush administration followed suit. During his administration, Chile entered the Free Trade Areas of the Americas in 2004 and Peru did so in 2007. In 2005 the Dominican Republic and Central America Free Trade Agreement with the United States was ratified as part of the same FTAA program.

And yet, in the 2003 meeting of trade ministers of the Americas held in Miami, it was agreed that the FTAA would not be extended beyond the countries that were at the time negotiating their adherence. This included Colombia and Panama beyond Chile, Peru and Dominican Republic and Central America. Hence, the boundaries of the Free Trade Area of the Americas were defined.

Security policies also continued to be emphasized during this period. US military and police aid to Latin American governments doubled during the Bush Administration, with Colombia receiving half of the value of such assistance. Bolivia, Peru and Mexico were also significant recipients. The fight against drugs was the main motivation, with Bogota receiving funds for the same broader objectives of Plan Colombia that, as seen, also included fighting left–wing insurgency.

At the end of 2007, Mexico's President Felipe Calderon and President Bush agreed on the Merida Initiative. According to the Initiative, the United States transferred significant military and economic resources to Mexico and Central American countries, to strengthen their capacity against drug cartels. Plan Colombia and the Merida Initiative became the only two relevant security projects of the US. government in Latin America. Bush's White House was supportive of democracy in the hemisphere. Nonetheless, its role in Venezuela's President Hugo Chavez brief ousting through a coup in 2002, did not follow suit. According to David R. Mares:

> "Breaking with the previous policy and with the Inter–American community, and amidst rumours of the US involvement, White House spokesman called for fresh elections instead of asking for the restitution of Chavez as President".[24]

Moreover, official documents declassified in accordance with the Freedom of Information Act, proved that the US government had knowledge of the upcoming coup.[25]

---

[24] Mares, DR (2004). El Multilateralismo y la Política Exterior de Bush en el Mundo post 11 de Septiembre. In , *Bajo la Mirada del Halcón: Estados Unidos-América Latina post 11-0-2001,* C Fuentes S (ed.), p.59. Santiago de Chile: FLACSO-Chile.

[25] Golinger, E (2005). *The Chávez Code: Cracking U.S. Intervention in Venezuela.* La Habana: Editorial José Martí.

During George W. Bush's term in office, relations between Latin America and the United States began to take a distance. Two considerations caused it. One preceded the Bush administration, while the other was clearly attributable to its actions. By this time, although still favoured by the White House, most of Latin America was rejecting the Washington Consensus. Having experienced, high social turmoil and low economic growth rates because of it, governments in the region were not willing to go ahead with its prescriptions.

As for the second consideration, there was a generalized regional malaise caused by the overbearing attitude that prevailed in Washington after September 11. Through threats, arrogance and verbal abuse, Washington tried to enlist Latin America in its fight against the real and imaginary demons that it was now confronting. Other subjects, like the pressures exerted upon Latin America to align with Washington in relation to the exemption of US troops from the jurisdiction of the International Penal Court, contributed to this drifting apart. Only Colombia, Dominican Republic and some Central American countries decided to follow Washington's lead, while the majority abstained from doing so.

But there was also a third consideration involved: China. The sudden and unexpected appearance of this huge market for its exports, empowered the region and gave reassurance to its voice. While China did not contest Washington's influence over the region, it was instrumental in providing a potent alternative to the United States.

According to Jorge I. Dominguez:

> "China's economic rise helps to explain the wider room for manoeuver in the international system and, more specifically, the Latin American economic boom of the century's first decade and the consequent empowerment of Latin American states to carry out their preferred domestic and foreign policies".[26]

Moreover, in Dominguez words:

> "China thus widened political opportunities for Latin America and other countries of the world…but it did so mainly through trade–created

[26] Dominguez, JI and RF de Castro (eds.), (2010). *Contemporary U.S.-Latin American Relations: Cooperation or Conflict in the 21st Century?* New York: Routledge, p. 6.

prosperity, not by countering the United States in Latin America — it would allow U.S. influence to implode on its own".[27]

The ease with which the United States accepted being displaced by China from the access to commodities which had always been under its privileged reach, is bewildering. Even if the United States could choose natural resources from global sources, the ones which had traditionally been considered secure, even strategic, were those located in its hemisphere. As China increased its share of world demand for commodities, huge competition for those located in Latin America became a new fact of life for the United States. According to Lauren Paverman:

> "China could be said to have jumped the fence into the United States' backyard in an attempt to capitalise on the impressive inventory of natural resources that the region has to offer".[28]

The arrival of Barack Obama to the White House was received with great optimism through the region, as it was believed to be in tune with the precedents of Franklyn D. Roosevelt and Jimmy Carter. Disappointment was thus generalized when the inertial follow through of ongoing policies became the main characteristic of his administration. In 2011, Colombia and Panama acceded to the FTAA as a result of long held negotiations.

In security, there was also a continuation of Bush policies. As Jorge I. Dominguez puts it:

> "When security concerns were not salient in a specific relationship…the US government gradually downgraded its attention. As for the near-neighbors in the Caribbean, Central America, Colombia, and Mexico, the US security obsession with terrorists and criminals became a dominant element of the relations between them and the United States. The United States 'saw' those bilateral relations through a security lens".[29]

---

[27] Ibid., p. 12.

[28] Paverman, L (2011). China looks to Venezuela for energy security. Worldpress.org, (11 October 2011). http://worldpress.org/Americas/3820.cfm. Accessed 15/02/2012.

[29] Dominguez, *op. cit.*, p. 23.

Hence, a period that could have created a rapprochement between Washington and Latin America, after the drifting away of the Bush years, simply faded away. Again, in Jorge I. Dominguez words:

> "By the end of the Bush presidency, the US claim to primacy and deference was no longer credible in the Americas. Barack Obama's understandable international distractions and inability to work with Congress did little to restore that credibility. The era of US–Latin America coordination flourished and died with that decade. The enhanced capacities thanks to economic growth, the self–imposed isolation of the Bush administration, and the volatility of the Obama administration generated Latin American foreign policies more markedly independent from the United States".[30]

On the Losing Equation

Not surprisingly, several regional multilateral institutions, that excluded the United States from membership, would take shape during those years. They became a good expression of disillusionment and new–found assertiveness in relation to Washington. Notwithstanding the US' indifference towards the region beyond security issues, there was a relative closer relationship with the countries that belonged to NAFTA or FTAA.

Surprisingly, in the second half of his administration, Obama opened the floodgates of a connection with Cuba. When nothing else could have been expected, he finally showed that he had something of F.D.R. and Jimmy Carter in him. Most of the steps that Obama took were directly related to his capacity to act within the authority granted by executive orders. Hence, they were limited in scope and could be reversed by any future US President. They included the opening of an American Embassy in Havana, the loosening of restrictions for US citizens to visit the island nation, and the easing of trade and financial barriers. It was perhaps late for him to capitalize on this initiative to improve relations with Latin America. Nonetheless, the door had been opened for his successor to do so.

---

[30] Ibid., p. 26.

But the successor was none other than Donald Trump. Even if it is too soon to write about his administration, some trends are already taking shape. The opportunity of improving relations with the region by further improving them with Cuba was foreclosed, as the new President soon began reversing some of the initiatives taken by Obama, tightening trade and travel rules in relation to the island. By aiming at the tourist industry, lifeline of the Cuban economy, Trump discouraged investments and developments in that sector.

As for the members of NAFTA or the FTAA, which were better positioned in relation to Washington than the rest of the Latin American countries, they seem to be on the losing side of the new political and economic equation. Mexico, the US' closest ally in the region is being targeted on several fronts. Moreover, all free trade agreements within the umbrella of the FTTA are to be reviewed. Free trade, indeed, has become a discredited proposition within the Trump Administration. Washington's sponsored Trans–Pacific Partnership, in which several Latin American Pacific Basin countries had placed positive expectations, was abandoned by the new administration.

As for the rest of Latin America, there seem to be no gains in sight within the prevailing state of things. With the United States relinquishing its leadership over the globalized economy, climate change and cooperative multilateralism, there are no reasons to look upon to Washington. Beijing's position in Latin America, hence, will be substantially strengthened. Not only because China is rapidly transforming itself in the main turbine of global trade, economic connectivity and climate change, but as a result of its impressive positioning in Latin America since the Millennium. This will probably take America's influence in the region to a historical low.

CHAPTER 8

THE REVENGE OF THE SOUTH

For the greater part of their independent history, relations between the United States and Latin America seem to have been guided by the following quote of Thucydides in the Melian Dialogue: "...while the strong do as they can and the weak suffer what they must". Which literally means that the powerful do what they want, while the weak endure what they must. Approaching the second decade of the new millennium, though, things have changed. As the United States and Latin America are increasingly drifting apart, the influence of Washington upon the latter is decreasing with every passing year.

Curiously, while the countries drift apart, society in the United States is becoming more and more "Latino American". By 2050 the total US population is projected to grow to almost 400 million, of which 28 per cent or about 112 million will be Latino. In other words, close to a third of its population will trace back their ascendancy to Iberian America. Indeed, population growth for Latinos is currently at 23 per cent versus seven per cent for the total population.[1]

The United States' national identity will inevitably be permeated by the sheer force of numbers. Not surprisingly, Samuel P. Huntington wrote

[1]Malavé, I and E Giordani (2015). *Latino Stats: American Hispanics by the Numbers,* p. 3. New York: The New Press.

about the strong possibility of the United States becoming a bifurcated society in

> "...terms of language (English and Spanish) and culture (the Anglo–Saxon and the Hispanic)...Substantial portions of the United States, particularly Florida and the Southwest, would end up being essentially Hispanics both in terms of culture and language with both cultures and languages coexisting. The United States, hence, would lose its cultural and linguistic unity transforming itself into a bilingual and bicultural society such as Canada, Switzerland or Belgium".[2]

If such a prediction materializes it would undoubtedly represent the revenge of the South.

Crossed by the Border

Much is said about Latin Americans, particularly Mexicans, entering the United States. This generates the impression that a great part of the population now based in the US is made up by current migration fluxes. That is certainly not the case. Latino population growth is driven by the children or grandchildren of immigrants, as the number of Latino immigrants in the country continues to decline. Two out of every three Latinos in the United States today were born there. Every year one out of four babies born in the United States is born to a Latino mother. Three–quarters of Latinos are thus US citizens.[3]

Moreover, many members of the Latino community trace their ancestry to places that were incorporated into the United States. In other words, their forefathers lived there before such territories became part of the United States. The descendants of families who inhabited what is now the Southwestern United States, could say "We didn't cross the border. The border crossed us". Hence, even if their traditions remain very much in tune with Hispanic America, they belong to families that for generations have enjoyed US citizenship.

---

[2]Huntington, SP (2004). *¿Quiénes Somos? Los Desafíos de la Identidad Nacional Estadounidense*, p. 45. Barcelona: Paidos Iberica Ediciones S. a.
[3]Ibid., p. 3.

However, even being American citizens, their ancestors were subjected, by their new fellow countrymen, to the same kind of self–righteous sense of superiority that the United States as a nation showed to Latin American countries. In Lars Schoultz words: “A belief in Latin American inferiority is the essential core of United States policy toward Latin America”.[4]

Let us take the cases of California and Texas to understand the above. The first Spanish town in California was Saint Augustine, founded in 1556. That is, 11 years before Jamestown was founded in Massachusetts. In the 1660s the “Camino Real” between San Diego and Sonoma was full of Jesuit or Franciscan missions, which gave rise to the first Californian towns, those of Los Angeles, San Francisco and San Diego, which in time were to become great cities.

In 1823, the Mexican government decreed the secularization of religious missions, whose vast land holdings were divided and allotted as ranches to numerous Mexican settlers. 80,000 Mexicans, or “Californios” as they called themselves, lived in California when the 1845–1848 War between Mexico and the United States ensued. As a result of the subsequent Guadalupe Hidalgo Treaty of 1848, these Californios not only became American citizens, but their property was to be guaranteed within their new country.

As it happened, when gold was discovered in California, Americans began arriving there in droves. Suddenly Californios not only found themselves engulfed by the newcomers, but became second class citizens in their own land. Moreover, as their properties were not respected by the newcomers, and taking their cases to court ended up by ruining them, their situation became dire.

The Treaty of Guadalupe Hidalgo covered “Tejanos” as well. That is, Texans of Mexican origin who had become American citizens and whose properties were also to be protected by law. Nonetheless, as Ray Suarez says: “Landless Americans were pouring into Texas, and town after town moved to expel its native-born Tejano Mexican residents”.[5] Tejanos

[4]Schoultz , L (1998). *Beneath the United States: A History of U.S. Policy toward Latin America.* Kindle Ed., Preface, Paragraph 15. Cambridge, Mass.: Harvard University Press.
[5]Suarez, R (2013). *Latino Americans: The 500-Year Legacy that Shaped a Nation.* Kindle Ed. Chapter 1, Loc 640. New York: Celebra.

became second class citizens in their own land as well, and subjected to all kinds of abuses.

The fact is that Californios and Tejanos, along with countless inhabitants of Mexican origin in Southwestern United States, were seen as a conquered people. Again, according to Ray Suarez:

> "That the United States was able to conquer Mexico so easily in the 1840s served to confirm Mexican inferiority in the eyes of many Americans...Anglos in places like Texas and New Mexico and California continued to affirm the basic terms of the US–Mexico war: That an inferior people had been conquered by a superior people. That democracy had won out over feudalism and backwardness. That progress was in the hands of the Americans, and Latinos...were simply destined to go away in the face of a superior American culture".[6]

Something similar applies to Puerto Ricans. Puerto Rico had been home to a resistance movement against the Spanish colonial rule since the early 1860s. As in Cuba, though, they got rid of it through the Spanish–American War of 1898. Nonetheless, theirs would be a simple change of colonial masters, as Washington substituted Madrid as the new imperial metropolis.

Unlike Cuba, which was occupied with the intention of promoting self–government, although under a Protectorate regime, Puerto Rico was to be directly owned by the United States. The population of Puerto Rico, which at the time numbered around a million, was thus subjected to great uncertainty in relation to its future.

Under the new circumstances Puerto Rican schools began teaching in English and the history of the United States became the official narrative. This was an outcome of the policy of assimilation. The island's status became highly ambiguous as the United States did not offer Puerto Rico independence or statehood.

Eventually, in 1917, citizenship was offered to its inhabitants through the Jones–Shafroth Act, albeit with limited rights. They would not have representation in the US Congress nor would they be able to elect their Governor. What they could do was to move freely into the United States.

[6]Ibid., Chapter 1, Loc 737.

And that they did by the thousands. Today there are more Puerto Ricans in New York than on the island itself. In their case, as well, they did not cross the border, the border crossed them.

Crossing the Border

But the opposite began happening in the first decades of the 1900s, when one million Mexicans crossed the border escaping from the Mexican Revolution. Such motivation was compounded by work opportunities. Among them were the construction of the great aqueducts in California and the agricultural industry in the Southwest United States. This migration came in handy for the United States, as cheap labour had stopped arriving from Europe because of World War I.

By the 1930s, 150,000 Mexicans had contributed to the urban expansion of Los Angeles by participating in the construction industry. Mexicans, who had originally built Los Angeles in colonial times, built it a second time in the 1920s. Without them the infrastructure of the city would have never materialized. This time, sadly, they were second class citizens in a land that had once belonged to their ancestors. As the African Americans in the South of the old Confederation, but not to the same extent, they too were segregated. Segregated schools and segregated public facilities. This was a common feature all over the Southwestern United States.

But if the 1920s had been good for the Mexicans in terms of working opportunities, the 1930s were grim. Economic depression brought with it intense competition for fewer jobs. American citizens were, indeed, ready to take occupations that had been allotted to Mexicans.

According to Ray Suarez:

> "Between 1931 and 1935, as American joblessness reached its Depression crescendo some four hundred thousand Mexicans, more than half of whom were American citizens, were 'repatriated' to a country that in many cases they had never seen. Carried on entirely without due process, the mass deportations were authorized by President Herbert Hoover, who gave the go–ahead to his Secretary of Labour".[7]

[7]Ibid., Chapter 2, Loc 1470.

During World War II a two–track process took place for Latinos. On the one hand, those with American citizenship went to fight abroad, mingling with fellow citizens from the most diverse background and geographical locations. Their courage in action and the interaction with other American citizens was a catalyst for civil rights advancement.

On the other hand, an agreement between the US and the Mexican governments was signed in 1942, for the supply of one million temporary farm workers. They were to fill the vacuum left by men at arms and came to be known as "braceros". 21 states received them for the purpose of harvesting the widest variety of agricultural products.

At the end of the war American farmers kept bringing this temporary labour force back, whose willingness for work had impressed them. From then on, they became a permanent fixture of the agricultural workforce of the United States. By the time the Bracero Program ended in 1964, five million legal crossings had taken place.

Even more so, during the post–war years large numbers of Mexicans crossed the border and went to work outside the framework of the Bracero Program. Estimates of such workers run as high as three million in 1951, according to the US Justice Department and the Immigration and Naturalization Service. They belonged to those who had crossed the border, and not to those whom the border had crossed. Both groups, though, were increasing their numbers with every passing year.

Cubans and Others

A few years later, with the arrival of the new decade, came the turn of the Cubans. Amid expropriations of private enterprises, leaning into the Soviet orbit and rumours of different kinds being aired, scores of people from Cuba began moving into Florida. Even if it just implied traveling 90 miles north, it represented a tremendous shift in the life of those affected.

Most of the newcomers had a higher sociocultural status than those of previous immigrants. Doctors, dentists, engineers or lawyers represented a different social group. Nevertheless, their professional standing dropped dramatically because their titles were not recognized in the United States. For the majority it was, thus, a fresh start under diminished circumstances.

For obvious reasons this was, and would remain for many years to come, a politically engaged immigration in relation to US policies towards Cuba and Latin America. As they grew in political importance within the host country, these immigrants became a fundamental factor in determining Washington policies in relation to Cuba. Normalizing such relations, and lifting the economic blockade imposed over the island at the beginning of the revolution, thus became extremely difficult under such circumstances.

By the end of the 1960s there were 300,000 Cubans living in Miami.[8] It had become a very successful immigration. In historian Maria Cristina Garcia's words:

> "No immigrant community in US history had gained so much economic and political power in the short time Cubans had. And all these gains were attained by not assimilating into the existing culture. In fact it is arguable that by remaining Cubans, and remaining focused on maintaining their heritage in the expectation of returning home, Cubans were able to succeed as they did". [9]

As Cubans grew in cultural influence and economic clout, the city became increasingly bilingual. Moreover, thanks to their presence, the city was transformed into the natural bridge between the United States and Latin America, becoming a favourite destination for the wealthy and mobile within the region. Large investments in real estate and in the banking sector resulted from this.

Unfortunately, for the good image of Cuban immigrants in American eyes, a new wave contributed to tarnishing the prevailing perception. Between April and October of 1980, around 125,000 Cubans reached south Florida. This refugee flow came to be known as the Marielitos, as they went on board at the Mariel port in Cuba. Faced with the pressure of countless of his citizens wanting to leave the island, Fidel Castro announced that Cubans who wished to do so were free to leave. Hundreds of boats streamed towards Florida. In the process, Castro opened the gates

---

[8] Ibid., Chapter 4, Loc 2480.

[9] Ibid., Chapter 4, Loc 2528.

of jails and mental hospitals so that all common prisoners and mental patients make their way to Florida as well.

In the end, only around 25,000 had criminal records and no more than four per cent of the immigrants were mentally ill.[10] Nonetheless, as the 1983 Brian De Palma film *Scarface* showed, this was a new face of Cuba. Shortly after, no wonder, the hit television series *Miami Vice* made its appearance. With it came a whole array of Latino characters, including drug dealers, prostitutes, pimps and money launderers.

But Cubans, thanks to the Cold War, enjoyed a privileged entry ticket to the United States, as all the citizens of the island who reached its shores could claim refugee status. The same was not the case for the rest of the region. Post–war immigration laws had limited the number of people who could come from Asia, Africa and Latin America. This formula favoured arrivals from Europe and within it from northern and western Europe. Nonetheless, the Immigration and Nationality Act of 1965 relaxed the situation.

According to the 1965 Act, national quotas designed to keep Latin Americans and Asians out were abolished. This was part of the broader push for civil rights, giving preference for immigration of relatives of US citizens and residents. Dominicans who had family members residing in the United States, were the first to take advantage of this situation.

Thousands of Dominicans arrived in New York during the second half of the 1960s and all through the 1970s. They were likely to occupy the spaces left by Puerto Ricans who were moving to better places in New Jersey, Connecticut and suburban New York counties. The same happened with economic niches. Dominicans essentially started up by buying the grocery stores left by the former. This is why it has been said that Puerto Ricans laid the foundations for Dominicans.

In the 1980s came the turn of Central Americans. As the low intensity war ravaged their countries, much of it with the support of the American government, almost a million people fled from El Salvador, Honduras, Guatemala or Nicaragua. The United States became their favourite destination.

Salvadorans, who represented the largest group, mostly headed to Los Angeles. When the Central American civil wars ended, there were

---

[10] Ibid., Chapter 6, Loc 3491.

also large and growing communities of those countries in Washington DC, Miami and Houston, among other places. Consequently, during the 1980s the Latino population of the United States grew a stunning 53 percent.[11]

In 1986, Ronald Reagan signed the Immigration Reform Act. Its purpose was twofold. On the one hand, it put the burden of illegal workers on employers, who would be fined for hiring alien citizens not allowed to work and live in the United States. On the other hand, it opened a path to legal residence to millions of immigrants who had illegally entered the country. In other words: "The United States would give people who had cheated under the old system a chance to get legal, and then slam the door behind them".[12] So it was that two and a half million people who had been living and working illegally, became legal residents.[13]

There would be another important influx of Latin American immigrants; from Mexico this time. The North American Free Trade Agreement was supposed to create jobs in Mexico, with the idea of containing illegal immigration. In many areas, it did. Nonetheless, it promoted exactly the opposite in an area as important as agriculture. The agreement placed an unbalanced competition between the Mexican communal farmers and the vast mechanized farms of the United States and Canada.

Countless Mexican farmers suddenly found that they could no longer make a decent living by growing a crop that was synonymous to the country's identity: corn. Eventually a million farmers gave up, resulting in a new migration wave into the United States.[14] But these new migrants were no longer going to Los Angeles or to the big metropolitan areas where they had been heading since the Mexican Revolution. This time they were moving to Georgia, Alabama, Nebraska, North Carolina, Iowa and New York. Competition among Latinos was increasing and new areas had to be found.

These last few years, on the other hand, more than a million Puerto Ricans moved to Florida. An important feature of Puerto Ricans' status is that while in the island they cannot vote in presidential elections, whereas once in the United States they have all the voting rights of American

[11] Ibid., Chapter 6, Loc 3613.

[12] Ibid., Chapter 6, Loc 3593.

[13] Ibid., Chapter 6, Loc 3598.

[14] Ibid., Chapter 6, Loc 3694.

citizens. These arrivals coincided with those of numerous Colombians, Venezuelans and people from other parts of the region.

Latino numbers kept increasing both from new immigration and from American new born babies. During the 1980s, this population had grown to more than 22 million, whereas in the 1990s it added ten million more.[15] Only 17 per cent of all Latinos are currently undocumented workers, while most are the children or grandchildren of immigrants. Today three–quarters of Latinos are US citizens, which is close to 40 million people. Moreover in 2012, almost 24 million Latinos were entitled to vote. Of the total Latino population, 55 per cent could not vote because they were not yet 18 years old or were non–citizens.[16]

As their numbers grew so did their political importance. However, this was not an easy process. Several decades of advocacy and political activism were required to give a voice to this diverse Latino population.

Latino Activism

The oldest Latino civil rights organization in the United States is the League of United American Citizens (LULAC). It was established in 1929 in Corpus Christi, Texas. Since the beginning, LULAC had an "assimilation" policy. According to this policy its members were encouraged to adapt to the dominant European–American culture.

Despite its philosophy, challenged in later years when pride in the Hispanic heritage was asserted, LULAC has a very important advocacy record. Through the years, the organization struggled to erase discriminatory laws and practices. Since the 1930s, its activities included voter registration education campaigns.

In the 1960s the duo Cesar Chavez and Dolores Huerta were pioneers in grassroots organization. Together they created the United Farm Workers (UFW), unionizing and giving voice to the previously destitute Latino farmworkers. They were responsible for bringing a new kind of attention to Latinos in the United States.

---

[15] Ibid., Chapter 6, Loc 3613 and Loc 3744.

[16] Malavé and Giordani, *op. cit.*, p. 3.

While the African–Americans were fighting for their civil rights in the south eastern United States, the UFW was simultaneously fighting for the Latinos civil rights in California. Like Martin Luther King, Chavez and Huerta insisted in non–violence, which is why UFW strikers did not fight back against the violence of strike–breakers. Several farmworkers were killed in shootings and beatings.

Fasting also became a powerful tool of resistance, with Chavez entering in several hunger strikes. While he did so, Huerta headed to different parts of the country to nationalize their struggle, urging Americans to boycott table grapes. Boycotting, fasting and non–violence against strike–breakers, became powerful nonviolent tactics that attracted national attention. The Catholic Church, Martin Luther King and Senator Robert Kennedy, were among those that lent their support to the "cause", as this movement was known.

Luther King sent Chavez a message after one of his fasts saying: "As brothers in the fight for equality, I extend the hand of fellowship and goodwill. Our separate struggles are really one. A struggle for freedom, for dignity, for humanity".[17] Kennedy travelled to California to meet Chavez and became an important voice of support for his struggle.

In 1968, Herman Gallegos, Julian Samora and Ernesto Galarza founded the Southwest Council of La Raza. In 1973, it became a national organization, henceforth known as the National Council of La Raza. The term "La Raza" refers to the Hispanic people of the New World, as defined by Jose de Vasconcelos. Initially focused on Mexican American issues, it expanded in 1975 to Latino issues in general. It is currently the largest Latino non–profit advocacy organization, promoting public policies that favour the Latino community. Such polices include immigration reform and a path to citizenship for immigrants living in the country illegally.

Also in 1968, the Mexican American Legal Defense and Educational Fund was created as a non–profit organization aimed at protecting the rights of Latinos in the United States. Founded in San Antonio, Texas, it is currently headquartered in Los Angeles. Its first years were devoted to legal aid cases in defense of Latino causes, such as fighting illegal discrimination

[17] Suarez, *op. cit.*, Chapter 5, Loc 3019.

or promoting financing for education. In later years, they set up several promotional campaigns on Latino issues. In 1994, they challenged California Proposition 187, a state–run citizenship screening system against illegal aliens and in 2010 they opposed Arizona SB1070, the broadest anti–illegal immigration measure in the United States in generations.

In 1971, the conference "Unidos" (Together), took place in Washington DC. It was the first concerted effort by members of the Mexican–American, Cuban–American and Puerto Rican communities, to joint efforts in the pursuit of common objectives. According to Armando B. Rendon, Mexican–American activist and author:

> "It was the first time in which Mexican–Americans took conscience of the severity of the discriminatory status of Puerto Rico or understood the socio–political views of the Cuban–Americans. Puerto Ricans and Cubans openly discussed about the preconceptions that separated them while the two of them got to understand the exploitation suffered by the Chicano population…The three groups discovered how much they had in common. Unidos was a turning point towards the consolidation of a Hispanic community in the United States".[18]

In 1976, the Congressional Hispanic Caucus was organized by five Hispanic Federal Congressmen: Herman Badillo, Baltazar Corrada del Rio, Kikode la Garza, Henry B. Gonzalez and Edward Roybal. Its goal was to address national and international issues of relevance for the Latino community. In addition to covering legislative action, the Caucus also monitors legislative, executive and judicial actions that impact the community. As the number of members of Latinos in Congress increased, so did the membership of the Caucus.

In the second half of the 1990s, the Republican Representatives decided to leave the Caucus in protest over its support for improved relations with Cuba. In 2003, the dissenting group created the Congressional Hispanic Conference, headed by Congressman Mario Diaz–Balart.

[18]Rendon, AB (1981). Latinos: Breaking the Cycle of Survival to Tackle Global Affairs. In *Ethnicity and U.S. Foreign Policy,* Abdul Said Aziz (ed.), p. 188. New York: Praeger.

Currently, the Caucus has 30 Democratic members of both houses, while the Conference has 13 Republican ones.

Willie Velasquez was a Texan with a long history of Mexican American activism who decided to concentrate his efforts in promoting Latino voting. He concluded that Latinos would only realize their full potential and acquire influence within. The American society, once they started to vote in great numbers. For many years, his efforts were thus devoted to registering millions of Latino voters. For such an endeavour he was posthumously awarded the Presidential Medal of Freedom in 1995.

In 2006 and 2007, massive protest marches in which millions participated, showed the organizational power enjoyed by the Latino community and in particular by the Spanish–language media outlets in the United States. The largest single demonstration took place in Los Angeles on March 25, 2006, with 500,000 marchers, while the largest nationwide march occurred on April 10, 2006, with marches in 102 cities around the United States.

Such initiatives responded to the House of Representatives' Border Protection, Antiterrorism and Illegal Control Act of 2005, better known as H.R. 4437. Passed in 2005, the Bill mandated fines for illegal immigrants, making the housing of illegals a felony while increasing the fact of being in the country illegally from a low–level civil infraction to a federal crime.

The overwhelming reaction to the Act surprised the Republican politicians, who had sponsored it. They had wrongly believed that the Latino community was split. On the one side, those that supported an easy path to a legal status or citizenship for Latino immigrants, and, on the other, those who opposed it. In assuming so, they grossly underestimated the level of solidarity prevailing within the community. Spanish–speaking TV, radio and written press mobilized the protests, which were considered a historic turning point in Latino politics.

From Political Power to Soft Power

Not surprisingly, after so many years of activism and mobilization, the Latino community has become a political force to be reckoned with. That translates into numerous high ranking positions occupied by its members. The list includes: US Supreme Court Judge Sonia Sotomayor; current US

Senators Ted Cruz, Marco Rubio, Bob Menendez and Catherine Cortez Masto, two of whom were Presidential pre–candidates (former US Senators Mel Martinez and Ken Salazar were also elected in the new millennium), and numerous members of the House of Representatives.

Also on the list, former US Cabinet members Alberto R. Gonzalez (Attorney General); Manuel Lujan Jr. and Ken Salazar (Secretaries of the Interior); Carlos M. Gutierrez (Secretary of Commerce); Hilda L. Solis and Thomas E. Perez (Secretaries of Labor); Henry Cisneros, Mel Martinez and Julian Castro (Secretaries of Housing and Urban Development); Federico Peña (Secretary of Transportation); Federico Peña and Bill Richardson (Secretaries of Energy); and Lauro F. Cavazos (Secretary of Education). Within the Executive branch there has also been a broad spectrum of Latinos at the level of Under Secretaries and Ambassadors.

Twelve current or former State Governors from California, Florida, New Mexico, Arizona, New Hampshire and Nevada; and numerous city mayors, including Antonio Villaraigosa from Los Angeles, should also be included in that list. The Chairperson of the Democratic National Committee is Tom Perez, while the Executive Director of the American Civil Liberties Union is Anthony Romero, both Latinos.

But beyond the institutional and political area, Latinos have also attained high visibility within the entertainment, cultural, scientific or fashion sectors. In other words, together with their emerging political power there is also a soft power in motion. This not only translates into the representativeness of this group within society, but expresses the insertion of their culture into mainstream values. Theirs is no longer a segregated culture, but a fundamental addition to the American one.

Names such as Dolores del Rio, Ramon Novarro or Lupe Velez became famous at the inception of Hollywood. During the 1940s, 1950s, 1960s and 1970s they were followed by Latino figures such as Anthony Quinn, Carmen Miranda, Katy Jurado, Fernando Lamas, Ricardo Montalban, Cesar Romero, Pedro Armendariz, Raquel Welch, Jose Ferrer or Rita Moreno. The latter two won Oscars, with Moreno also wining an Emmy, a Tony and a Grammy Award.

Together with his wife Lucille Ball, Desi Arnaz made history on American TV in the 1950s with "I Love Lucy". His Cuban–American accent and characterization introduced a Latino figure for the first time into the homes of Americans. Puerto Rican Freddie Prinze would replicate a similar level of TV celebrity during the 1970s.

What differentiates the situation today, is the sheer impact of combined Latino talent. In the movie industry we may mention a long list of names, including Salma Hayek, Jessica Alba, Cameron Diaz, Benicio Del Toro, Guillermo Del Toro, Alejandro Gonzalez Iñarritu, Alonso Cuaron, Michelle Rodriguez, Zoe Saldana, Eva Mendes, Selena Gomez, Andy Garcia, Guillermo Arriaga, Robert Rodriguez, Oscar Isaac, Rosario Dawson, John Leguizamo, Edgar Ramirez, Michael Peña, Gael Garcia Bernal, Ruben Blades, Edward J. Olmos, Ana De Armas, Rosie Perez, Hector Elizondo, Emmanuel Lubezki and Jennifer Lopez, to mention just a few.

The superstar status of Jennifer Lopez also translates into the music industry, where she alternates with other Latino icons such as Shakira, Christina Aguilera, Mariah Carey, Thalia, Carlos Santana, Mark Anthony, Ricky Martin, Juanes, Pitbull, Arturo Sandoval, Willie Colon, Gloria Estefan, Linda Ronstadt or Ruben Blades. Broadway's icon Lin-Manuel Miranda and TV industry names such as Sofia Vergara, Eva Longoria, Ana Ortiz, Catalina Sandino Moreno, George Lopez, Demian Bichir, Alexis Bledel, Karla Souza, Jimmy Smits, Naya Rivera, David Zayas, Jorge Garcia and Geraldo Rivera.

There is also a long list of famous sportspeople in particular in the country's main sport, baseball. Numerous Latinos have been Major League players with many attaining the Hall of Fame. Within the latter Roberto Clemente, Martin Dihigo, Al Lopez, Juan Marichal, Luis Aparicio, Orlando Cepeda, Tony Perez, Jose Mendez, Alex Pompez, Cristobal Torriente, Roberto Alomar, Ron Santo, Joe Torre, Pedro Martinez and Ivan Rodriguez.

In the cultural sector, we find authors such as Pulitzer Prize winner Junot Diaz, world acclaimed author Isabel Allende, Julia Alvarez, Sandra Cisneros, Alisa Valdes–Rodriguez, Luis Alberto Urrea, Rudolfo Anaya or Luis J. Rodrigez. In opera, the towering figure of Placido Domingo shines, while in classical music the Los Angeles Philharmonic Orchestra Conductor Gustavo Dudamel, The Miami Symphony Orchestra Conductor Eduardo Marturet or the pianist Gabriela Montero enjoy wide recognition.

In the visual arts, Marisol Escobar, Olga Albizu, Frank Romero, Baruj Salinas, Jose Bedia, Richard Serra, Julio Larraz, Soraida Martinez, Tomas Sanchez and Rupert Garcia, are widely respected. Dana Goia served as

Chairman of the National Endowment for the Arts, Mari Carmen Ramirez is the Director of the International Center for the Arts of the Americas; Monica Ponce de Leon won the National Design Award and is the Dean of the School of Architecture at Princeton University.

There are also scientists such as Rafael Reif, President of the Massachusetts Institute of Technology; Nobel Prize laureates Baruj Benacerraf, Mario J. Molina or Cesar Milstein; France Cordova, Director of the National Science Foundation; Helen Rodriguez–Trias, former President of the American Health Association; Regina Benjamin, former Surgeon General of the United States; futurist and technology divulger Jason Silva; Jaime Escalante; Gustavo Adolfo Romero; Alfredo Quinones–Hinojosa; Evelyn Miralles and Ysrael Seinuk. Astronauts like Frank Chang–Diaz, John D. Olivas, Jose Hernandez and Ellen Ochoa; the latter being the current Director of the Johnson Space Center.

Reputed scholars like Ernesto Zedillo, Director of the Center for the Study of Globalization at Yale University; Ricardo Hausmann, Director of the Center for International development at Harvard University; Moises Naim, former Editor of *Foreign Policy*; Sebastian Edwards, Henry Ford Professor of International Business Economics at the University of California, Los Angeles; Jorge I. Dominguez, former Director of the Weatherhead Center for International Affairs at Harvard; Arturo Valenzuela former Director of the Center for Latin American Studies at Georgetown and former Under Secretary of State for Hemispheric Affairs; Guillermo O'Donnell, leading world theorist on authoritarianism and democratization; David L. Carrasco, Neil L. Rudensteine Professor on religious studies at Harvard; Angelo Rivero Santos Academic Director of the Georgetown Center for Latin American Studies; Harold Trinkunas, Assistant Director for Research at the Center for International Security and Cooperation of Stanford University; Gustavo Perez Firmat, David Feinson Professor in the Humanities at Columbia, to mention but a few. Within the community there have also been numerous MacArthur Fellows and Guggenheim recipients.

Fashion designer icons such as Carolina Herrera, Oscar de la Renta, Narciso Rodriguez, Isabel Toledo, Alejandro Ingelmo or Angel Sanchez, must be added as well.

But beyond the political power and the soft power realms, Latinos are also present in the business sector. Several CEOs of Fortune 500 companies are Latinos. Amid them Mary T. Barra of General Motors; Oscar Muñoz of United Airlines; Marcelo Claure of Sprint; Carlos Rodriguez of Automatic Data Processing; Robert E. Sanchez of Ryder System; George Paz of Scripts; Richard A. Gonzalez of AbbVie; Nina Vaca of Pinnacle Technical Resources; J. Paul Raines of GamesStop; Joseph Alvarado of Commercial Metals Company or J. Mario Molina of Molina Healthcare. But also, world class businesspeople, like Gustavo Cisneros, Chairman of Cisneros Group; Andres Gluski, CEO of AES Corporation; Nina Tassler Chairman of CBS Entertainment; Hilda Ochoa–Brillembourg, CEO of Strategic Investment Group; Jorge Perez, real estate developer; Betro Perez, founder of Zumba Fitness or Jordi Munoz, founder of 3D Robotics.

Gross Numbers and Republican Myopia

Latino figures, as seen, are everywhere amid mainstream America. But besides famous or well reputed names we find the argument of gross numbers. With more than 56,592,000 people, representing 17.61 percent of the total population, Latinos are the largest minority of the country. The growth of the United States Latino population is part of a demographic shift of tectonic scale. They are thus not only increasingly influential but they represent a fundamental electoral force. Being a fairly young population, its voting numbers will keep increasing with every passing election.

According to *The Economist* of January 31, 2004: "The 50/50 division of the electorate represents a historical gain for Republicans. Until such a recent date as the 70s, Democrats enjoyed of a thirty point lead in terms of party identification". Indeed, as the gap between both parties has shrunk to parity level, the electoral power of a massive group such as Latinos increases substantially.

In 2016, 27.3 million Latinos, representing 12 per cent of all eligible voters, could cast their ballots. Since 2012 their numbers increased by four million, accounting for 37 per cent of the growth in all eligible voters.[19] By 2030 the number will increase to 40 million as 17 million Latinos

[19]Krogstad JM (2016). Key facts about the Latino vote in 2016. Pew Research Center, 14 October 2016. http://www.pewresearch.org/fact-tank/2016/10/14/key-facts-about-the-latino-vote-in-2016/. Accessed 15/07/2017.

under the age of 18 get older. It must be outlined that more than 90 per cent of Latinos under the age of 18 were born in the United States and are therefore eligible to vote.[20] Let us not forget, indeed, that in the next 30 years the United States population will increasingly feature a growing cohort of young Latinos amid white elderly. And in 2050 one in every three Americans will be a Latino.

Their numbers though just tell part of the story. The other part derives from its block power. The 2006 and 2007 massive protest marches in reaction to H.R. 4437, proved that it is a relatively close community and therefore one which is easy to mobilize. Within it, the presence of issues of converging nature combines with that of Spanish–language media outlets with direct capacity to target the community. As Samuel P. Huntington reminds us, most Latinos emphasize that their children are proficient in Spanish: this varies between 66 and 85 per cent according to the different national groups.[21]

In contrast to other national communities such as German Americans, Norwegian Americans or Polish Americans, which have diluted into mainstream America to the point of not been easy to target or mobilize, Latinos tend to act and react as a block. This substantially increases the Latino political impact.

Republicans have had very limited success in winning over such voters in presidential elections. Since 1972 they never reached the 40 per cent mark except in the 2004 election, when George W. Bush obtained 44 per cent of the Latino vote. The reason for such success was that Bush supported a comprehensive immigration reform and promised to act on it in during his second term. He did as offered, but the reform did not get through Congress, because his own party did not support it.

Ronald Reagan had the following line about Latinos: "Hispanics are Republicans. They just don't know it yet". Referring to it, Garry Segura, Political Sciences Professor at Stanford adds:

> "There are two things that Republicans look at to make that conclusion. They look at entrepreneurial behaviour among Latinos, which is very

[20]Cillizza, C (2013). The Republican problem with Hispanic voters (18 March 2013). *The Washington Post*.

[21]Huntington, *op. cit.*, p. 271.

high…Latinos are starting businesses left and right. The second is that this is a very churchgoing, family–oriented subculture that would appear to be consistent with the family–values segment of the republican coalition".[22]

It could be added, though, that the Republicans' attitude towards Latinos is not in tune with such references. On the contrary, as David McNew says: "Latino' is a coherent political identity largely because of republican attacks".[23]

Time and again, Republicans have taken aim at Hispanic immigrants and, by extension, at the Latino community. From California's Proposition 187 to Arizona's SB1070, from the House of Representatives Bill 4437 to Trump's harsh ejection of Hispanic undocumented immigrants, Republicans keep widening the gap that separates them from Latinos.

Besides George W. Bush's good intentions, there was a second occasion when Republicans could have emended their relations with this community. Explaining the reasons why Mitt Romney lost the 2012 Presidential Elections, David Frum concluded in a well–researched piece in *The Atlantic*, that the fundamental problem came from having proposed a harsh immigration policy.[24] Having received just 27 percent of the Latino vote seriously hampered Romney's chance of winning the election. Not surprisingly, this gave rise to a subsequent serious attempt to reach out to Latinos.

According to Chris Cillizza:

"The Republican National Committee's 'Grow and Opportunity Project', a 100–page autopsy of what went wrong in 2012, is an attempt to re–start a party that has stalled out nationally — having come up short in consecutive presidential elections and having suffered popular vote defeats out of the last five contests. Much of the document is dedicated to addressing the demographic problems that confront Republicans with a shrinking white population and rising number of Hispanics entering

[22] Suarez, *op. cit.*, Chapter 5, Loc 4104.

[23] McNew, D (2016). This is the year of the Latino vote, (7 November 2016). *Vox.* http://www.vox.com/policy-and-politics/2016/11/7/13515248/latinos-vote-2016-clinton. Accessed 05/05/2017.

[24] Frum, D (2016). Will the Republican Party survive the 2016 election? *The Atlantic*, January-February 2016.

> the electorate. 'We are not a policy committee, but among the steps Republicans take in the Hispanic community and beyond, we must embrace and champion comprehensive immigration reform', reads the report. 'If we do not, our party's appeal will continue to shrink to its core constituencies only'".[25]

The Republican Party leadership attempted to proceed accordingly. But the immigration reform in question had to be abandoned, thanks again to the resistance of Republican constituencies and the unwillingness of much of the Republican bench. Moreover, Eric Cantor, who as Leader of the Republican Majority in Congress and had promoted the initiative, had to face the premature end of his career. His protagonist role in this matter was partially responsible for such an outcome. Senator Marco Rubio would also have to pay a high price in his presidential aspirations, as the base line of his party did not forget or forgive his leading role in the contentious immigration reform.

But in the same way in which Senator Rubio was punished, Donald Trump strengthened his candidacy thanks to his harsh rhetoric against Latinos. Once more Republican batteries found a good target to pound. In the short term, this seems to have worked on their behalf, as Trump's electoral success shows. The price tag, though, is huge. Republicans may have alienated, perhaps irreparably, their relationship with the Latino community. And with "a shrinking white population and rising number of Hispanics entering the electorate" as Chris Cillizza referred, there is no medium to long term win in this position.

Let us remember that besides their huge numbers in states that represent 72 per cent of the electoral vote, Latinos are rapidly increasing their population in battleground states such as Florida, Nevada, Colorado and Arizona. Moreover, according to John Micklethwait and Adrian Wooldridge, before the end of this decade, the population of Texas will be dominated by them.[26] In other words, a traditional blue state with 36 electoral votes, will have a Latino majority.

---

[25] Cillizza, *op. cit.*

[26] Micklethwait J and A Wooldridge (2004). *The Right Nation: Conservative Power in America.* London: Penguin Books.

In the 2016 election, it was reported that 67 per cent of Latinos voted for Hillary Clinton versus 31 per cent for Donald Trump. That represents a decrease in Latino votes for Democrats, as compared with 2012. On that occasion 71 per cent of the Latino vote went to Barack Obama and 27 per cent for Mitt Romney. That being so, rejection against Trump's rhetoric was not as obvious as it could have been. Nonetheless, these numbers are firmly contested by Latino Decisions, a pollster specialized in the Latino vote.

According to the pollster, Latino turnout not only grew substantially compared to 2012, but Hillary Clinton obtained 79 per cent of such vote versus 18 per cent for Donald Trump. If this was the case, it would have been the lowest level on record for any Republican presidential candidate. The difference given by Latino Decision is derived, according to them, by the following reason: "Exit polls get results from a small, non–representative sample of a handful of precincts. By contrast, the Latino Decision election poll includes a random state wide sample of all Latino voters across each state".[27]

Hence, in their words:

> "Nationally, Clinton received a record–high 79 percent to 18 percent for Trump, with 3 percent voting for one of the third–party candidates. This 61 percent gap is the largest we have recorded at Latino Decisions, outpacing the 2012 Obama advantage over Romney…In Florida, influenced by the more conservative Cuban vote, Clinton won 67 percent and Trump 31 percent — which still gave her a large increase over Obama who won Florida Latinos 58 to 40 percent".[28]

If the above numbers are correct, Republicans should be really worried. Going against a rising tide is never a wise decision.

---

[27] Sanchez, G and MA Barreto (11 November 2016). In record numbers, Latinos voted overwhelmingly against Trump. *Washington Post.*
[28] Ibid.

CHAPTER 9

WHEN CHINA ARRIVED FROM NOWHERE

For many years now the influence of the United States in Latin America has been decreasing, as the two have been drifting apart. Meanwhile, since the millennium China has been able to acquire a privileged standing in the region, becoming the main trade partner and lender of many of its countries. This requires some background, especially so because as late as the 1990s China was totally absent from the Latin American scene, while the United States saw this region as its backyard. Let us go back in time to properly frame this situation.

Latin American countries opted for free trade and access to international capital markets since the beginning of their independent life. As the new states began to stabilize, the ruling elites decided that the future development of the region was linked to the export of natural resources and the import of needed capital goods. When traditional exports recovered from the chaos caused by the independence wars, additional products were incorporated to the exports list.

From the mid-19th century onwards, Latin American exports began to expand, bringing with them economic growth. During the half century between the 1860s and 1910s, Latin American economies performed fairly well. Even if they grew less than the big winners of the period, such as the United States or Germany, they grew more than other peripheral regions and kept pace with European growth.

According to Victor Bulmer–Thomas, John H. Coastworth and Roberto Cortes Conde:

> "The integration of the Latin American economies between 1850 and World War I was unprecedented in scale and complexity. The fall in transportation costs attributable to technological innovations was the key factor in Latin American exports reaching the European and North American markets...This became possible through the dramatic fall in ocean freight rates and land transportation costs from the interior to the ports made possible by the construction of a very wide railway network".[1]

Latin America, thus, moved into the 20th century full steam ahead. Its raw materials provided important economic growth rates and some of the countries of the region were among the richest of the world at the time. Between 1870 and 1913, Latin American GDP grew 3.5 per cent while world GDP grew 2.1 per cent.[2] Brazil generated 70 per cent of the planet's coffee exports, while in terms of meat, cereal and wool, Argentinean exports had very few competitors worldwide. Uruguay, a much smaller country than Argentina, was also booming with the same export commodities.

With the introduction of cold storage, during the first decade of the century, profits from meat exports multiplied by four. Silver export booms in Mexico, Peru and Bolivia had their equivalent in copper export booms in Chile and Peru. But there was also saltpetre in Chile and Peru. The latter also exported sugar and guano. Sugar was prevalent in the tropical countries in the northern part of the region, as was banana.[3]

Indeed, this first era of globalization, resulting from the falling of transportation costs, the rising of the capital flows and increased of labor

---

[1] Bulmer–Thomas, V, Coatsworth JH and R Cortes Conde (2006). *The Cambridge Economic History of Latin America, Volume II: The Long Twentieth Century,* p. 4. Cambridge: Cambridge University Press.

[2] Loser, C (2012). Latin America in the Age of Globalization: A Follower or a Force of its Own? *The Impact of Globalization on Latin America Task Force,* p. 4. Miami: University of Miami Center for Hemispheric Policy (11 June 2012).

[3] Halperin Donghi, T (1997). *História Contemporánea de América Latina.* Buenos Aires: Alianza Editorial.

mobility, greatly benefited the exploitation of Latin American natural resources. However, World War I interrupted the globalization process both in Latin America and elsewhere.

At the end of the 1920s, Latin American countries had re–established the primacy of the export sector, after the disruptions brought by World War I. Capital streams began flowing in to Latin America again, but this time not so much from Great Britain but mainly from the United States.

Latin American Style Industrialization

And then, suddenly, the Great Depression of the 1930s hit the region. The fragility of the economic world order to which Latin America had incorporated itself, not only as a reliable commodities supplier but as a relevant importer of manufactured goods, became evident. Indebted and in a bad economic situation as a result of the global crisis, the primary productive sector had to be subsidized by the state. Not surprisingly, industrialization began to be seen as the appropriate medicine to provide firmer economic ground. Light industry began to take shape in the region to compensate for the import needs that the international crisis left uncovered.

World War II gave new impetus to this industrialization process. Even if significant by Latin American standards this process was modest for international ones, especially so in view of the limitations for importing capital goods. Its aim was to manufacture those goods that could no longer be imported and not to compensate for the shortcomings of a primary industry, which, due to the war, was booming again.

Already in 1947, the industrial sector had a bigger percentage of Argentina's GDP than the primary sector. At the end of the war what was already a fact — the import–substituting industrialization process — was duly conceptualized. Since 1948, indeed, the theoretical framework for the import–substituting industrialization process began to take shape. Two economists and an organization were basically responsible for it. The economists were Raul Prebisch and Sir Hans Wolfgang Singer. The organization was the Economic Commission for Latin America, ECLA, a regional institution dependant on the United Nations and established in 1948.

The first steps in import substitution industrialization were, thus, largely non–theoretical and based on pragmatic choices of how to face the limitations imposed by manufactured needs left uncovered. The second phase, on the other hand, would have a strong theoretical foundation.

Prebisch, a well–known Argentinean economist who had been the first General Director of the Argentinean Central Bank and who in 1949 worked for ECLA, was requested by the Secretary General of this organization to write an analysis on the deterioration of the terms of trade of raw materials. Having written the first draft of a long text he came to read Singer's recent paper "Post-War Relations between Under–developed and Industrialized Countries", which complemented his own ideas.

Prebisch changed the first version and proceeded to print the fresh material extensively quoting Singer in his conclusions. The latter, a German, had been a protégé and a pupil of both Schumpeter and Keynes and at the time was one of the few economists at the new Economics Department of the United Nations. The result was a book called *The Economic Development of Latin America and Some of its Main Problems*, published in 1949. Without collaborating directly, and having arrived at similar conclusions separately, both economists gave birth to what was called the Prebisch–Singer Hypothesis.

The above proposal was to be extensively spread throughout the region by the Economic Commission for Latin America, ECLA. Since 1950 and until 1963 its Secretary General would be Prebisch himself. Under the auspices of ECLA, a group of outstanding Latin American economists would follow the ideas of Prebisch and Singer, elaborating on the need of developing a substitutive manufacturing base.

The so called "hypothesis" was made up of two sub–hypotheses. The first had to do with the fact that the prices of primary products had a declining tendency over time. Countries specialized in their production were thus condemned to lag behind the industrial ones, and the terms of trade between them would be detrimental to raw material producers. As for the second one, as Daniel Yergin and Joseph Stanislaw point out:

> "They argued that the world economy was divided into the industrial 'center' — the United States and Western Europe — and the commodity

producing 'periphery'. The terms of trade would always work against the periphery".[4]

In order to face this double negative situation ECLA's oriented economists, with Prebisch at their helm, argued that the answer was to create a substitutive manufacturing base. In Daniel Yergin and Joseph Stanislaw words:

> "So instead, the periphery would go its own way. Rather than exporting commodities and importing finished goods, these countries would move as rapidly as possible towards what was called 'import–substituting' industrialization. This would be achieved by breaking the links to world trade through high tariffs and other forms of protectionism... Currencies were overvalued, which cheapened equipment imports needed for industrialization; all other imports were tightly rationed through permits and licenses".[5]

To put in motion such a process, a set of guidelines was indeed required: an active industrial policy to subsidize and orchestrate the production of strategic substitutes; protective barriers to imports; an overvalued currency to help manufacturers import the capital goods they needed; promotion of domestic private sector investments and discouragement of foreign direct investments; etc. Unlike Asia, where an "outward–oriented industrial growth" would be emphasized since the 1960s, Latin America visualized industrialization as an "inward–oriented process". Products that would otherwise have to be imported were to be manufactured domestically.

The Eternal Infancy

The import–substituting industrialization presented three important flaws. The first was to visualize this process as permanent in time. In doing so they did not proceed like all major developed economies have done, that is, using

---

[4]Yergin D and J Stanislaw p. 234.

[5]*Ibid.*,p. 234.

interventionist economic policies to promote industrialization and protect national companies until they were prepared to compete internationally.

Thus, domestic industries were indefinitely isolated from international competition. The "industries in their infancy", a protectionist thesis developed by Alexander Hamilton at the end of the 18th century, assumed a permanent character in the Latin America of the 20th century. This implied creating a gap between highly competitive companies abroad and highly protected ones inside. In as long as domestic companies were cut off from the outside world by thick walls there was no problem. Nonetheless, if those walls were ever to suddenly fall, industrial massacre would follow.

The second flaw was not to have given enough consideration to the fact that the unequal distribution of income generated small national markets. Markets were too small to sustain the industrialization effort. With the exception of larger countries such as Brazil or Mexico, this flaw posed an important problem for the majority of Latin American nations. To overcome such difficulties, and enlarge consumer markets, ECLA's economist suggested two alternatives.

On the one hand, better income distribution within each country, so as to bring the enormous disenfranchised population into the consumer market. On the other hand, regional or sub–regional economic integration mechanisms, which would allow for the products of one country to be sold in the others. Consequently, the "inward–oriented growth" evolved from a national to a regional or a sub–regional level.

Unfortunately, insofar as Latin American countries had engaged in building the same type of industries, the scenario turned out to be more competitive than complementary, making integration a difficult task. Moreover, when each country showed different levels of inflation or of payment of its manpower or of its exchange rates against the dollar, the competition tended to become destructive in many ways. Despite the great obstacles faced, though, advances were very important and integration never ceased to be a fundamental goal.

The third flaw was that the dependency on commodities continued to be fundamental, as they were the ones generating the currency that nurtured this whole process. Indeed, while local products were sold inside the protected trade area, commodities were sold abroad, thus becoming the fundamental source of currency. The whole import–substituting industrialization structure became thus dependant on the same commodities from which it wanted to gain independence.

Notwithstanding its flaws, though, the system provided results. Some qualified opinions can attest to it. According to Kevin P. Gallager and Roberto Porzecanski:

> "It will be easy and tempting to look backward to the period roughly between 1940 and 1970. During that period Latin America was indeed able to build innovation and industrial capabilities. Indeed, that period was certainly the 'golden age' of economic growth in Latin America that is yet to be matched".[6]

Joseph Stiglitz's opinion is in the same direction:

> "In earlier decades, Latin America had had notable success with strong government interventionist policies...focused more on the restriction of imports than on the expansion of exports. High tariffs were placed on certain imports, to encourage the development of local industries — a strategy often referred to as import substitution. While its success did not match that of East Asia, Latin America's per capita income still grew at an average of more than 2.5 percent annually from 1950 to 1980. Brazil, whose government intervened more aggressively in the economy, grew at an average of 5.7 percent...".[7]

Greg Grandin on his part adds: "If we take Latin America in its entirety we find that between 1947 and 1973 (the state-dominance stage) the per capita income grew by 73% in real terms".[8]

The success of the model, based on the Keynesian doctrine, mirrored the unprecedented prosperity that these policies brought to the Western World between 1945 and 1975. However, between 1950 and 1973 Latin America grew even faster than the world average: 5.4 per cent versus 4.9

---

[6] Gallagher K and R Porzecanski (2010). *The Dragon in the Room,* p. 140. Stanford: Stanford University Press.

[7] Stiglitz, J (2006). *Making Globalization Work* p. 35. London: Allen Lane.

[8] Grandin, G p. 198.

per cent. Moreover, in 1981, shortly before the system began to crumble, Latin America's share of the world´s GDP was 11 per cent, while its GDP per capita exceeded the world´s average by 10 per cent during the third quarter of that year.[9]

The collapse of the import–substituting industrialization model would be closely linked to the end of Keynesianism in Western economies, where a combination of inflation and stagnation, known as stagflation, would lift von Hayek's neoliberal ideas from the dusty bookshelf.

A Fatidic Duo

The inherent vulnerabilities within the import–substituting industrialization model were ready to concatenate when the right set of international conditions appeared. And they did as a result of the debt crisis. It all began during the 1970s, when an international banking system overflowed with petrodollars, resulting from the sudden hike in oil prices, devoted itself to grant plentiful loans.

This easy access to international credit, actively promoted by lenders themselves, was seen by Latin American governments as an excellent opportunity to invest in infrastructure and the modernization of its state industries. As a consequence, the region got massively in debt under the assumption, prescribed by the conventional wisdom of the day, that interest rates would remain low for the foreseeable future.

But they did not. As Joseph Stiglitz points out:

"In 1980, fighting its own problem of inflation, the United States initiated interest rate increases climbed to over 20 percent. These rates spilled over to loans to Latin America, triggering the Latin American debt crisis of the early 1980s, when Mexico, Argentina, Brazil, Costa Rica, and a host of other countries defaulted on their debt".[10]

The debt crisis hit Latin America very hard and between 1975 and 1982, the regional debt increased from US$45.2 billion to US$333 billion.[11] Needless to say that this increase had much to do with the snowball

---

[9] Loser, *op. cit.*, p. 2.

[10] Stiglitz, *op. cit.*, p. 36.

[11] Yergin and Stanislaw, *op. cit.*, p. 234.

effect derived from the combination of interest rates over 20 per cent, and short–term loans and credits to pay the old debt.

But while interest rates were rising, the price of primary products was going down. The reasons behind these two phenomena were very much the same. Faced with the hike in the oil prices in 1979, the new governments of Ronald Reagan and Margaret Thatcher decided to fight inflation not only through monetary tools (such as interest rate increases), but also by reducing fiscal expenditure.

Those policies resulted in a recession that increased unemployment and precipitated the fall in the demand, and by extension in the prices, of commodities. Such an unexpected downturn in the prices of primary products gravely affected the capacity of Latin American governments to meet their debts. While the sources of currency income were dropping significantly, the external debt was growing exponentially as a result of the interest rates hike.

This situation of extreme weakness was compounded by the appearance of a new economic paradigm brought in, again, by the duo of Reagan–Thatcher: neoliberalism. Just when Latin American governments were in need to renegotiate their debts and acquire fresh loans to pay for the old ones, they were confronted by this all–powerful ideology. With its negotiating leverage collapsed, the region had no other option but to bow to the Washington Consensus and the directives of its executive arm, the International Monetary Fund, IMF.

The Washington Consensus agenda, as mentioned in Chapter 4, resulted from the convergence of positions of a group of institutions based in Washington DC, chiefly the US Treasury Department, the World Bank and the IMF. The agenda included structural reforms such as trade liberalization, privatization of public assets, economic deregulation, fiscal discipline, fiscal reform, etc.

The acceptance of this agenda became unavoidable given the confluence of several factors. First: "As part of the rescue packages, the International Monetary Fund became...a sort of international bankruptcy receiver".[12] As such, indebted countries willing to renegotiate their debts had to accept the IMF conditions. Second, because international credibility or ostracism parameters, tied to the acceptance or rejection of the

[12] *Ibid.*, p. 132.

neoliberal credo. Third, because of the influence of the so called "Chicago boys" (a term broadly applied to Ivy League graduates imbued with market economy ideas), in leading economic positions within Latin American governments.

Genghis Khan´s Hordes

All of the above led to the sudden and widespread opening of Latin American trade barriers. That forced a totally unprepared industrial sector to compete with the most efficient companies of the world. The impact of such measures upon jobs is clearly described by Joseph Stiglitz:

> "It is easy to destroy jobs, and this is often the immediate impact of trade liberalization, as inefficient industries close down under pressure from international competition. IMF ideology holds that new, more productive jobs will be created as the old inefficient jobs that have been created behind protectionist walls are eliminated. But that is simply not the case".[13]

As for the industries themselves, Rubens Ricupero, Secretary General of the United Nations Commission for Trade and Development (UNCTAD), pointed out that this opening of protective barriers resulted in an accelerated and premature disappearance of an important part of the Latin American industrial base.[14]

Transforming the infant–industry logic into a mature–industry logic, that indefinitely isolated local industries from outside competition, had indeed been a huge mistake. But the corrective medicine should never have been the sudden opening of trade barriers. As Joseph Stiglitz remarks:

> "The most successful developing countries, those in East Asia, opened themselves to the outside world but did it slowly and in a sequenced way. These countries...dropped protective barriers carefully and systematically".[15]

---

[13] Stiglitz, JE (2002). *Globalization and its Discontents,* p. 59. London: W.W. Norton & Company.

[14] Hardy, AT (2004). *¿Tiene Futuro América Latina?* Bogotá: Villegas Editores.

[15] Stiglitz, *op. cit.,* 2002, p. 60.

No one doubts that Latin America had an important catch–up process ahead. Nonetheless, the reform process should have been guided by common sense and not by ideology. If there was much to be dismantled, there was much to be preserved as well. What happened, though, was the equivalent to the brutal throwing down of the protective walls to let Genghis Khan´s Hordes in. Companies that had thrived under the old system began to be slaughtered on mass.

On the other hand, and under the ideological commands of the Washington Consensus, an irrational privatization process of state–owned companies took shape. Again, in Joseph Stiglitz words:

> "Unfortunately, the IMF and the World Bank have approached the issues from a narrow ideological perspective — privatization was to be pursued rapidly...those who privatized faster were given the high marks".[16]

As a result of this fast–paced logic, the very same state companies and public utilities whose expansion had indebted the governments of the region, started to be sold at laughable prices. Usually the beneficiaries of this process were transnational corporations.

Thus, while Latin American governments were facing a foreign debt that had grown out of all proportion in relation to the originally granted loans, the assets resulting from such loans were been bargained to the transnational companies. This involved a net and massive transfer of wealth overseas.

An additional part of the problem had to do with the fact that privatized companies were disconnected from their traditional domestic suppliers and reconnected with intra–corporate chains of supply. The result being that the national productive chains were totally disrupted and supplanted by foreign chains of supply. Big local companies, precisely those bought by foreign corporations, ceased to be the turbines of industrial development that they had been so far, and became disconnected islands within their domestic economies. Amid these islands, numerous medium and small size enterprises that had hitherto been linked to them began to disappear.

---

[16] Ibid., p. 54.

Not surprisingly, the effects of the neoliberal policies were devastating for the Latin American industrial base, which between 1980 and 2002 suffered a significant contraction. In Argentina, the industrial participation in the country's GDP went down from 29 per cent to 15 per cent; in Brazil from 31 per cent to 19.9 percent; in Uruguay, from 28.6 percent to 17 percent; in Peru, from 29.3 percent to 14.4 percent; in Colombia from 21.5 percent to 13.5 percent and in Ecuador from 20 percent to 7 percent.[17]

But not only was the industrial base shrinking. The technological capabilities that had been associated with those industries, dramatically contracted as well. During the import–substituting industrialization phase, a great effort in Research and Development had taken place. The industrial development strategy had required the build–up of endogenous technological capacities. Through the implementation of the Washington Consensus not only were regional R&D efforts abandoned, but the whole idea of generating local technology began to be seen as useless.

Henceforth, imported technology became the aim and it was assumed that this would naturally come by way of trade or foreign direct investments. According to the neoliberal dogma, the market would automatically allocate such capabilities. But, as it happened in Mexico, the most extreme case in this area, more than 40 years of sustained technological efforts were swept away and supplanted by an "enclave" assembly sector.

Nevertheless, the most serious impact of these reforms was felt in the social area. In Greg Grandin's terms:

> "If we take Latin America in its entirety we find that between 1947 and 1973 (the state-dominance stage) the per capita income grew by 73% in real terms. By contrast, during the era of the free market fundamentalism, the average per capita income stagnated at 0%. By the late seventies, 11% of Latin Americans could be considered as poverty-stricken...By 1996, the number of indigents rose to a third of its total population. That is, 165 million people. And by 2005, 221 million people lived below the poverty line, an increase of 20 million in just a decade".[18]

[17] Sader, E, Jinkings, I *et al.*, coord. (2009). *Latinoamérica: Enciclopedia Contemporánea de América Latina y El Caribe,* p. 471. Madrid: Clacso-Ediciones AKAL, S.A.
[18] Grandin, *op. cit.,* p. 198.

Neoliberal policies had, thus, a profoundly regressive effect on Latin America in their industrial, technological and social sectors. Had Latin America followed a common–sense approach to reform, as was the case in China during the same period, the history of the region would have evolved in a very different direction. If instead of applying a shock therapy to change the system, they would have adopted the famous economic reform dictum by Deng Xiaoping, of "crossing the river by feeling the stones", many good things could have been preserved. At the same time, inefficiencies could have been purged in a rational way. However, that became impossible as neoliberals, with their "level playing field" notion, rejected as unfair competition the natural tools of industrial policies.

While during those years, Latin America witnessed an accelerated downward tendency, both economically and socially, China showed a spectacular upward one. These reverse tendencies would become evident when China and Latin America's roads crossed at the beginning of the millennium. When Latin America´s industries were beginning to redress the impact caused to them by the neoliberal tsunami, the avalanche of Chinese low–cost products came along. It was a second shock that pushed those Latin American industries that had been able to survive into a corner.

Redeeming Virtue

China had a redeeming virtue though that the Washington Consensus never did: it was a voracious consumer of commodities. Thanks to this voraciousness the price of natural resources began booming everywhere. According to the International Monetary Fund, between 2002 and 2006 the general index of commodities worldwide, excluding oil, increased by 60 per cent in real terms. Moreover, in the areas of oil and metals the increases reached 150 per cent and 180 per cent, respectively. Conversely, before China's boom and for the five previous decades the price of commodities had been falling at an annual rate of 1.6 per cent in relation to manufactured goods.[19]

---

[19] Kosacoff, B and S Campanario (2007). *La Revalorizacion de las Materias Primas y sus Efectos en América Latina* (May 2007). Santiago de Chile: CEPAL, p. 11.

While the regional industrial base got hammered, the commodities sector thus began to blossom in an unexpected way. For this sector, a gigantic market suddenly appeared from nowhere. In Kevin P. Gallager and Roberto Porzecanski words:

> "In the recent boom, Latin American export growth, which was considerably faster than GDP growth, was being driven by a commodities boom. Indeed, 70 percent of the growth in Latin American countries exports was due to growth in commodities exports, and commodities exports comprised 74 percent of all Latin American countries growth. China had both indirect and direct effects in this trend. Directly, Latin American countries exports to China have increased 370 percent since 2000...Indirectly, Chinese consumption of global commodities was making them scarcer and boosting global prices and leading somewhat to more Latin American countries exports".[20]

As a result, growth rates soared in countries that represented 69 per cent of Latin America's GDP, which were precisely those dependant on commodities. Moreover, and much to the contrary of the experiences resulting from the Washington Consensus policies, there were tangible social benefits. Between 2002 and 2011, a period in which sales to China grew exponentially, the GDP per capita in the region increased by almost 25 per cent. Poverty rates in Latin America declined sharply between 2002 and 2008, with more than 50 million people being lifted out of moderate poverty.[21] In a speech delivered shortly before leaving the World Bank presidency, Robert B. Zoellick went even further when he said: "Between 2003 and 2010, the income of the average Latin American increased by more than 30 percent. About 73 million Latin Americans have been lifted out of poverty since 2003".[22]

Unfortunately, there was a price tag attached to this bonanza: the region had to redefine its role within the international distribution of labor. This meant that Latin America had to go back in time to the beginning of the

---

[20] Gallager and Porzecanski, *op.cit.*, p. 37.

[21] World Bank (2011). *Latin America and the Caribbean's Long Term Growth: Made in China?* Washington D.C.: September 2011, p. 12.

[22] Zoellick, RB (2012). Globalization: Made in the Americas. (7 June 2012). *30th Anniversary Celebration of the Inter-American Dialogue.* Washington D.C.

20th century, when it had shined as a producer of commodities. 80 years of industrializing efforts essentially disintegrated. Not surprisingly, relations between China and Latin America became complex, entailing benefits as well as costs and engendering winners as well as losers.

Indeed, for some countries and sectors of the region, China not only subtracted export markets but also foreign direct investments. For others, though, China represented the opportunity of high and sustained economic growth within a framework of clear complementarities. For the latter, China became an important market and a significant source of investment and financing. Amid these two clear cut positions we found the in between: countries that benefited in certain areas and were affected in others. To be classified in one group or another, or in the middle, depended on the respective export items.

In Robert Devlin's and Theodore Kahn's words:

> "The dynamism of the Latin America–China trade since 2002 has been much discussed, and for good reasons. Trade increased at an annual average rate of 27 percent between 2003 and 2013, reaching $289 billion that year. However, the Sino–Latin American story is really the tale of two regions".[23]

The Inter–American Development Bank refers to Mexican–type countries and Brazilian–type countries. The former are mainly net commodity importers and highly exposed labor intensive manufacturing exporters to the United States. The latter are commodity exporters with lower dependence on developed countries in terms of exports. The Mexican group includes Central America, Dominican Republic and, of course, Mexico itself. The Brazilian group contains all South American countries plus Cuba in the Caribbean. Within those two groups, the first was badly affected while the second benefited.[24]

The Mexico–Brazil distinction refers to three different elements. The first involved countries that exported commodities and hence benefited

---

[23] Devlin R and T Khan. (2016). Latin American trade with India and China: The region needs a business plan. In Roett, R and G Paz (eds), *Latin America and the Asian Giants*, p. 151. Washington D.C.: Brooking Institution Press.

[24] Izquierdo, A and E Talvi, coord. (2011). *One Region, Two Speeds?* (March 2011). Washington D.C.: Inter-American Development Bank.

from the high prices attached to it, versus countries that imported commodities and were harmed as a result of those same high prices. The second involved net exporters of labor intensive products in direct competition with China, versus economies that were essentially outside the frame of competition.

The third difference mirrored, in a Latin American context, Ian Bremmer's categorization between "pivot states" and "shadow states". Pivots are those that have been able to build profitable relationships with multiple economic partners without becoming overly reliant on any of them. Shadows are those that have tied their economic possibilities almost entirely to a single powerful partner. As a consequence, "pivot states" can be more resilient and strong, given the diversity of their options, while "shadow" ones simply follow the fortune of their dominant partner.[25]

While South American countries diversified their economic partners, Mexico and Central America became overly reliant on the United States. It has been estimated that between 2009 and 2011, Latin America ceased to export US$250 billion to the United States because of the latter's economic contraction.[26] Mexican–type countries were disproportionally affected by this situation.

Brazil, the rest of South America and Cuba not only benefited from its condition of net exporters of commodities, but by their wider access to other markets, with particular reference to China.

But this clear cut distinction between net winners and losers was not straightforward, as Brazil and Argentina did not only export commodities but products as well. Even though the overall economy of such countries benefited from the hike in the price of commodities, their industrial sectors were damaged as a result of Chinese competition.

The Maquila System

Let us begin with the losers. After the massacre caused in the industrial base of the region by the neoliberal policies, the maquila system took hold

---

[25] Bremmer, I (2012). *Every Nation for Itself: Winners and losers in a G-Zero World*. New York: Portfolio.

[26] Secretaría Permanente del Sistema Económico Latinoamericano y del Caribe (2012). Relaciones Económicas de Estados Unidos con los Países de América Latina y el Caribe en Época de Transición, (May 2012). Caracas.

in some Latin American countries. It was an export–oriented system based on labor intensive assembly lines dependent on foreign technology and supply chains. Mexico, Central American countries and the Dominican Republic followed this frame.

Given the devaluation of Mexico's currency in 1994 and the North American Free Trade Agreement, it made very good sense to locate maquila factories in this neighboring country to the United States. On the other hand, the proximity and the special access to the American market derived from the 2005 Dominican Republic and Central America Free Trade Agreement (with the United States), were the reason for investing in maquila factories in these countries.

Nations heavily involved with the maquila system were hit harder than anyone else by Chinese competition. In Mauricio Mesquita Moreira's and Theodore Kahn's words:

> "The second group of countries consists of Mexico and Central America, which had the bad luck of having relatively similar productive structures to China during the trade boom. These economies suffered from direct competition with China's low–wage manufacturing juggernaut while lacking the natural resource base to export to China in a large scale. They experienced heavy losses in the US market, particularly in labor–intensive goods, but avoided total economic disaster thanks to what is arguably their strongest comparative advantage: geography. Proximity to the United States gives them an edge on bulk, transport–intensive and time–sensitive goods".[27]

Indeed, in the United States the imports coming from China grew by 1,600 per cent between 1990 and 2005.[28] In 2003, China displaced Mexico as United States' second commercial partner and according to a Latin American and the Caribbean Economic System 2012 report: "Mexico and China are rivals in the United States market, where both countries are the second and first surplus's trade partners of the United States".[29]

---

[27] Moreira, MM and T Khan (2016). Future Scenarios for Latin America's Relations with China and India. In R Roett and G Paz (eds.), p. 296.

[28] *Newsweek*, 9 May 2005.

[29] Sistema Económico Latinoamericano (2012). Las relaciones entre China y América Latina y el Caribe en la actual coyuntura económica mundial, p. 4 (September 2012). Caracas.

There was, though, a line of defense as Kevin P. Gallager and Roberto Porzecanski pointed out:

> "Mexico is losing out in sectors abundant in unskilled labour where value–to–transport costs are cheap. It is holding steady, instead, in assembly sectors such as trucks and autos, where transport costs are more significant and NAFTA's rules of origin serve as local content rules mandating that production stay in North America".[30]

In 2006, 80 per cent of all Mexican exports to the United States' market (which represented 85 per cent of total Mexican exports) were constituted by maquila manufactured products, which were precisely the most affected by China's competition.[31] According to Kevin P. Gallager and Roberto Porzecanski: "Ninety-nine percent of Mexico's manufacturing exports are under threat from China, representing 72 percent of Mexico's entire exports".[32]

It would be interesting to add that Mexico was also overflowed by Chinese products, while its exports to China were modest. In 2010, Chinese exports represented US$41.4 billion while Mexican exports to China were just US$8.3 billion.[33] In 2011, China represented less than two per cent of total Mexican exports while 15 per cent of its imports came from this Asian country. As a matter of fact, Mexico's trade deficit with China became responsible for Latin America's trade deficit with China. Otherwise trade equilibrium between China and Latin American economies had been the case.[34]

---

[30] Gallager and Porzecanski, *op. cit.*, p. 93.

[31] González Peña, JM (2011). Una aproximación a las relaciones económico-comerciales entre China y América Latina y el Caribe (13 September 2011). *Observatorio de la Política China.*

[32] Gallager and Porzecanski, *op. cit.*, p. 51.

[33] González Peña, *op. cit.*

[34] CEPAL (2012). *La República Popular China y América Latina y el Caribe: Diálogo y Cooperación ante los Nuevos Desafíos de la Economía Mundial,* p. 30. (June 2012). Santiago de Chile.

A Tale of Two Giants

On the other side of the fence were the winners from China's sudden appearance from nowhere. For them, exports expanded threefold between 2003 and 2013.[35] The convergence between two giants — a commodities consumer and a commodities producer — made of this relation a very particular one. On the one hand, the consumer giant represented by China was responsible in 2011 for the following percentage of world demand: [36]

Iron ore:	47.7%
Coal:	49.9%
Pigs:	46.4%
Steel:	45.4%
Lead:	44.6%
Zinc:	41.3%
Aluminium:	40.6%
Copper:	38.9%
Eggs:	37.2%
Nickel:	36.3%
Rice:	28.1%
Soybeans:	24.6%
Wheat:	16.6%
Chickens:	15.6%
Oil:	10.3%
Cattle:	9.5%

Among the many commodities of which China was the world's largest consumer were copper, lead, zinc, tin, nickel, aluminium, meat, soy, rice, wheat, tea, rubber, raw wool, cotton, oil seeds and coal, while it was the second larger consumer of oil and corn.[37]

---

[35] Devlin and Kahn, *op. cit.*, p. 145.

[36] *Connect the Dots*, 4 July 2011, http://ctdtoday.com/2011/07/04/chinas-demand-world-commodity-prices-and-the-australian-economy/. Accessed 10/03/2012.

[37] The Economist (2012). *Pocket World in Figures: 2012 Edition.* London: Profile Books Ltd.

According to the International Energy Agency, in 2035 China will be consuming a fifth of the global energy, which would represent a 75 per cent increase in relation to 2008. There is also the need to feed a population of 1.3 billion with rapidly escalating living standards. Moreover, an ongoing infrastructure and urbanization development process has been described by James Kynge in the following terms:

> "In China, the urbanization is still an infant. There are approximately 400 million people living in big and small cities at this moment, but by 2050 this number is expected to rise to 600 or 700 million, to reach a billion or 1.1 billion people. The investment required to accommodate so many people in an urban environment is impossible to calculate precisely, but it is clear that the global demand of steel, aluminium, copper, nickel, iron, oil, gas, carbon and many other raw materials and resources will remain strong as long as urbanization in China reaches its limits".[38]

Between 2005 and 2011 commodity prices, pushed in large extent by China's consumption, increased in the following percentages: rubber 330.8; cotton 280.8; tin 250.0; sugar 248.0; palm oil 212.7; corn 210.1; cooper 199.7; coconut oil 197.2; soya oil 186.1; wheat 169.7; soybeans 159.7; coffee 149.5; lead 144.0; oil 116.3; tea 103.2, cocoa 98.8; rice 89.2; nickel 69.1; lamb 66.7; beef 31.7; aluminium 30.9.[39] Moreover, since 2004, China exceeded the United States as the largest world consumer of grain and meat.[40]

South America, on the other hand, is a commodities producing giant, whose might is felt in several fields. The first of them is food. As Mariano Turzi explains:

> "America's economic power, in particular, rested on a secure and steady supply of oil from the Middle East...And countries like Saudi Arabia, Iran and Iraq became important to US foreign policy. An underappreciated parallel is developing in the world's political economy today — but this time, grain replaces oil, China stands in for the United States, and South

---

[38] Kynge, J (2006). *China Shakes the World*, p. 29. London: Phoenix.

[39] *The Economist*, *op. cit.*

[40] González Peña, *op. cit.*

> America plays the Middle East's role. Indeed, as climate constrains and demographic imperatives make food security an ever more critical issue, agricultural resources may become the new linchpin in international relations. In a world where soil trumps oil, South American agricultural producers, with their vast amounts of fertile land and water, might see their geopolitical positions greatly improved".[41]

Since 1990, the productivity of the farming sector in Latin America has grown faster that of the United States and East Asia. Latin America represents 40 per cent of global agricultural exports while, according to the General Director of the Inter–American Institute for Agricultural Cooperation, Victor Villalobos, 42 per cent of the world's potential for growth in agriculture lies in Latin America.[42]

A good example of this is Brazil, which represents 43 per cent of the global soy export market.[43] Brazil ranks number one worldwide, as well, in the production of coffee, sugar and orange juice.[44] But food in South America is not only agricultural products as the region also tops the world in several animal exports items. In poultry export ranking, Brazil occupies the number one global position.[45] The same happens with beef where Brazil is the world's leading exporter. Between 1994 and 2006, Brazil expanded its national herd by 24 per cent and its exports increased over 450 per cent in volume and 385 per cent in value. In 2006, Argentina's herd volume was around 50 to 55 million heads with exports reaching 720,000 tons.[46]

---

[41] Turzi, M (2012). Grown in the Cone: South America's Soybean Boom. *Current History*, 111 (742), p. 50.

[42] Verghese, SG (2012). The Latin America-Asia Partnership (3 October 2012). *Latin Asia Business Forum 2012*, Singapore; Agencia EFE (2012). Latinoamérica reúne el 42% del potencial de expansión agraria (2 June 2012).

[43] Newman, J and J Bunge (2012). America's agricultural dominance is ending (21 April 2017). *The Wall Street Journal.*

[44] It's only natural, Special Report: Latin America (11 September 2010). *The Economist.*

[45] Sesti, L (2012). Brazilian broiler production. http://www.polutrymed.com/Poultry/SendFile.aspDBID=1&LNGDID=1

[46] Steiger, C (2006). Modern beef production in Brazil and Argentina (Second Quarter 2006). *Choices: The Magazine of Food, Farm and Resources Issues.*

In 2007, exports to China from Brazil and Argentina had multiplied by ten in relation to 2003. That year those two countries accounted already for 20 per cent of the Chinese import of meat, while Peru fulfilled 45 per cent of China's animal food consumption.[47]

Regarding oil, Venezuela's proven oil reserves surpassed those of Saudi Arabia in 2010 when 296.5 billion barrels in reserves where certified.[48] Nonetheless the estimates of those reserves are substantially bigger, doubling those of Saudi Arabia:

> "Scientists working for the US Geological Survey say Venezuela's Orinoco belt holds twice as much petroleum as previously thought. The geologists estimate the area could yield more than 500bn barrels of crude oil. The USGS team gave a mean estimate of 513bn barrels of 'technically recoverable' oil in the Orinoco belt".[49]

But it is not only Venezuela. According to some experts Brazil's gigantic offshore oil reserves could reach up to 100 billion barrels of oil. Moreover, "Colombia's oil production is climbing so fast that it is closing on Algeria's and could hit Libya's pre–war level in a few years. Exxon Mobil is striking new deals in Argentina, which recently heralded its biggest oil discovery since the 1980s. For the first time in decades, the emerging prize in global energy may be the Americas...As said by Amy Myers Jaffe, associate director of Rice University's Energy Program in Houston 'This should make the world's megasuppliers nervous, since the pendulum has already begun to move in this direction'".[50]

Indeed, the bulk of oil reserves is beginning to shift from the Middle East to the Americas. As Andrés Cala clearly explains: "So while the US is preoccupied with containing Chinese surging ambitions in Asia...the biggest contributors to oil production in the future, are just south of its

---

[47] Kosacoff and Campanario, *op.cit.*, p. 14.

[48] Faucon, B (2011). Venezuela's oil reserves topped Saudis in 2010 (18 July 2010). *The Wall Street Journal.*

[49] Venezuela oil 'may double Saudi Arabia' (23 January 2010). http://news.bbc.co.uk/2/hi/8476395.stm. Accessed 28/02/2012.

[50] Romero, S (2011). The Americas regain the title of oil titans (21 September 2011). *International Herald Tribune.*

border".[51] In addition to oil there are also other sources of exportable energy where South America enjoys a very relevant position. In 2012, Brazil was the international leader and the largest world exporter of ethanol while, with seven billion tonnes, it also has the 10th largest coal reserves in the world. Within South America, Colombia follows in world coal reserves with the number 12 position representing 6.6 billion tonnes. Regarding gas proven reserves, Venezuela is ninth in the world with 178 billion cubic feet.[52]

As for mining, few regions can compete with South America. Chile is the number one copper producer in the world while Peru is number three. At the same time, the latter is the world's largest producer of silver, the second of zinc, the fourth of lead and the sixth of gold. Brazil, on its part, ranks third in the world in the production of iron ore, manganese, aluminium and ferroalloys, fourth in tin, sixth in gold, eighth in steel and represents 92.4 per cent of the world's production of columbium. Cuba ranks sixth in the world in nickel production and accounts for eight per cent of global cobalt production.[53]

In conclusion and as Xulio Rios clearly points out:

> "Beijing requires huge amounts of natural resources to nurture its amazing growth rates. It cannot pass over the fact that Latin America possesses 15 percent of the world oil reserves, 25 percent of the world agricultural lands, 30 percent the world water and 40 percent of the world gold and copper reserves". [54]

---

[51] Should the US worry about China's Latin American inroads? (31 October 2011). *Energy Tribune.*

[52] Frayssinet, F (2012). Biocombustibles luego de la euforia (12 February 2012). *IPS*; World Energy Council (2010. *2010 Survey of Energy Resources.* London; Countries with the largest coal proven reserves, aneki.com: rankings and records; World's top 22 natural gas proven reserves holders (1 January 2011). *Petroleum Insights.* http://petroleuminsights.com/2011/03/worlds-top-22-natural-gas-proven.html. Accessed 5/04/2012.

[53] Toovey, LM (2011). Copper mining in Chile (3 February 2011). *Copper Investing News*; Toovey, LM (2012). Copper mining in Peru (13 February 2012). *Copper Investing News*; Brazil mining and industry (14 November 2011). *Zimbio; MBendi Information Services*, 22 November 2011.

[54] Zhonguuo, J (2012). Crédito y descrédito en América Latina, p. 23. *Análisis y Pensamiento Iberoamẽricano sobre China.* Número 2 (Primer Trimestre 2012).

For the Latin American group of commodities exporters to China, China also became a prime source of investments. This reached new momentum on 9 March 2007, when the Chinese government announced the creation of a special agency, the China Investment Corporation. The purpose of such an institution was investing an important part of its international reserves abroad, which in 2010 amounted to US$2.45 trillion. According to Jim Yardley and David Barboza:

> "Analysts say that the agency could assign hundreds of billions of dollars to acquire strategic assets around the world, particularly in developing countries of Africa and Latin America. 'They are not looking for financial assets, but for assets of energy, minerals and natural resources, things that China desperately needs', pointed out J. Ulrich of J.P. Morgan".[55]

Chinese loan commitments to Latin America's commodities exporters within the region, totalled more than US$130 billion during the period 2005–2013. The greatest part of that amount was dedicated to infrastructure and energy projects.[56] Moreover, since 2005 China has lent more to Latin America than the World Bank, the Inter–American Bank and the US Export and Import Bank together. A good example of it was given in 2010, when China lent US$37 billion to Latin America while the other three institutions combined lent US$30 billion to the region.[57]

China's loans come with no macroeconomic or ideological strings attached which, for a region that was ravaged by the impositions of the International Monetary Fund, is a refreshing situation. The only risks faced by South America's countries are those derived from an asymmetrical power of negotiation and by China's toughness as a negotiator. As for such toughness, the following remarks by former German Minister of Foreign Affairs Joschka Fisher are enlightening: "China will become a largely inward–looking superpower, which — precisely for that reason — will

[55] China acts to become a huge global investor (10 March 2007). *International Herald Tribune*.

[56] Guajardo, J (2016). A Latin American Perspective on China's growing presence in the region. In Roett, R and Paz G (Eds). p. 69.

[57] China presto más a América Latina que los entes multilaterales (17 February 2012). *El Universal*.

pursue its foreign policy interests in a completely unsentimental manner".[58] In other words its raw national interest precludes any other consideration, making it a very tough interlocutor.

The In Between

But between the two previous positions we found an intermediary one: countries that benefited from China's trade in certain areas but were affected in others. Indeed, on one hand are the so called Mexican–type countries that were negatively affected by China's emergence and, on the other hand, the Brazilian–type countries that benefited not only from its commodities export but also from China's investments and loans. In between those two groups there was another one that combined both commodities and manufacturing. Such was the case of Brazil itself and Argentina. While being top commodities exporters, they still retained a relevant industrial base which was impacted by China´s competition.

Over 90 per cent of Brazilian and Argentinean manufactured exports are under threat due to China's competition. But while manufacturing exports in Mexico represents 72 per cent of its total exports, they represent just 39 per cent in the case of Brazil and 27 per cent in the case of Argentina.[59] But even if the impact of such a threat is substantially lower than in the case of Mexico, and the benefits deriving from the exports of their commodities is substantially higher, it nonetheless implies the potential destruction of a significant part of its manufacturing base.

Chinese products not only compete in their export markets, but also in their domestic ones.

> "Latin American manufacturing imports from China grew much more between 2000 and 2006 than manufacturing imports from the rest of the world. In fact, while the rate of growth on average for the top twenty Chinese imports was 570 percent for China, it was only 89 percent for the rest of the world for those same twenty products".[60]

[58] China a different type of superpower (7 October 2010). *The Straits Times.*

[59] Gallager and Porzecanski, *op. cit.*, p. 51.

[60] Ibid., p. 55.

Not surprisingly, the great majority of anti–dumping investigations initiated in Latin America originated in the three countries with the larger manufacturing capacity: Brazil, Mexico and Argentina. The nature of the bilateral trade aggravated such situation as in 2010, 83.7 per cent of Brazilian exports to China where commodities and 97.5 per cent of imports from China were products, while 95.8 per cent of Argentinean exports to China where commodities and 99.3 per cent of the imports coming from China were products.[61]

So, while domestic and export markets for products from both Brazil and Argentina were overwhelmed by Chinese goods, China mainly imported commodities from them. For a country such as Brazil, where a percentage of its manufacturing base is sustained by high–tech products, this became a very sensible issue. Responding to Brazil's political pressure, in 2011, China agreed to acquire 135 "Embraer 190" airplanes.[62]

For Brazil and Argentina, therefore, the relationship with China was not essentially determined by costs as in the case of Mexico or only by benefits as in the case of countries such as Chile, Venezuela or Peru. It was, on the contrary, a complex relationship that entailed both benefits and costs.

The Paper Giant

The complexity or the value added of the commodities business should not be downplayed, though. To be globally competitive in the commodities sector is by no means an easy or elemental task. According to the World Bank:

> "Latin American countries have been not only moving towards the production of more sophisticated and higher–value–added products within its natural resource based industries but clustering and production chains are being developed".[63]

---

[61] González Peña, *op. cit.*

[62] Higueras, G (2011). El gigante asiático devora las materias primas de la región (8 November 2011). *El País.*

[63] World Bank, *op. cit.*, p. 37.

Nonetheless, countries overly dependent on natural resources tend to deindustrialize as exports of such resources drives up the value of their currencies, making the export of products less competitive. It is the "Dutch disease". That creates a vicious circle where industries are increasingly threatened. As the history of the region clearly shows, to become dependent on commodities is to be at mercy of economic cycles and high volatility.

Alternatively, it could be argued that dependence on commodities would just reflect a classical international distribution of labor based on comparative advantages. In David Ricardo's terms, every country or region must emphasise those productive sectors where it can become really competitive, letting their own consumers benefit from imports coming from the lower cost producers. If the economy grows, positive trade balances are obtained, strong accumulation of reserves takes place and domestic consumers have access to more affordable goods, then the benefits exceed the costs of jobs suppression in the manufacturing sector.

According to the World Bank the extreme regional dependence on natural resources should not be seen as a "curse" but, on the contrary, as a development opportunity. For this institution, there is not much evidence to support the idea that commodities represent an area of slow growth in productivity or that they have a lower potential for generating a positive economic outcome. In the long run, what is important is to administer well the periods of bonanza, investing benefits in human development, infrastructure and innovation to guarantee sustainable growth.[64]

Since 2013, though, the commodities boom has ceased. In Francisco Rojas Aravena's words:

> "The export value of the region's products shows an important contraction which, according the Inter–American Development Bank, reached 14%. The most affected countries by such export contraction have been those from South America, whose basic products, oil and mining products, have fallen as a result of Asia's lower demand. In 2015

---

[64] Sinnot, E, Nash, J and A de la Torre (2010). *Natural resources in Latin America and the Caribbean: Beyond Booms and Busts?* Washington D.C.: The World Bank.

> South American exports reached minus 21%, a rate that doubles that of world trade".[65]

According to Anthony Spanakos, the downturn percentage in the price of global commodities since the boom ended, has been the following: energy products –31 per cent; base metals and minerals –18 per cent; agricultural products –4 per cent.[66] Hence, not all Latin American commodity exporters have been equally affected. Venezuela tops the list of the most affected as the overwhelming majority of its exports come from oil, while Argentina or Uruguay are on the safer side with most of their exports coming from the food sector. Brazil is punished more in energy, metals and minerals than in agricultural products, but is in a better position than Venezuela thanks to its wider offer of commodities.

Between 2003 and 2013, as mentioned before, South American merchandise exports expanded threefold amid the boom of commodities generated by China. That allowed not only high economic growth rates but also impressive social advancement. Nonetheless, the export contraction of South American commodities is rapidly eroding such social gains.

According to Francisco Rojas Aravena:

> "It is important to remember that during the decade 2003–2013, as mentioned in the last UNDP report...72 million people were lifted from poverty and close to 94 million were incorporated into the middle classes. Nonetheless, these substantial social gains are in danger. The current global crisis could take millions of people back to poverty. It is estimated that between 25 and 30 million people could relapse into poverty...".[67]

Several factors have triggered such a downfall in the price of commodities, particularly oil and mining products. A common denominator,

---

[65] Aravena, FR (2016). América Latina en un ciclo de baja, pero con señales esperanzadoras (January 2016). *Pensamiento Iberoamericano*. Tercera Época, p. 58.

[66] Spanakos, A (2017). One Tightening Belt, One Bumpy Road: Chinese Extension to Latin America at a Time of Increased Political and Market Risk (9 June 2017). East Asia Institute, National University of Singapore.

[67] Aravena, *op.cit.*, p. 57.

though, has been the slowing down of the insatiable demand for natural resources in China. The rebalancing towards domestic consumption in China means that industry grows less rapidly than in the past, while the service sector expands. This generates a positioning away from commodity–heavy sectors, where production over–capacity exists.

As Guadalupe Paz states:

> "Although the China–driven commodity boom clearly helped the region weather the global financial crisis that erupted in 2008–2009, Latin America's policymakers are increasingly preoccupied with the unbalanced nature of their trade relationship with China, particularly as the Asian giant faces an economic slowdown and global commodity prices are on a downward trend". [68]

Natural resources should not be seen as a curse, as much depends indeed in the way in which periods of bonanza are administered. If its benefits are invested in human capital, infrastructure and innovation, much can be attained despite volatility in prices. Nonetheless, one thing seems to be certain: being a natural resources giant per se, is tantamount to being a paper giant.

As we will see in the next chapter, though, the road for commodities producers does not seem to be closed. And Asia, with very special reference to China, may still have a very important role to play. Actually, for natural resources producers, Asia is the only place to look to.

---

[68] Paz, G (2016). Assessing Latin America's Relations with the Asian Giants. In Roett, R and G Paz (eds.) *op.cit.*, p. 1.

CHAPTER 10

LATIN AMERICA'S OPTIONS

Where can Latin America go to from here? One fact seems to be clear: Latin Americans cannot look forward to industrialization as a panacea, as they once did. Indeed, this road appears to be blocked not only at the top but increasingly so at the bottom as well. And that not only includes South American economies but also Mexican–type economies.

Latin America's total factor productivity, which is a proxy for technological innovation, higher skills and improved methods of production, has evolved in a negative way during the last 30 years.[1] Latin Americans are not able to compete in the high–tech manufacturing sector. But, at the same time, they are finding it extremely difficult to maintain competitiveness in the labour–intensive sector. Not even geographical proximity and free trade agreements have been able to overcome the problems faced in the latter case.

Caught in the Middle

In that sense, Latin American countries are in a typical middle–income trap situation. Indeed, their economies are unable to compete with advanced economies in highly skilled innovations. At the same time, they are under continuous competitive pressure by Asia's lower wage economies. As Latin American wages rise and competitiveness declines, possibilities at the bottom end of the equation are becoming increasingly

[1] Loser, C (2012). Op. Cit. p. 9.

reduced. Conversely, they do not have the capabilities to compete at the top through technological innovation.

Only Brazil, Cuba and Argentina have a presence in certain high–technology niches. Such is the case of aeronautics, microchips or products associated with deep–water oil drilling in the case of Brazil, and biotechnology in the three countries. This is the exception, though, not the rule. And although Brazil has been at the top of innovative manufacturing in Latin America, its relative place towards other emerging economies has decreased in the last few decades. In 1987, it was level with South Korea, while Malaysia only reached 60 per cent of its level and Thailand, 30 per cent. By 2009, South Korea's technology level was 60 per cent higher than Brazil, Malaysia had almost caught up with it and Thailand had gone up 55 per cent.[2]

For most of the region, indigenous generated technology is a closed door. As shown in Chapter 9, market liberalization policies imposed under the umbrella of the Washington Consensus, forced Latin American countries to abandon their efforts in research and development. Today Mexico exhibits a whole array of high–tech export products, but theirs is foreign generated technology. And even though Mexico annually produces an impressive number of engineering graduates, indigenous generated high–tech seems to be out of reach.

In Kevin P. Gallagher's and Roberto Porzecanski's words: "In the case of Mexico, more than 95 percent of all high–tech firms —and their suppliers — are foreign assembly plants".[3] To which they add: "Moreover, Mexico remains a low–wage assembly haven for US products and is not showing much of an increase in the sophistication of high–tech exports".[4]

At the other extreme, intensive–labour manufacturing has also proved to be increasingly difficult. Competition with China, as explained in the previous chapter, has been a true nightmare for the Mexican–type economies. And not even China's contraction in labour–intensive manufacturing represents a solution, as other Asian economies such as Vietnam, Indonesia,

[2] Ibid., p. 9.
[3] Gallager, KP and R Porzecanski (2010). p. 74.
[4] Ibid., p. 81.

Philippines or Bangladesh will be taking its place at the bottom. Asia's supply chain of production is simply unbeatable.

In Robyn Meredith's words:

> "But during the 1990s, companies began searching for the lowest–cost place to make each component of their products. At the same time, sophisticated technology made reality of what had once been a logistical pipe dream: creating a seamless connection between multiple factories... The last time a manufacturing revolution of this magnitude occurred was in the early twentieth century, when Henry Ford revolutionized the business world by popularizing the assembly line...In the twenty–first century, everything has changed...The new system — call it a disassembly line — is the result of companies rushing to break up their products into specialized subassemblies to drive down costs...The manufacturing process is so different from the last century that the term 'assembly line' has been replaced by the phrase 'supply chain'". [5]

Moreover, as Meredith adds:

> "The disassembly line has let companies become extremely efficient, by building each piece of a finished good in the country where it is cheapest, then moving the part on to the next factory in line".[6]

So, with parts passing from Vietnamese factories to Indonesian ones, to be followed by Bangladeshi ones, always in the search of the cheapest wage cost for every manufactured component, it will be extremely difficult for Latin America to keep pace.

Latin American economic integration though can provide a certain protection against Asia's supply chains. Rules of origin deriving from agreements such as MERCOSUR, Andean Community of Nations or Central American Common Market, can cushion against lower foreign production costs. The combination of such rules of origin with higher

---

[5] Meredith, R (2007). *The Elephant and the Dragon*, p. 99. New York: W.W. Norton & Company.

[6] Ibid., p. 101.

transport costs from East Asia (in areas where transport costs are significant), have proven to be effective.

Not surprisingly, a growing percentage of manufacturing exports remains within the region. Let us take as an example the case of Argentina which in 1985 directed 31 per cent of its manufacturing exports to other Latin American nations while in 2006 such regional exports reached 69 per cent.[7]

It is not strange, then, that threatened with a NAFTA renegotiation by the Trump Administration, Mexico is now aiming at increasing its exports to Latin American markets. Nonetheless, having been transformed into a shadow economy to that of the United States, Mexico cannot easily overcome a trade tightening of the screws by Washington.

The same would apply to the Dominican Republic and the Central American countries, which are entirely dependent on their respective Free Trade Agreements with the United States. As President Trump announced that all Free Trade Agreements signed by his country will be reviewed, the economic frailty of Mexico, Dominican Republic and the Central American nations has become evident. Living in the shadow of an inconsistent giant can indeed become a very risky affair.

As seen in Chapter 9, Latin America's commodity producers are in an extremely difficult situation because of the fall in prices. However, when compared with countries dependent on labour–intensive manufacturing they seem to have much better options. For Mexican–type economies, the road ahead looks more limited than for South American commodity producers. For the latter, several sources of potential advancement appear to be available.

Commodities Widening Horizons

The first of these areas is the Trans–Pacific Partnership (TPP). The TPP would allow its Latin American members a much better positioning in relation to Asian developed and emerging markets. A market share expansion, resulting from the opening of new opportunities, could somehow compensate for the contraction of commodities' prices. Unfortunately, this option was greatly reduced as the United States exited the agreement. Even if the Latin American member countries of the TPP are inclined to go through with it, their options are not the best.

[7] Gallager and Porzecanski, *op. cit.*, p. 52.

The only good thing resulting from the US abandoning the partnership, though, is that Latin American countries can be more relaxed in relation to China. While Washington was at its lead, the TPP looked like a geopolitical effort driven by the United States to isolate China. This placed Latin American commodity producers in a very delicate position in relation to its main market.

India could offer an even brighter opportunity. This Asian country is beginning to emerge as a potential important market for Latin American commodities. According to the Inter–American Development Bank: "Any cursory analysis of the complementarity between the two economies shows that the potential for massive bilateral trade is there".[8]

Up to now, India has followed a similar trade pattern as China, buying natural resources from Latin America while selling manufactured goods to the region. The value of Latin American exports to India expanded threefold between 2003 and 2013, while imports from India rose nearly fivefold. Exports are very much dominated by natural resources, while imports are dominated by manufactured goods.[9]

Moreover, Indian trade growth with Latin America is comparable to that of China, albeit from a much lower base. Bilateral trade between India and Latin America grew 22 times between 2000 and 2014 whereas that of China and Latin America grew 24 times during the same period.[10]

Even though, if both the pattern of trade and the trade growth lines between India and Latin America were to follow that of China and Latin America, the numbers are not the same. According to Robert Devlin and Theodore Kahn:

> "Trade with India, by contrast has yet to reach a critical mass. Though growth has been fast…total trade reached only $43 billion in 2013, about 15 percent of the region's trade with China".[11]

On the other hand, India's balance of trade with Latin America is more beneficial to the region than that of China. In 2014, for example,

[8] Moreira, MM (2010). *India: Latin America's Next Big Thing?* ix. Washington D.C., Inter-American Development Bank.

[9] Devlin, R and T Kahn (2016). p. 145.

[10] *Op. Cit.*, p. 11.

[11] Devlin and Khan, *op. cit.* p. 153.

India bought US$29 billion in goods from the region, while it sold it US$17.53 billion. By comparison that same year China bought US$95.3 billion from Latin America but its sales were US$190.38 billion.[12]

It seems clear that Latin America's commodities producers can highly benefit from this emerging Asian market. And yet, the question, is whether as stated by the Inter–American Developing Bank, the "potential for massive bilateral trade is there"? This requires some analysis.

It could be argued, prima facie, that with 1.3 billion people and a growth rate of more than seven per cent, India could follow China's place in relation to Latin America. Nonetheless that is far from certain. On the one hand India's development model did not follow the classic Asian strategy of a labor intensive–export oriented economy.

On the contrary, it emphasised services over industry and high technology over low–skilled manufacturing. As a result, it has been successful in high–end services and capital and knowledge intensive manufacturing, but has not been able to create a broad industrial base. Hence, it may never become a magnet for commodities producers on China's scale.

On the other hand, should India promote a second green revolution with ambitious agribusiness developments, it could not only become self–sufficient in food production but also transform itself into a competitor in some Latin American export markets.

Conversely, though, the Indian government is currently aiming at reaching China's level of investment in infrastructure, which would be nine per cent of its GDP. A good example of this objective is represented by the project known as the Delhi–Mumbai Industrial corridor that has been in discussion for the last few years. It would be an infrastructural corridor larger in land size than Japan, stretching from New Delhi down to Mumbai. This US$90 billion plan envisages numerous infrastructural and industrial developments, susceptible of tripling industrial output across the six states through which it runs.[13]

---

[12] Ellis, ER (2017). Indian Chinese engagement in Latin America and the Caribbean: A Compatative Assessment. Washington D.C.: Strategic Studies Institute and U.S. Army War Caller Press (March 2017). p. 11.

[13] Williams, M and L Prickitt (2011). Project will 'change lives' in India (5 November 2011). *thestar.com.* http://www.thestar.com/news/world/article/1081409--project-will-change-lives-in-india. Accessed 12/06/2017.

The need for infrastructural modernization is evident as shown at the end of July 2012. On that occasion, 600 million citizens, in 20 states and union territories, were affected by a huge electricity blackout that plunged half of India into darkness. If India materializes its infrastructure development ambitions, overcoming the limitations imposed by its boisterous political system, staggering bureaucracy and traditional land battles, it could indeed become a second China.

Another area that Latin America's natural resources exporters can look forward to is China's One Belt, One Road Initiative. Of the different potential options on the table, this seems to be the most auspicious. A mega infrastructure development plan whose clout could cover more than 65 countries in Asia, Africa and Asia and whose price tag is estimated at one trillion dollars. Comprising a land route ("Silk Road Economic Belt") and a maritime route ("Maritime Silk Road"), it aims at building highways, railways, pipelines, ports and industrial ports. The land route will go from Lianyungang in China to Rotterdam in the Netherlands, while the maritime one will depart from Quanzhou in China and end in Venice, Italy.

Referring to China's reasons behind the One Belt, One Road Initiative, Hugh White states:

> "China wants to consolidate its position at the center of the global supply and manufacturing networks which will be the key to the global economy over the coming decades. Beijing understands that as China's economy matures and its income levels rise, the lower–wage industries which have fueled China's growth so far will migrate to less–developed countries where labor costs are lower. China's economic planners want to fight that trend, but turn it to China's advantage by building itself an inexpugnable place at the center of the expanding supply–chain web which will result from it".[14]

The One Belt, One Road project encompasses 65 per cent of the world's population, about one third of the world's gross domestic product and about a quarter of the world's trade.[15] Making this bold vision a reality will require

[14] China's One Belt, One Road to challenge US-led order (27 April 2017). *The Straits Times*.
[15] Goh, SN (2017). "China makes tracks on modern Silk Road" (11 May 2017). *The Straits Times*.

an extraordinary alignment of financial resources, political commitment, technical skills and international cooperation. It is by no means an easy task. However, the benefits that it may bring to so many are so significant, that numerous countries have shown their interest in this project.

Not surprisingly 110 countries were represented, some of them at the highest level, at the mid–May 2017 Beijing meeting to discuss the initiative. With commodities showing their lowest prices in more than a decade, the incentive to build an intercontinental web of infrastructure and trade links has been greatly enhanced. The China Development Bank alone has earmarked US$890 billion for some 900 projects herein involved.[16]

Concomitant to such a megaproject is the estimation by the Asian Development Bank that the Asian region alone, needs US$1.7 trillion worth of infrastructure building annually from 2016 to 2030 to maintain its growth momentum.[17]

There is a caveat, though, for Latin American producers of natural resources, as many of the countries through which the land and maritime routes would pass are themselves important commodities producers. As such they would naturally be the primary beneficiaries of this megaproject. Nonetheless, even if a competition of commodities sources may ensue, there should be ample possibilities for everybody to get a share of the cake. Especially since the prices of natural resources would rise accordingly for everybody.

Neither the TPP, the Indian market or the One Belt, One Road Initiative, are assured bets for Latin American commodities exporters. However, they represent potential expansive markets. This is more than what labor–intensive assembly lines from Mexico, the Dominican Republic and Central America can look forward to. Mexico, though, is in a better position than the Dominican Republic and Central America, as in addition to its manufactured exports it is also an exporter of commodities, of oil in particular.

It is obvious, though, that both groups of exporters — of products and commodities — have to widen their export horizons. Services will count as an important option in this sense, given that this sector is becoming the new export frontier.

---

[16] Projects span rail, ports, industrial parks (15 May 2017). *The Straits Times.*

[17] Ibid.

The New Export Frontier

According to Saurabh Mishra, Susanna Lundstrom and Rahul Anand:

> "Services have grown as a share of the world's GDP in the last decade accounting for 70 percent of the global GDP, and service exports in developing countries have almost tripled between 1997 and 2007. Even though manufacturing continues to be a dominant driver of growth, recent developments suggest that we must include the service sector in the debate. Services are no longer exclusively an input for trade in goods but have become a 'final export' for direct consumption".[18]

Latin America has proven to have great strength and potential in the service sector, which represents the main economic activity of the region. In 2010, it reached 74.2 per cent of the regional GDP (including the Caribbean). Moreover, the service sector generates 80 per cent of the region's urban employment.[19] In telecommunications, energy, engineering, entertainment, air transport, finance or real state, among other service areas, Latin American multinational companies are growing in importance, giving a boost to this sector.

Within the service sector there is, though, an area of particular relevance. We refer to the global chains of value. Until recently many services were difficult or impossible to supply beyond their frontiers, but this has changed because of the exponential advance in information and telecommunication technologies.

Thanks to them distance has disappeared and many previously domestically encapsulated services have become global. Within the frame of the Information Technology Enabled Services (ITES) an immense variety of services can be provided at a distance, giving a tremendous boost to the offshoring of white–collar jobs.

Several reasons are behind this process: a) the strong diffusion in the technologies of information and telecommunications; b) the globalization

---

[18] The World Bank, South Asia Region (2011). Service Sophistication and Economic Growth (March 2011). Policy Research Working Paper 5606, p. 20.

[19] Sistema Económico Latinoamericano (2012). Informe sobre el proceso de Integración Regional 2011-2012 (August 2012). Caracas.

of competences that has allowed companies to look for the best available talent at the lowest possible costs wherever they can be found; c) the homogenization of practices of consumption, production and management induced by globalization; d) the tendency within corporations to outsource or offshore non–core areas.

Within the context of non–core areas we witness the appearance of the "back office", which implies the outsourcing of numerous activities traditionally performed inside the company. Such activities include, among others, accounting, client management, salary payments, data processing, etc. Whenever quality can be maintained and costs can be reduced, outsourcing tends to give place to offshoring, that is, the transference of jobs abroad.

Dematerialization of companies has become a fact of life in developed economies. Assembly lines and "back office" services are being scattered and offshored around the world, in the search of the lowest manpower costs. Research and Development activities are also being sent to subsidiaries abroad, particularly to Asia. But while corporations stick to brands and patents as their core areas, the bulk of their activities is being outsourced and offshored.

According to *Bloomberg/Businessweek*:

> "Some observers even believe Big Business is on the cusp of a new burst of productivity growth, ignited in part by offshore outsourcing as a catalyst...As executives shed more operations, they also are spurring new debate about how the future of corporation will look. Some management pundits theorize about the 'totally disaggregated corporation', wherein every function not regarded as crucial is stripped away...The rise of the offshore option is dramatically changing the economics of reengineering. With millions of low–cost engineers, financial analysts, consumer marketers, and architects now readily available via the Web, CEOs can see a quicker payoff. 'It used to be that companies struggled for a few years to show a 5% or 10% increase in productivity from outsourcing', says Pramod Bhasin, CEO of Genpact, the 19,000–employee back–office–processing unit spun off by GE last year. 'But by offshoring work, they can see savings of 30% to 40% in the first year' in labor costs...Professor Mohanbir Sawhney of

Northwestern University's Kellogg School of Management, a self–proclaimed 'big believer in total disaggregation', says: 'One of our tasks in business schools is to train people to manage the virtual, globally distributed corporation.'"[20]

Latin America and the Global Chains of Value

Chains of value imply the interconnection between manufacturing and services within the context of global processes of production and trade. Moreover, according to experts, in the future more products will be sold based on attached services as the lines between manufacturing and services are blurring. Increasingly, the level of knowledge and responsibility of the services sent abroad tends to be higher.

So far more than 70 per cent of offshore white–collar jobs have remained within OECD countries, with India and China strongly emerging from the outside.[21] Nonetheless that should be seen as the first step in a process that inevitably leads to equilibrium between job quality and the lowest possible job salaries. As India and China are showing, emerging economies can become unbeatable in this area.

According to Alan Blinder, Director of the Center for Economic Policy Studies at Princeton University, impersonal services are on the brink of a gigantic revolution. Such services, which are those that do not require a face–to–face interaction with the customer or patient, will be transferred in their tens of millions to emerging economies, where a gigantic pool of talent converges with much lower costs.[22] In another study that Blinder co–authored together with Alan B. Krueger, the conclusion was that jobs that require a high degree of education and qualification are, if anything, more offshorable than the rest[23]

---

[20] The future of outsourcing (30 January 2006). Bloomberg/Businessweek.

[21] López, A, Ramos, D and I Torres (2009). *Las Exportaciones de servicio y su integración a las Cadenas Globales de Valor*, p. 16 (March 2009). Santiago de Chile: Comisión Económica para América Latina y el Caribe.

[22] Offshoring: The Next Industrial Revolution (2006). *Foreign Affairs*. New York. (March/April 2006). Volume 85 (March/April 2006), pp. 113–128.

[23] Alternative Measures of Offshorability (2009). *National Bureau of Economic Research*, Working Paper 15287 (August 2009), http://www.nber.org/papers/w15287. Accessed 15/05/2012.

According to Saurabh Mishra, Susanna Lundstrom and Rahul Anand:

> "The mid 1990s saw two seemingly separate but related developments. First was the revolution in information and communication technology (ICT) and, second, rapid growth in the global forces often referred to as the 3Ts — technology, transportability, and tradability — with the advent of internet age. Both events had a profound impact on the nature, productivity, and tradability of services. This has resulted in rapid growth of what can be called *modern impersonal progressive services*... These services differ significantly from the *traditional personal services*, which demand face–to–face interaction".[24]

We are, thus, talking of the massive migration of impersonal services jobs to the developing world in the next few decades. From accountants to software engineers, from designers to architects, from doctors to researchers, from financial consultants to lawyers, the areas of service jobs here involved can become countless.

Latin America could offer several advantages within this process of dematerialization of companies, among which five stand out. First is the fact that Latin America is part of Western civilization and, for all its particularities, it still shares such heritage and background. As evidenced by the fact that the majority of services offshored jobs have so far remained within OECD countries, it would seem that cultural affinity with Western values still plays an important role. If that were to be the case Latin America enjoys of a comparative advantage for companies of the Western world.

Second is the fact that Latin America shows a strong online culture. According to Basil C. Puglisi, a digital brand marketing consultant formerly with AOL:

> "Although Latin America makes up only 8.2% of the world's population, they are the second largest consumer of social media. The online behavior of Latin Americans is evolving right along with the rest of the world, but in many cases, a bit faster".[25]

---

[24] Mishra, S, Lundstrom S and R Anand (2011). Op. cit, pp. 2–3.

[25] Puglisi, B C (2011.). Social networking statistics in Latin America (October 5, 2011). *Digital Doughnut*, http://digitaldoughnut.com/social-networking-statistics-in-latin-america. Accessed 20/3/2012.

Third would be Latin America's unique know–how and experience in productive sectors associated with commodities. Such knowledge can be projected internationally through the aforementioned Information Technology Enabled Services. Among them we could mention agro-industry in Brazil, Argentina Chile or Colombia; hydrocarbons in Venezuela, Mexico and Brazil; mining in Brazil, Chile and Peru; cattle management in Brazil, Argentina or Uruguay. And so on.

Fourth are the Western time zones. These work in favor of Latin America, as the region shares the same timeframe with most of the United States does and is just a few hours behind that of Western Europe. That allows work to be developed in a simultaneous way permitting a more direct control of foreign operations.

Five is the fact that English is a widely spoken language in the region, as a result of the closeness to the United States. Even if not attaining the general use that characterizes Indian middle classes, it is nonetheless a familiar second language for the majority of Latin America's middle class.

Latin America has a tremendous challenge ahead if it wants to become a relevant participant in the projected wave of offshore service jobs. The preparations herein involved should aim at several directions: English proficiency, online infrastructure, tertiary education and the creation of an institutional base for supporting private efforts in this area. Global chain of values could become a good export addition to that of manufactures and commodities.

The Fourth Industrial Revolution

While favorable conditions seem to be visible on the horizon, it is impossible not to notice an approaching thunderstorm as well. This is represented by the incoming disruptive technologies. This phenomenon, which has been labeled in different manners — "Fourth Industrial Revolution", "Cambrian moment", etc. — represents the greatest threat to the stability of the region in the coming decades. And even if this is a worldwide challenge, the implications for Latin America can be simply devastating.

In 1991, Alvin Tofller wrote about a world divided into quick–moving and slow–moving nations. This implied a decoupling between countries with advanced economic and technological systems and outpaced economic and technological nations, submitted to huge economic limitations and social problems.[26]

The millennium brought with it, though, the inclusion into the global labor equation of 1.3 billion Chinese and 1.2 billion Indians, within a context of a race to the bottom of production costs. As a result, Western nations began transforming themselves into embattled fortresses. Moreover, in 2008, Western nations unleashed an international recession of which they emerged amid a concatenation of high indebtedness, sluggish growth and lack of confidence. A decoupling, very different from that predicted by Toffler, began to take shape. Indeed, developing nations, lifted by China's phenomenal emergence, continued to grow despite the crisis of the developed world.[27]

However, the Fourth Industrial Revolution in sight will bring back the kind of decoupling envisaged by Toffler. Within it, the distinction between high and low cost producing countries, or between emerging and mature markets, will become increasingly irrelevant. What will matter is the capacity to innovate shown by each country. And a group of developed economies led by the US, this time with the presence of China as well, will run the show.

This decoupling could be particularly tough for slow–moving nations, as technologically advanced economies will become much more autonomous in relation to commodities, products and services, coming from the developing world. While globalization loses standing, as a result of the increasing autarchy of developed countries, emerging nations will become dramatically stressed.[28]

The caveat for rapidly moving nations, however, would be a tremendous polarization within their societies. Let us just consider, well–known 2013 Oxford University report predicts, that up to 47 per cent of existing

---

[26] Tofller, A (1991). *El Cambio de Poder.* Barcelona: Plaza y Janés Editores.

[27] Hardy, AT (2013). *The World Turned Upside Down: The Complex Partnership between China and Latin America.* Singapore: World Scientific

[28] Hames, TX (2016). *The end of globalization? The international security implications* (2 August 2016). https://warontherocks.com/2016/08/the-end-of-globalization-the-international-security-implications. Accessed 12/02/2017.

employments in the United States will disappear within the next one to two decades as a result of digital technology.[29]

According to Klaus Schwab, companies and people that survive or thrive amid this scenario,

> "will need to maintain and continually sharpen their innovative edge. Businesses, industries and corporations will face continuous Darwinian pressures and as such, the philosophy of 'always in beta' (always evolving) will become more prevalent".[30]

As MIT scholars Erik Brynnjolfsson and Andrew McAfee have amply explained, when a technological leap surpasses the adjustment capabilities of societies, social havoc might ensue.[31] Especially so when radical changes not only affect a single productivity sector, but all of them at the same time. Digital technology, referred to as the great disruptor by the abovementioned Oxford University report, is indeed just one of the several converging leaps leading to radical changes in the market place.

Again, in Klaus Schwab's words:

> "Contrary to previous industrial revolutions, this one is evolving at an exponential rather than linear pace…It builds on the digital revolution and combines multiple technologies that are leading to unprecedented paradigm shifts in the economy, business, society, and individually. It is not only changing the 'what' and 'how' of doing things but also 'who' we are. It involves the transformation of entire systems, across (and within) countries, companies, industries and society as a whole".[32]

---

[29] Frey, CB and ME Osborne (2013). *The Future of Employment: How Susceptible are Jobs to Computerization* (17 September 2013). Oxford University. http://www.oxfordmartin.ox.ac.uk/downloads/academic/The_Future_of_Employment.pdf. Accessed 05/02/2015.

[30] Schwab, K (2017). *The Fourth Industrial Revolution,* p. 63. London: Portfolio Penguin.

[31] Brynnjolfsson, E and A McAfee (2014). *The Second Machine Age: Work, Progress, and Prosperity in a Time of Brilliant Technologies.* New York: W.W. Norton and Brynnjolfsson, E and A McAfee (2011). *Race against the Machines: How Digital Revolution is Accelerating Innovation, Driving Productivity, and Irreversibly Transforming Employment and the Economy.* Lexington Mass.: Digital Frontier Press.

[32] Schwab, *op. cit.,* p. 3.

And he adds: "The danger is that the fourth industrial revolution would mean that a winner–takes–all dynamic plays out between countries as well as within them".[33]

To understand the meaning of exponential pace we must read what Ray Kurzweil, Director of Engineering at Google and founder of the Singularity University, has to say:

> "Exponentials are quite seductive because they start out sub–linear. We sequenced one ten–thousand of the human genome in 1990 and two ten–thousand in 1991. Halfway through the genome project, 7 and a half years into it, we have sequenced 1 percent. People said, 'This is a failure. Seven years, 1 percent. It's going to take 700 years'. Seven years later it was done, because 1 percent is only seven doublings from 100 percent — and it has been doubling every year. We don't think in these exponential terms".[34]

But even if this Fourth Industrial Revolution creates immense social problems for quick–moving nations, it may become devastating for slow–moving ones. Within this "only the paranoid survives" scenario — Andy Grove's dixit — developing economies can simply be left aside and robbed of an economic future.

As seen in Chapter 9, during the past decades Latin America was confronted by two sudden and superlative economic challenges: the opening of its previously protected domestic markets to foreign competition and the appearance of Chinese low–cost competition. What lies ahead, though, will dwarf by comparison such changes to the point of irrelevance. But while the previous two shocks took the region by surprise, this one is announcing its arrival with ample anticipation.

The Incoming Tsunami

As a result of the two previous economic tsunamis (as well as a consequence of NAFTA and the Free Trade Agreement with Dominican

[33] Ibid., p. 47.

[34] Parker, L (2016). Google, Singularity University visionary Ray Kurzweil on the amazing future he sees (6 September 2016). *Silicon Valley Business Journal* http://www.bizjournals.com/sanjose/news/2016/09/06/exclusive-google-singularity-visionary-ray.html. Accessed 19/12/2016.

Republic and the Central American nations), Latin American countries bifurcated. On the one hand, labor–intensive export oriented economies and, on the other hand, natural resources exporters. Domestic oriented service sectors were of course present in both cases, with some scattered examples of export–oriented services as well. In all three cases — labor-intensive assembly lines, commodities and services — the approaching technological leaps may produce devastation.

The convergence of digital technology and robotics; nanotechnology; biotechnology and genomics; additive manufacturing (3D printing); the Internet of things, autonomous vehicles and energy technologies, to mention just some of the most relevant leaps, will project its impact in every imaginable direction. Even if affecting the whole world this disruptiveness will be particularly felt in emerging economies, like those of Latin America.

Latin America's assembly lines could be flattened because of robotics. Indeed, robots are becoming an economic alternative even in labor–intensive China. According to Martin Ford, in 2017 China will be number one worldwide in robotic manufacturing capacity.[35] As robots become more adaptive, flexible and inexpensive, no measure of cheap labor will be able to keep pace with them. This will propitiate onshoring manufacturing processes, as robotic low-cost production will take factories back to the United States and to other rapidly advancing economies.

Assembly lines in the region will also be totally disrupted by additive manufacturing or 3D Printing. This consists in creating physical objects by printing layer upon layer from a digital 3D model. It is the opposite of traditional subtracting manufacturing, which is how things have been done until now: with layers being removed from a piece of material until the desired shape is obtained.[36]

This will lead to the mass customization and design for purpose of industrial parts and pieces. Not only inventories will become unnecessary, but numerous intermediary manufacturing steps will become redundant. Rather than stocking a wide variety of parts, these will be printed on demand. And instead of manufacturing multiple smaller parts to be joined together, a single final one can be directly printed. The result will be the

---

[35] Ford, M (2015). China's troubling Robot Revolution (10 June 2015). *The New York Times*.

[36] Klaus Schwab, *op. cit.*

obsolescence of labor–intensive manufacturing, with the consequent onshoring of manufacturing activities.[37]

Latin American mining as well as iron and steel industries will lose much ground, as the introduction of new materials by nanotechnology materializes in the next few decades. According to K. Eric Drexler:

> "A nanoscale technology revolution has already arrived, bringing with it the radical abundance we call the information Revolution…The same profound digital principles will enable a parallel revolution that will enable radical abundance, not just in the world of information, but in the world of tangible, physical products as well". [38]

Some examples speak for themselves: carbon nanotubes with higher strength than any other known materials which result, at the same time, more conductive than copper; lightweight material as stiff as aircraft aluminum but 100 times stronger; heavier material, stronger than steel, yet only one–fifth as dense. And what to say about a nanomaterial such as graphene, which is about 200 times stronger that steel, a million times thinner than a human hair, and an efficient conductor of heat and electricity?[39]

Again, in Drexler's words:

> "The extraordinary lightness and strength of materials like these has far–reaching consequences (…) In aerospace technology and a range of other spheres of engineering, the prospect of removing more than 80 percent of the structural mass promises a revolution in performance and efficiency. Performance aside, making products less massive reduces materials consumption, with a proportional impact on production costs".[40]

Farming and livestock sectors in the region can be turned upside down as genome technology advances in the direction of producing

---

[37] T.X. Hammes, *op. cit.*

[38] Drexler, KE (2013). *Radical Abundance: How Revolution in Nanotechnology will Change Civilization.* Kindle Ed. Chapter 1, Loc 274. New York: Public Affairs.

[39] Klaus Schwab, *op. cit.*

[40] Ibid., Chapter 11, Loc 2876.

vegetables, fruits and meat "in vitro". In other words, genetically designed food that would be engineered from the ground up and then industrially produced. In addition to fruit and vegetables created in laboratories, this implies cultured meat or tube steak: a flesh product that has never been part of a complete, living animal. This technology, which is already scientifically viable, shall become financially viable in the second half of the 2020s.[41]

But together with such advancements in genome technology, there will be many others leaps in sensors, production automation, robot farming or engineering, which will radically transform the multi millenarian relation between human beings and soil. While those technologies materialize, indoor farms are beginning to take shape in the United States. Such farms do not require herbicides or pesticides, use 97 per cent less water, use 40 per cent less power, waste 50 per cent less food and are not subject to weather irregularities. [42]

Latin American hydrocarbons reserves run the risk of remaining underground, as a result of technological leaps coming from all directions. In addition to technological advances in fracking and horizontal drilling, there have been impressive advances in clean energies. Solar and wind technologies, whose prices have fallen 85 per cent since the beginning of this century or the last years of the preceding one, are duplicating their capacity every two years within the parameters of the Moore Law. According to well–known futurologist Jeremy Rifkin, such technologies are moving towards the zero marginal costs stage. Biomass — now entering its second generation — evolves rapidly, as rapidly as geothermic and wave technologies. Lithium batteries, whose price has fallen 40 per cent since 2009, and whose storage capacity has augmented dramatically, are beginning to provide profitability to electric cars. Chemical systems that can replicate photosynthesis artificially and on a grand scale – and hence

---

[41] Hammes, *op. cit.*

[42] Zappa, M (2015). 15 emerging agriculture technologies that will change the world (6 May 2015). *Policy Horizons Canada.* http://www.businessinsider.sg/15-emerging-agriculture-technologies-2014-4/#18EzrTcMUDhrlBtw.97. Accessed 12/04/2017; Garthwaite, J (2014). Beyond GMOs: The rise of synthetic biology (25 September 2014), *The Atlantic;* Watson, B (2015). The science of sustainability: what we've learned from artificial photosynthesis and synthetic meat (30 June 2015). *The Guardia*n; Hammes, *op. cit.*

create solar collectors that produce fuel — are on the way. Biotechnology is also in its way to substituting oil in the production of plastics. Self–fertilizing plants, deriving from synthetic biology, could decouple agriculture from the oil industry fertilizers. Moreover, such technological changes move in tandem with the decarburization requirements of the 2015 Paris Agreement on Climate Change.[43]

Meanwhile the region's service sector is threatened by digital technologies in every possible way. Not only repetitive and routine jobs will be displaced by such technologies. Jobs that require analytical thinking and high educational levels are being targeted as well by "big data", the Internet of things and the automation of knowledge work. This will not only abort Latin America's possibilities of integrating into global value chains, but may lead to a substantial contraction of its middle classes. Autonomous vehicles, on the other hand, will affect industries dedicated to the mobilization of merchandise and people.[44]

More diversified economies within Latin America will be undoubtedly better prepared to handle this challenge. The examples of Brazil and Paraguay at the beginning of the 20th century come to mind. The economy of Paraguay was devastated when US cotton surpluses took out of the market its mono–production of cotton. Meanwhile, Brazil's more diversified economy could withstand much better the disappearance of its rubber exports, resulting from the sudden emergence of lower cost competition from British Malaya. Even if the Fourth Industrial Revolution bears no relation to such examples, diversified economies will be always better prepared to endure the impact of disruptive technologies. Especially so because not all the technological leaps will arrive at the same time or be equally disruptive.

---

[43] Rifkin, J (2014). *The Zero Marginal Cost Society, and the Eclipse of Capitalism.* New York: Pelgrave; McKinsey Global Institute (2013). *Disruptive technologies: Advances that will transform life, business, and the global economy* (May 2013); Garthwaite, *op. cit.*, Watson, *op. cit.*,. Hammes, *op. cit.*

[44] Brynnjolfsson and McAfee, *op. cit.*; Steiner, C (2012). *Automate This: How Algorithms Took over Our Markets, Our Jobs, and the World.* New York: Portfolio/Penguin; Ford, M (2015). *Rise of the Robots: Technology and the Threat of a Jobless Future.* New York: Basic Books.

Shortcomings and Comparative Advantages

The Fourth Industrial Revolution will make evident Latin America's shortcomings and comparative advantages when dealing with drastically changing environments. It is a subject related to the region's characterological traits, expressed at the end of Chapter 5. Lacking in method and systematic action, Latin Americans run the risk of not anticipating and preparing sufficiently for the incoming disruptions. Conversely, the region excels in lateral thinking, unorthodox approaches to difficult situations and capacity for improvisation, which will serve it well when faced with the drowning of certainties and conventional wisdom.

The implications of the Fourth Industrial Revolution have been essentially absent from the agenda or the debate of decision–makers, scholars, business people or public intellectuals in Latin America. Even if the only positive aspect of this incoming tsunami is that it will not take the region by surprise, its potential destructiveness seems to be out of the regional radar. More immediate and pressing problems and challenges are obstructing the view of Latin American elites in relation to this subject.

The truth is that decision–makers should be elevating this subject to regional forums, while discussing common strategies and policies. Governments should be dealing with this incoming threat by creating strategic thinking teams. Universities, think–tanks, business federations, unions, professional associations, should be focusing their attention on the implications herein involved. Economic diversification processes, the search for niches outside the boundaries of technological leaps and extensive educational reforms, should have been included in regional and national agendas. But nothing of the sort has happened. The region seems to be oblivious to what lies ahead.

On the other hand, though, Latin Americans are resilient by nature. They possess adaptive and improvisational talents when confronted by rapidly evolving situations. And events will indeed move rapidly. A good example of such velocity and of Latin American responsiveness capacity may be found in education.

According to Margie Warrell, up to 40 per cent of what college students learn today will become obsolete in a decade.[45] Alternatively, and

[45] Warrell, M (2014). *Learn, Unlearn and Relearn* (3 February 2014). Forbes.

according to Cathy Davison, 65 per cent of children entering into the educational system in 2011 will end up working in careers that have not been invented yet.[46] Even if continuous education is the obvious response when confronted with such challenges, there is more to it than meets the eye. Indeed, being able to unlearn what has been learned will become fundamental.

As existing paradigms are to become the bigger obstacles to rapid movement, being able to surpass what was conventional knowledge until the day before, will become a necessity. Margie Warrell provides the example of painting a wall surface, asserting that as painters know well, 70 per cent of the work involved consists in removing the old painting.[47]

A highly advanced educational system such as that of Finland, is changing its traditional educational curriculum to emphasize creativity and critical thinking, at the expense of the accumulation of knowledge. Within that process, critical thinking, lateral thinking and imagination will become essential tools to learn, unlearn and relearn in rapid succession. It comes without saying that the capacity to improvise shall also become fundamental.

Such traits seem to be in line with the Latin American mindset. Indeed, with its characteristic fluid and open mind and its capacity to adapt to changing and stressful environments, always at odds with rigidity, Latin Americans seem to be in tune with the resilience requirements of this emerging whirlwind world. Let us remember Charles Darwin's dictum: "It is not the strongest of the species that survives, nor the most intelligent. It is the one that is most adaptable to change".[48]

---

[46] Davison, C (2012). *Now You See It: How Technology and Brain Science will transform Schools and Business for the 21st Century.* London: Penguin Books.

[47] Warrell, *op. cit.*

[48] Ibid.

CONCLUSION

Latin America is made up of those non–Anglo or Dutch components of the Americas formed in the common mould of the Catholic religion, the Latin cultural heritage and the romance languages. Iberian America and Haiti would naturally fit into this description. The former because of its Spanish and Portuguese ancestry, the latter because of its French one.

However, if we were to take this argument to its logical conclusion, we would have to include in the notion of Latin America not only the Catholic and French speaking province of Quebec in Canada, but also France itself by virtue of its overseas territories in the Americas. Indeed, such territories are not considered to be colonies, but integral parts of the French state.

Nevertheless, when the term Latin America is used, its meaning is more restricted as it just covers the Iberian American countries. That is, Brazil and the 19 Hispanic American nations. That is, the Iberian American countries.

Why then the term Latin America?

The notion of Latin America originated in France, at a time when the French Emperor Napoleon III held hegemonic aspirations at the other side of the Atlantic, particularly in Mexico. To provide a framework of legitimacy to these aspirations, he needed to underline a common link between his country and Iberian America. The so–called "Pan–Latin" thesis, which amalgamated within a common identity the countries situated on both shores of the Atlantic that could trace their origins back to ancient Rome, became the solution.

Despite France's retreat from Mexico in 1866 and the fall of Napoleon III's own Empire in 1870, the "Pan–Latin" notion persisted in the region.

It is quite surprising that the term Latin America survived despite its origin and imperialistic connotations. For their own reasons, though, regional elites found the term conveniently useful and adopted it as the new symbol of identity of the region.

The end of the era of Napoleon III coincided with the emergence, all over the Iberian American countries, of a powerful Positivist movement which saw France as the epitome of civilization. Both Brazil and Spanish America found it convenient to call themselves by a name that enhanced their connection to France. In Hispanic America, this move had a further motive: establish a direct parentage with Western civilisation skirting round Spain.

As a result, the region came to be known as Latin America, obviating a more descriptive notion of its origins. Nonetheless, as aforementioned, that term refers specifically to Iberian America.

The notion of Iberian America comprises those countries of the Americas which were former colonies of Spain and Portugal, and where Spanish or Portuguese is spoken. The prefix "Iberian" derives from the fact that those two European countries share the Iberian Peninsula, located in the foremost western part of that continent.

Both Spain and Portugal share an old, rich and complex civilization. This civilization was the result of many centuries of physical co–existence and fusion of cultures among Christians, Muslims and Jews and before that of the interaction with many other civilizations. Spain and Portugal were part of the same Roman Province, Hispania, and could have evolved as a single state if political and military factors, in the 10th and 11th centuries, had not decided otherwise. No two other countries in Europe are probably as similar as these two are.

Starting with these common denominators Spaniards and Portuguese would have to go through the same process of racial mixture and cultural fusion when they reached the New World, thus giving rise to a new human group of similar characteristics.

In the process, the indigenous people they encountered were confronted by the same shattering experiences: defeat, submission, servitude, conversion to their overlords' religion and massive human loses resulting from the infectious diseases brought by the Iberians.

The demographic crumbling of the Indians, as a consequence of their lack of resistance to alien illnesses, generated a lack of workforce. This led to the introduction in America of its third human protagonist: the African slave. If the fate of the Indian had been dramatic, that of the African slave was by no means any better.

The human identity of Iberian America would be the result of the miscegenation and acculturation of these three groups: the Iberian, the Indian and the African slave. Notwithstanding this fusion, the Iberians were the prevalent force, imposing upon the rest language, religion, law and hegemonic ideas. Moreover, those sectors of the social structure which preserved their "whiteness" through inbreeding, became its leading force.

These similarities aside, however, there are relevant differences between Brazil and Spanish America. To begin with, because of the more pragmatic and conciliatory character of the Brazilians, when compared to that of the Hispanic Americans. The history of Brazil displays a process of moderate evolution, devoid of the epic deeds and sudden shocks so typical of Hispanic America.

It has been correctly pointed out that the Brazilians fell asleep one night as a colony and woke up to find themselves an independent Empire and, sometime later, woke up again to find themselves a Republic. The history of Hispanic America, on the other hand, looks more grandiose and traumatic.

In Brazil conditions were created for the colony to become a unitary State after independence from Portugal. In Hispanic American colonies, the opposite happened: the soil was paved for its fracture into numerous countries after its liberation from Spain. Moreover, prevailing conditions in Brazil allowed the country to emerge as an independent monarchy with a Prince of Portuguese royal blood on the throne. Conversely, Spanish America underwent harrowing and bloody wars of independence against the Spanish monarch, which led to a Republican system.

Brazil's monarchical regime provided power legitimacy and allowed for the arbitration of conflicting interests and visions. Independent Hispanic American nations, on the contrary, were faced with the beheading of the established order and to profound institutional disorientation. Moreover, civil wars plagued Spanish America, as conflicting societal interests and visions could not be reconciled.

As Brazil became a Republic at the end of the 19th century, it entered greater political tune with Hispanic American nations, with which it shared similar challenges. A curious form of synchronism with many of those nations materialized, within a pendulum movement that alternated between democratic and military governments. Even so, Brazil has always shown a more moderate and pragmatic evolution than its Hispanic American cousins.

There are, thus, commonalities and differences between Brazilians and Hispanic Americans. A natural convergence arises from what they have in common. The ways in which they are different, constructively complement each other. All being said, Brazil and Spanish America share a common destiny and a strong sense of solidarity.

But what about Hispanic America itself? Are there sufficient common denominators within it? Spanish America, as is to be expected, shows elements of homogeneity and heterogeneity.

Many homogeneous elements are present within this group of nations. There is a common language, which implies possessing the most powerful instrument for the transmission of a cultural identity. There is a shared religion which represents not only an attachment to the same spiritual values, but also similar cultural expressions of that faith. There is a synchronism of historical events which projects itself to a common past beyond the Ocean and to shared experiences once in the Americas. The latter projects itself over a period of more than 500 years. There are the same social values, which revolve around the family as the fundamental building block of society.

But beyond their commonalities, Hispanic Americans also show differences. Two of them turn out to be of particular relevance. The first are those which derive from the variety of latitudes, topography and climate. The second one emerges from the diverse racial mixtures or from the lack of them.

Hispanic America is a wide and diverse region. Its countries coexist within different geographical contexts, which translates into dissimilar attitudinal characteristics. But together with geography we also find ethnicity and by extension cultural identity. As the three original human components of Hispanic America brought with them different cultural traits, it is logical to assume that their mixture or lack of it produced different outcomes.

The indigenous and black elements of society that mixed with the Spanish one, were highly heterogeneous in nature. Not only the indigenous populations were extremely diverse, but also the black ethnicity derived from a wide range of sources. Consequently, while the Spanish ethnicity played a centripetal role, being the glue that held the group together, the Indian and African ones played a centrifugal one.

But in addition to such centrifugal forces in play, Hispanic America can be divided in three basic areas according to their ethnicity. There is a Spanish America of strong indigenous roots, another one of deep African roots and, finally, one mostly white. Each showing a distinct personality.

The diverse countries of the region give different connotations to the phenomenon of miscegenation. Some look at it favorably and give proper recognition to its ethnic diversity, while others, nowadays the minority, see it with pejorative eyes.

Notwithstanding the differences amid Hispanic Americans the shared elements clearly prevail. The solidarity shown between their different countries is rarely seen in other parts of the world.

With such a complex background and characteristics, can Iberian Americans claim to be part of Western Civilization? The answer is not clear cut. To begin with, some scholars maintain that Spaniards and Portuguese are not properly Westerners. Besides having been conquered by the Moors for many centuries, arguments in that direction insist that the two movements which were responsible for some of the essential features of Western thought — the Renaissance and the 18th Century Enlightenment — scarcely reached Spain and Portugal.

The Iberian Peninsula remained "eccentric" (far from the centre) in relation to the nucleuses of Western Civilization, as symbolized by countries such as France or England. This not only has a cultural meaning but a geographic one as well, as Portugal and Spain stand on the most extreme points of the European landmass.

Hence, the starting point of Latin American cultural heritage is a fringe model, as both Spain and Portugal were "eccentric" countries. But then, upon their arrival to the Americas, Iberians did not conform to a settler's society as the English did in North America, Australia or New Zealand. On the contrary, they mixed themselves with indigenous and African elements giving rise to an acculturated society.

In other words, Latin America represents a sort of fringe version of the Iberian fringe model itself. Not surprisingly then, Latin Americans harbor so many doubts in relation to their own identity. These doubts have led to a soul–searching attitude that has permeated several schools of thought.

In order to properly assess the inclusion of Latin America in Western civilization, though, some background is required. Western civilization was the result of the interweaving between the Classical tradition — meaning Greek and Roman — and the Judeo–Christian world. Other elements were added to this mix — particularly in the case of Renaissance and Enlightenment — but the previous two remained as the central ones.

What entitlement have Latin Americans then to such heritage?

Colonization was a process of incorporation into Western values. Iberian America inherited such values (state, family, home, urbanization, social relation, the status of women and children, property, crime and punishment, etc.) directly from Roman Law. For five centuries, with a few localized exceptions, Iberian Americans were subjected to an overwhelmingly predominant Western culture.

However, Latin Americans have a particular way of being Westerners. Theirs, as mentioned, is an acculturated society in which powerful identity influences moved in every direction. Not all its three original components, though, contributed in equal measure to the final product. The Iberians remained the undisputed guiding force within the mix, determining language, religion, law, family values and architectural traditions. In other words, a Roman–Christian heritage. Latin Americans, hence, have sufficient elements to be included within Western Civilization.

Nonetheless, those clearly dominant Roman–Christian set of values coexist, sometimes peacefully, sometimes wistfully and even belligerently, with the values of the other cultural identities. As a result, Latin Americans can look at Western civilisation from within and from outside. In other words, they can be at once entitled to and critical of Western civilisation. A very intriguing position to be in indeed.

Latin America, a peripheral Western region, shares the same hemisphere with the United States, a country that epitomizes today's the Western World. The astonishing development attained by the

Anglo–Saxon society of the North, and the continuous but unfulfilled quest toward development by the Latin societies of the South, are immersed in profound cultural differences.

Both began as overseas colonies of European countries. Both were amply endowed with natural resources. Both achieved their independence during the Age of Revolutions in the late 18th or beginning of the 19th centuries. In the case of United States and Spanish America, revolutionary wars were needed to consolidate separation from their respective metropolises. But at this point their similarities end.

Why was one so successful while the other mired in so many problems and limitations? Even if this great dichotomy took shape after independence, the reasons behind it were forged during their respective colonial periods.

Endless rules, norms and regulations, within a bureaucratic and legalistic environment, defined the Iberian colonial relations with their metropolis. In contrast, English colonies in North America enjoyed wide political autonomy.

Trade regulations imposed by Madrid and Lisbon worked against the development of intercolonial trade and the creation of a network of ports across the region. Transporting the colonies' bullion and agricultural products to the metropolis was the only interest of the latter. British North America not only promoted the creation of numerous ports but allowed each to compete for trade. This not only provided invaluable commercial experience but led to an economic specialization that sowed the seeds of industrialization.

Preventing intellectual inquisitiveness and religious, social or moral deviations, was the main role of the colonial church in Iberian America. Church and state worked in tandem with the Inquisition being an adjunct to both. In the Anglo–Saxon North, competition to attract colonists implied the existence of a broad spectrum of religious denominations to choose from. In fact, English colonization arose from the search of religious freedom.

Iberian American essentially urban societies were marked by highly stratified structures. By comparison, they dwarfed the European class system. North American colonists not only wanted to leave behind the English class system, but being in their majority Protestants they presented a homogeneous profile. Moreover, theirs was an essentially rural environment in which manual labor prevailed, leaving little room for social distinctions.

Iberian American conquerors wanted to be “hidalgos”, gentry. That meant not having to work, but making others work for them. It meant obtaining glory at war to be rewarded with land and a workforce. North American Protestants were austere, industrious and disciplined. Moreover, Calvinists, Lutherans or Baptists believed in predestination, in that nothing could change what was preordained. Material success was interpreted, though, as a sign of divine favor and hence of eternal salvation. A compulsive pursuit of material success was thus integral to their identity.

Not surprisingly, the United States and Iberian America evolved in different directions. Political institutions, economic development, freedom of thought, intellectual inquisitiveness, democratic spaces and work ethic in both, took divergent routes.

The asymmetric evolution of these two spheres produced an asymmetric relationship as well. Such a relationship was formed by well–defined chapters. Initially the United Stated defined a sphere of influence in the hemisphere that foreclosed any further European penetration. Even if still unable to enforce such perimeter at the time, the Monroe Doctrine would become a paramount piece of US foreign policy.

Another chapter of this saga was the Manifest Destiny period, which defined the US’ continental expansion ambitions. During this time, the United States took half of Mexico’s territory, what nowadays are the states of California, Colorado, Utah, Nevada, New Mexico, Arizona and Texas.

After the successful war with Spain in 1898 the United States entered a new chapter: Empire. During this phase Puerto Rico became an American colony, Cuba a Protectorate, Panama was separated from Colombia and transformed into another Protectorate, with its Canal Zone falling under American legal jurisdiction. US troops invaded countries from the Caribbean Basin on 34 occasions, occupying some of them for extended periods.

Suddenly a new phase arrived with the election of Franklyn Delano Roosevelt: The Good Neighbourhood chapter. A policy of absolute non–intervention in Latin American affairs was put in place, while Washington tolerated a wide degree of political and economic manoeuvring in the region. Respect for their governments prevailed in what became the best moment in the relationship between both parties.

The following chapter, Cold War, was a ghastly one. Under the spell of ideological demons and seeing the threat of communist penetration at every corner, Washington was instrumental in promoting human rights violating dictatorships throughout the region. In the middle of this extremely difficult time, the parenthesis represented by the Administration of Jimmy Carter became a breath of fresh air for Latin America.

Trade and drugs was the subsequent chapter, as those two issues absorbed the attention of the United States towards Latin America. This phase, which arrived with the collapse of Communism was to be followed until the Obama Administration.

President Trump seems to be opening a new chapter, the contours of which are still in the making. The drifting apart of the United States and Latin America, a trend that began materializing during the trade and drugs period, will probably consolidate during the current Administration. The US' closest partners in the region seem, indeed, to be on the losing side of the political and economic equation introduced by Trump.

During the major part of their independent history, relations between the United States and Latin America seemed to have been guided by a Thucydides quote in the Melian Dialogue, according to which the powerful do what they want, while the weak endure what they must. Approaching the second decade of the fresh millennium, though, things have changed.

While the United States and Latin America are increasingly drifting apart, the influence of Washington upon the latter is decreasing with every passing year. Curiously enough, the United States is following an opposite route with its society becoming more and more "Latino American". By 2050 the total US population is projected to grow to almost 400 million, of which 28 per cent or about 112 million will be Latino. In other words, close to a third of its population will trace their ascendancy back to Iberian America.

Nowadays, Latino figures are everywhere in mainstream America. Their names are highly visible in the political, entertainment, academic, business, and fashion sectors. But besides famous or well reputed names we find the argument of numbers even more convincing. With more than 56,592,000 people, representing 17.61 per cent of the total population, Latinos are the largest minority of the country. They are thus not only progressively more influential but they represent a fundamental electoral force. Being a young population, its voting numbers will keep increasing with every passing election.

In 2016, 27.3 million Latinos, representing 12 per cent of all eligible voters, were able to cast their ballots. By 2030 that number will increase to 40 million as 17 million Latinos under the age of 18 get older. It must be outlined that more than 90 per cent of Latinos under the age of 18 are born in the United States and are therefore entitled to vote.

Their numbers though only tell half of the story. Its block power tells the other half. In contrast to other ethnic communities such as German Americans, Norwegian Americans or Polish Americans, which have diluted into mainstream America to the point of not being easy to target or mobilize, Latinos tend to act and react as a block. This, needless to say, increases substantially the Latinos political impact.

The United States' influence in Latin America has thus been decreasing, while the two have drifted apart. Meanwhile, since the millennium China has been able to acquire a privileged standing in the region, becoming the main trade partner and lender of many of its countries. This requires some background, especially so because as late as the 1990s China was totally absent from the Latin American scene, while the United States saw it as its backyard. Let us go back in time to properly frame this situation.

Since the very beginning of their independent life, Latin American nations had opted for free trade and free markets. As a result, from the mid-19th century onwards, Latin American exports began to expand bringing with them economic growth. The region moved into the 20th century full steam ahead. Its raw materials provided important economic growth rates and some of the countries of the region were among the richest in the world at the time.

Indeed, this first era of globalization, which came about as transportation costs fell, capital flows rose and labour mobility increased, greatly benefited the exploitation of Latin American natural resources. However, World War I interrupted the globalization process both in Latin America and elsewhere. When the region was beginning to redress itself from the negative impact of the war, the Great Depression of the 1930s hit.

The fragility of the economic world order that Latin America had tried to incorporate itself into, not only as a reliable commodities supplier but as a relevant importer of manufactured goods, became evident. Not surprisingly, industrialization began to be the appropriate medicine to provide a firmer economic ground.

World War II gave new impetus to this industrialization process. With the end of the war, what was already a fact — the import–substituting industrialization process — was duly conceptualized. Since 1948 the theoretical framework of that process began to take shape through the Economic Commission for Latin America, ECLA.

The import–substituting industrialization presented, nonetheless, important flaws. In the long run, two of them proved to be catastrophic. The first was to see the foreclosure of national markets as permanent in nature. Thus, domestic industries were indefinitely isolated. The second was that the dependency on commodities continued to be fundamental, as they were the ones generating the currency that nurtured this whole process. This generated an immense vulnerability for the whole import–substituting industrialization structure.

Notwithstanding its flaws, the system produced impressive results. Between 1950 and 1973 Latin America grew faster than the world average: 5.4 per cent versus 4.9 per cent. Moreover, in 1981, Latin American share of world's GDP was 11 per cent while its GDP per capita exceeded the world's average by 10 per cent during the third quarter of that year.

Unfortunately, the inherent vulnerabilities within the import–substituting industrialization model produced a domino effect when the right set of international conditions appeared. And they did because of the debt crisis. It all began during the 1970s, when the international banking system overflowed with petrodollars, derived from the sudden hike in oil prices, devoted itself to grant plentiful loans. This easy access to international credits was seen by Latin American governments as an excellent opportunity to invest in infrastructure and the modernization of its state industries.

In 1980, fighting its own problem of inflation, the United States initiated interest rate increases that climbed to over 20 per cent. These spilled over to Latin American loans who between 1975 and 1982, saw its debt increase from US$45.2 billion to US$333 billion.

To make matters worse, while interest rates were rising, the price of natural resources began to fall. The reasons behind these two phenomena were very much the same. Faced with the climb in oil prices in 1979, the new governments of Ronald Reagan and Margaret Thatcher decided to fight inflation not only through monetary tools (such as interest rate increases), but also by reducing fiscal expenditure.

Those policies caused a recession that projected elsewhere, increasing unemployment and precipitating the fall in the demand, and by extension in the prices, of commodities. Such an unexpected downturn in the prices of primary products gravely affected the capacity of Latin American governments to meet their debts. While the sources of currency income were dropping significantly, the external debt was growing exponentially because of the interest rates hike.

This period of extreme weakness was combined with the appearance of a new economic paradigm brought in, again, by the duo of Reagan–Thatcher: the neoliberal model. Just when Latin American governments were facing the need to renegotiate their debts and acquire new loans to pay the old ones, they were confronted with this ideological juggernaut. With its negotiating strength reduced to its minimum, the region was faced with the premise of the Washington Consensus and the directives of its executive arm, the International Monetary Fund.

All of the above lead to the sudden and widespread opening of Latin American markets. That forced a totally unprepared industrial sector, to compete with the most efficient companies of the world. This resulted in an accelerated and premature disappearance of an important part of the Latin American industrial base.

Indefinitely isolating local industries from outside competition had indeed been, a huge mistake. But the corrective medicine should never have been the sudden opening of trade barriers. What happened was the equivalent to the brutal throwing down of the protective walls to let Genghis Khan's hordes in. Companies that had thrived under the old system began to be slaughtered on mass.

On the other hand, and under the ideological commands of the Washington Consensus, an irrational privatization process of state–owned companies took shape. The very same state companies and public utilities, the expansion of which had indebted the governments of the region, started to be sold at laughable prices. Basically, to transnational corporations. Thus, while Latin American governments were facing a foreign debt that had grown out of all proportion in relation to the originally granted loans, the assets resulting from such loans were bargained against transnational capital. This involved a net and massive transfer of wealth overseas.

But there was not only the shrinkage of the industrial base, but also of the technological capabilities that had been associated with it. During the import–substituting industrialization phase, a great effort in Research and Development had taken place. The industrial development strategy required, the build-up of endogenous technological capacities. Through the implementation of the Washington Consensus not only regional R&D efforts were abandoned, but the whole idea of generating local technology began to be seen as useless. Henceforward, imported technology became the aim and it was assumed that this would naturally come by way of trade or foreign direct investments.

Neoliberal policies had a profoundly regressive effect for Latin America. Had Latin America followed a common–sense approach to reform, as was the case in China during the same period, the history of the region would have evolved in a very different direction. But, while Latin America was experiencing an accelerated downward tendency, China showed a spectacular climbing one.

These reverse tendencies would become evident when China's and Latin America's roads crossed at the beginning of the millennium. When Latin America's industries where beginning to redress from the impact of the neoliberal tsunami, the avalanche of the Chinese low–cost products came along. It was a second shock that pushed Latin American industries into a corner.

China though, had, a big redeeming virtue that the Washington Consensus never had. The Asian country was a voracious consumer of commodities. Between 2002 and 2006 the general index of commodities worldwide, excluding oil, was increased 60 per cent in real terms. Moreover, in the areas of oil and metals such an increase surge reached 150 per cent and 180 per cent, respectively. This phenomenon cannot but be attributed to China, a country that imported 20 times more commodities between 1993 and 2013.

As a result, while the regional industrial base got hammered, the commodities sector unexpectedly began to blossom. The Inter–American Development Bank refers to Mexican–type countries and Brazilian–type ones. The former are mainly labour–intensive export oriented economies. The latter are essentially commodity exporters. The Mexican group includes Central America, the Dominican Republic and, of course,

Mexico itself. The Brazilian group contains all South American countries plus Cuba in the Caribbean. Within those two groups, the first was badly affected by China's sudden appearance in the region, while the second greatly benefited.

After the massacre caused in the industrial base of the region by the Washington Consensus policies, the maquila system took hold in the Mexican–type economies. It was an export–oriented system based on labor–intensive assembly lines dependent on foreign technology and in a fundamental market: the United States. China's low–cost competition in the latter, implied an important displacement of their own export products.

Brazil–type economies reacted to the Washington Consensus policies essentially by emphasizing the export of commodities. Hence, they clearly benefited from China's voracious demand and for many of them the Asian country became its first export market. Nonetheless, both Brazil and Argentina had retained a significant industrial base. Even if in terms of total exports their products played a secondary role, they were still relevant within their domestic market where displacement by China's competition took place. Thus, for Brazil and Argentina the balance resulting from China's appearance was mixed: while greatly benefiting in their commodities export markets, they were negatively impacted in their manufacturing sector.

Besides trade, China has played a leading role in foreign direct investments and loans in Latin America, especially in Brazilian–type economies. Between 2010 and the end of 2014, such investments accounted for US$106 billion, while its loans reached more than US$130 billion during the period 2005–2013.

However, since 2013 the commodities boom ceased. Several factors have triggered such a downfall in their prices, particularly in the case of oil and mining products. The common denominator, though, has been the slowing down of the insatiable demand for natural resources in China. It's rebalancing towards domestic consumption means that industry grows less rapidly than in the past, while the service sector expands. This generates a positioning away from commodity–heavy sectors, where production overcapacity exists.

As a result, Brazilian–type economies have seen a substantial contraction in their exports, while its economic growth has slowed. Concurrently, the very important social gains obtained during the commodities export boom are being significantly eroded.

What are the region's economic options then? Latin American countries are in a typical middle–income trap situation. Indeed, their economies are unable to compete with advanced economies in high skill innovations. Only Brazil really shows some high–tech manufacturing niches, but still insufficient to be meaningful. Conversely, as Latin American wages rise and its competitiveness declines, possibilities at the bottom end of the manufacturing equation are becoming increasingly difficult. Not even China's contraction in labour–intensive manufacturing represents a solution, as other Asian economies such as Vietnam, Indonesia, Philippines or Bangladesh are taking its place at the bottom. Asia's supply chain of production is simply unbeatable.

Mexican–types economies are definitively on the wrong side of the equation. Especially so when its main export market, the United States, is abhorring from the free trade policies and agreements that paved the way for their conversion into labour–intensive exporters. Cornered between its declining possibilities of remaining competitive at the bottom, and the pressures imposed by its main trade partner for its low costs exports, room for manoeuvre is simply disappearing.

Notwithstanding the current contraction in the price of commodities, Brazilian–type economies seem to have more options. These options point to Asia. The Trans–Pacific Partnership, India's increasing demand of commodities and the One Belt, One Road Initiative, present themselves as sources of potential advancement. Especially so the last of them.

The One Belt, One Road project encompasses 65 per cent of the world's population, about one third of the world's gross domestic product and about a quarter of the world's trade. Moreover, it is backed by China's economic might and its ambition to consolidate its position at the center of the global supply and manufacturing networks. With 110 nations manifesting its adhesion to the Initiative and serving as stakeholders of its success, there is room for optimism. If the One Belt, One Road materializes, commodities will bloom again.

It is obvious, nonetheless, that not only product exporters but commodities exporters as well, will have to widen their horizons. Not only because there are not assured bets are on the table, but because their current vulnerabilities are very high. Services, which is becoming the new export frontier, looks the best way forward.

Within the service sector the global chains of value, acquire particular relevance. Until recently many services were difficult or impossible to supply beyond their frontiers, but this has changed because of the exponential advance in information and telecommunication technologies. Thanks to them distance has disappeared and many previously domestically encapsulated services have become global.

According to Alan Blinder, Director of the Center for Economic Policy Studies at Princeton University, impersonal services are on the brink of a gigantic revolution. Such services, which are those that do not require a face–to–face interaction with the customer or patient, will be transferred in their tens of millions to emerging economies, where a gigantic pool of talent converges with much lower costs.

We are, thus, talking of the massive migration of impersonal services jobs to the developing world in the next few decades. From accountants to software engineers, from designers to architects, from doctors to researchers, from financial consultants to lawyers, the service jobs herein involved could countless. This is an area where Latin America could play an important role.

However, in the same way there are promising signs in the horizon, there are also threatening ones. The incoming Fourth Industrial Revolution presents itself as the greatest challenge to the stability of the region in the coming decades. And even if this is a worldwide phenomenon, the implications for Latin America can be simply overwhelming.

The convergence of digital technology and robotics; nanotechnology; biotechnology and genomics; additive manufacturing (3D printing); the Internet of things, autonomous vehicles and energy technologies, to mention just some of the most relevant leaps, will project its impact in every imaginable direction. As a result, assembly lines, mining activities, farming and livestock sectors, hydrocarbons developments, service sectors can all be disrupted in dramatic ways.

A huge sign of interrogation hangs on the future of Latin America. Only time will provide the answer.

BIBLIOGRAPHY

Arana, M (2013). *Bolívar: American Liberator.* New York: Simon & Schuster Paperbacks.

Arciniegas, G (2001). *Cuando la América Completó la Tierra.* Bogotá: Villegas Editores.

Aziz, AS (ed.) (1981). *Ethnicity and U.S. Foreign Policy.* New York: Praeger.

Baigent, M and R Leigh (2000). *The Inquisition.* London: Penguin Books.

Bauer, AJ (2001). *Goods. Power, History: Latin America's Material Culture.* Cambridge: Cambridge University Press.

Bendiner, E (1995). *The Rise and Fall of Paradise: When Arabs and Jews Built a Kingdom in Spain.* New York: Barnes & Noble Books.

Bethell, L and I Roxborough (eds.) (1992). *Latin America between the Second World War and the Cold War.* Cambridge: Cambridge University Press.

Blinder, A (2006). "Offshoring: The Next Industrial Revolution". *Foreign Affairs.* 85 (March/April).

Borja, R (1997). *Enciclopedia de la Política.* México: Fondo de Cultura Económica.

Bremmer, I (2012). *Every Nation for Itself: Winners and Losers in a G–Zero World.* New York: Portfolio.

Brown, SR (2009). *Merchant Kings.* New York: Thomas Dunne Books.

Brynnjolfsson, E and A McAfee (2011). *Race Against the Machines: How Digital Revolution is Accelerating Innovation, Driving Productivity, and Irreversibly Transforming Employment and the Economy.* Lexington, Mass: Digital Frontier Press.

Brynnjolfsson, E and A McAfee (2014). *The Second Machine Age: Work, Progress, and Prosperity in a Time of Brilliant Technologies.* New York: W.W. Norton.

Bulmer–Thomas, V and J Dunkerley (eds.) (1999). *The United States and Latin America: The New Agenda.* Cambridge, Mass: Harvard University Press.

Bulmer–Thomas, V, JH Coastworth, and R Córtes Conde (eds.) (2006). *The Cambridge Economic History of Latin America, Volume II: The Long Twentieth Century.* Cambridge: Cambridge University Press.

Carmagni, M (2004). *El Otro Occidente: América Latina desde la Invasión Europea hasta la Globalización.* México: El Colegio de México/Fondo de Cultura Económica.

CEPAL (2012). *La República Popular China y América Latina y el Caribe: Diálogo y Cooperación ante los Nuevos Desafíos de la Economía Mundial.* Santiago de Chile: Junio.

Clark, K (1969). *Civilization.* New York: Harper & Row Publishers.

Coastworth, H. "The Cold War in Central America, 1975–1991", https://www.scribd.com/doc/109666536/The-Cold-War-in-Central-America-1975-1991-John-H-Coastsworth-Ch-10

Comblin, J (1977). *Le Pouvoir Militaire en Amerique Latine: L'idéologie de la Sécurité Nationale.* París: Jean–Pierre Delarge Editeur.

Davison, C (2012). *Now You See It: How Technology and Brain Science will Transform Schools and Business for the 21st Century.* London: Penguin Books.

Debouzy, M (1972). *Le Capitalisme Sauvage aux Etats–Unis.* Paris: Éditions du Seuil.

De Mesquita, B and H Roots (eds.) (2000). *Governing for Prosperity.* New Haven: Yale University Press.

Diamond, L, J Hartlyn, JJ Linz and SM Lipset (eds.) (1999). *Latin America: Democracy in Developing Countries.* London: Lyenne Rienner Publishers.

Dominguez, JI and R Fernandez de Castro (eds.) (2010). *Contemporary U.S.–Latin American Relations: Cooperation or Conflict in the 21st Century?* New York: Routledge.

ECLAC (2015). "Economic Relations between Latin America and the Caribbean and the Republic of Korea: Advances and Opportunities". Santiago de Chile: April.

Ellis, ER (2017). "Indian and Chinese Engagement in Latin America and the Caribbean: A Comparative Assessment". Washington D.C.: Strategic Studies Institute and U.S. Army War College Press. March.

Ferguson, N (2004). *Colossus: The Rise and Fall of the American Empire*. London: Allen Lane.

Fernández–Armesto, F (2005). *The Americas: A Hemispheric History*. New York: The Modern Library,.

Flagg Bemis, S (1959). *John Quincy Adams and the Foundations of American Foreign Policy*. New York: Knopf .

Frey, CB and M E Osborne (2013). "The Future of Employment: How Susceptible are Jobs to Computerization" (17 September 2013). Oxford University. http://www.oxfordmartin.ox.ac.uk/downloads/academic/The_Future_of_Employment.pdf.

Fuentes CS (ed.) (2004). *Bajo la Mirada del Halcón: Estados Unidos-América Latina post 11–0–2001*. Santiago de Chile: FLACSO–Chile.

Fuentes, C (1992). *El Espejo Enterrado*. México: Fondo de Cultura Económica.

Gallager, KP and R Porzecanski (2010). *The Dragon in the Room*. Stanford: Stanford University Press.

Golinger, E (2005). *The Chávez Code: Cracking U.S. Intervention in Venezuela*. La Habana: Editorial José Martí.

Grandin, G (2006). *Empire's Workshop: Latin America, the United States, and the Rise of the New Imperialism*. New York: Metropolitan Books.

Halperin Donghi, T (1975). *Historia Contemporánea de América Latina*. Madrid: Alianza Editorial.

Harrison, LE (2013). *Jews, Confucians and Protestants: Cultural Capital and the End of Multiculturalism*. Plymouth: Rowman & Littlefield Publisher, Inc.

Harrison, LE (2000). *Underdevelopment is a State of Mind: The Latin American Case*. Plymouth: Madison Books.

Harvey, R (2000). *Liberators: South America's Savage Wars of Freedom 1810–1830*. London: Robinson.

Harvey, R (2001). *A Few Bloody Noses: The American War of Independence*. London: John Murray.

Harvey, R (2011). *Romantic Revolutionary: Simón Bolívar and the Struggle for Independence in Latin America*. London: Constable.

Hawthorn, G (1993). *Plausible Worlds: Possibility and Understanding in History and Social Sciences*. Cambridge: Cambridge University Press.

Holland, T (2005). *Persian Fire: The First World Empire and the Battle for the West*. London: Little Brown.

Huntington, SP (2004). *¿Quiénes Somos? Los Desafíos de la Identidad Nacional Estadounidense*. Barcelona: Paidós.

Huntington, SP (1996). *The Clash of Civilizations and the Remaking of World Order*. New York: Simon & Schuster.

Inter–American Development Bank (2016). *A Virtuous Cycle of Integration: The Past, Present, and Future of Japan–Latin American and the Caribbean Relations*. Washington D.C.

Izquierdo, A and E Talvi (Coordinators) (2011). *One Region, Two Speeds?* Washington D.C.: Inter–American Development Bank, March.

Kicza, JE (2004). *The Indian in Latin American History*. Oxford: SR Books.

Kissinger, H (1994). *Diplomacy*. New York: Simon & Schuster.

Kosacoff, B y S Campanario (2007). *La Revalorizacion de las Materias Primas y sus Efectos en América Latina*. Santiago de Chile: CEPAL, mayo.

Krauze E (2013). *Redentores: Ideas y Poder en América Latina*. México: Debolsillo.

Kynge, J (2006). *China Shakes the World*. London: Phoenix.

Levitsky, S and KM Roberts (2011). *The Resurgence of the Latin American Left*. Baltimore: The Johns Hopkins University Press.

López, A, D Ramos, y I Torres (2009). *Las Exportaciones de servicio y su integración a las Cadenas Globales de Valor*. Santiago de Chile: CEPAL, marzo.

Loser, C (2012). *The Impact of Globalization on Latin America Task Force* (11 June 2012). Miami: University of Miami Center for Hemispheric Policy.

Loveman, B (2016). U.S. Foreign Policy towards Latin America in the 19th Century., Oxford: *Oxford Research Encyclopaedia of Latin American History*, July. http://oxfordindex.oup.com/view/10.1093/acrefore/9780199366439.013.41.

Lynch, J (1983). Simon Bolivar and the Spanish Revolutions (7 July 1983). *History Today*, 33 (7). http://historytoday.com/john-lynch/simon-bolivar-and-spanish-revolutions.

Lynch, J (2006). *Simón Bolívar: A Life*. New Haven: Yale University Press.

Malavé, I and E Giordani (2015). *Latino Stats: American Hispanics by the Numbers*. New York: The New Press.

Mann, CC (2011). *1491: New Revelations of the Americas before Columbus*. New York: Vintage Books.

Manseau, P (2016). *One Nation under Gods: An American History.* New York: Back Bay Books.

Marsh Smith, R (1965). *Spain: A Modern History.* Ann Arbor: University of Michigan Press.

Martínez, JL (1983). *Pasajeros a Indias, Viajes Trasatlánticos en el Siglo XVI.* Madrid: Alianza Editorial.

Maura, JF (2002). Adelantadas, virreinas y aventureras en los primeros años de la conquista de América. *Revista de Literatura Española Medieval y del Renacimiento*, Número 6.

Maura, JF (1995). Mujeres hispanas en el Nuevo Mundo: a la vanguardia de los acontecimientos. *Revista de Estudios Hispánicos*, Número 15.

Maurois, A (1972). *Historia de los Estados Unidos*. Barcelona: Círculo de Lectores.

Mesquita Moreira, M (Coordinator) (2010). *India: Latin America's Next Big Thing?* Washington D.C.: Inter–American Development Bank. .

Mishra, S, S Lundstrom and A Rahul (2011). *Service Sophistication and Economic Growth*. The World Bank, South Asia Region, Policy Research Working Paper 5606. Washington D.C.: March.

Molina, S y A Rosas (2014). Alejandro. *Érase Una Vez México: 2*. México: Editorial Planeta Mexicana, S.A.

Morant, I *et al.* (2005). *Historia de las Mujeres en España y América Latina.* Madrid: Ediciones Cátedra.

Paz, O (1992). *El Laberinto de la Soledad.* México: Fondo de Cultura Económica.

Peña. JMG (2011). Una aproximación a las relaciones económico–comerciales entre China y América Latina y el Caribe (13 September 2011). *Observatorio de la Política China.*

Pollak–Eltz, A (1991). *La Negritud en Venezuela*. Caracas: Cuadernos Lagoven.

Raudzens, G (1999). *Empires: Europe and Globalization 1492–1788*. London: Sutton Publishing.

Ribeiro, D (1995). *O Povo Brasileiro.* Sao Paulo: Companhia das Letras.

Rifkin, J (2014). *The Zero Marginal Cost Society, and the Eclipse of Capitalism.* New York: Palgrave,.

Ridley, J (1992). *Maximilian & Juarez*. London: Phoenix Press.

Ríos, X (2012). Crédito y descrédito en América Latina. *Jiexi Zhonguo: Análisis y Pensamiento Iberoaméricano sobre China*, Número 2., Primer Trimestre 2012.

Roberts, JM (1985). *The triumph of the West: The Origins, Rise and Legacy of Western Civilization*. Boston: Little, Brown and Company.

Sader, E, I Jinkings, Ivana *et al.* (Coordinators) (2009). *Latinoamérica: Enciclopedia Contemporánea de América Latina y El Caribe*. Madrid: Clacso–Ediciones AKAL, S.A.

Schoultz, L (1988). *Beneath the United States: A History of U.S. Policy toward Latin America*. Cambridge, Mass.: Harvard University Press.

Secretaría Permanente del Sistema Económico Latinoamericano y del Caribe. (2012) *Relaciones Económicas de Estados Unidos con los Países de América Latina y el Caribe en Época de Transición*. Caracas: Mayo.

Sinnot, E, J Nash, and A de la Torre (2010). *Natural Resources in Latin America and the Caribbean: Beyond Booms and Busts?* Washington D.C.: The World Bank.

Sistema Económico Latinoamericano (2012). *Informe sobre el proceso de Integración Regional 2011–2012*. Caracas: Agosto.

Sistema Económico Latinoamericano (2012). *Las relaciones entre China y América Latina y el Caribe en la actual coyuntura económica mundial*. Caracas: Septiembre.

Sistema Económico Latinoamericano (2012). *La Crisis en la Zona del Euro, su impacto en el proceso de integración europeo y en las relaciones birregionales entre América Latina y el Caribe. Líneas de acción desde la perspectiva latinoamericana y caribeña*. Caracas: 17 al 19 de octubre.

Schwab, K (2017). *The Fourth Industrial Revolution*. London: Portfolio Penguin.

Stein, S J and BH Stein (1970). *The Colonial Heritage of Latin America*. New York: Oxford University Press.

Steiner, C (2012). *Automate This: How Algorithms Took over Our Markets, Our Jobs, and the World.* New York: Portfolio/Penguin.

Stiglitz, J (2002). *Globalization and its Discontents*. London: W.W. Norton & Company.

Stiglitz, J (2006). *Making Globalization Work*. London: Allen Lane

Suarez, R (2013). *Latino Americans: The 500-Year Legacy that Shaped a Nation.* New York: Celebra.

Swanson, P (ed.) (2014). *The Companion to Latin American Studies*. New York: Routledge.

The Economist (2012). *Pocket World in Figures: 2012 Edition*. London: Profile Books Ltd.

Toffler, A (1991). *El Cambio de Poder*. Barcelona: Plaza y Janés Editores.

Thomas, H (2003). *Rivers of Gold.* New York: Random House.

Toro Hardy, A (1988). *El Desafío Venezolano: ¿Cómo Influir las Decisiones Políticas Estadounidenses?* Caracas: Instituto de Altos Estudios de América Latina de la Universidad Simón Bolívar.

Toro Hardy, A (2002). *The Age of Villages: The Small Village vs. the Global Village.* Bogota: Villegas Editores.

Toro Hardy, A (2004). *¿Tiene Futuro América Latina?* Bogotá: Villegas Editores.

Toro Hardy, A (2013). *The World Turned Upside Down: The Complex Partnership between China and Latin America*. Singapore: World Scientific.

Turzi, M (2012). Grown in the Cone: South America's Soybean Boom. *Current History*, 111 (742), No. 742, February.

Uslar Pietri, A (1982). *Fachas, Fechas y Fichas*. Caracas: Editorial Ateneo de Caracas.

Uslar Pietri, A (1979). *Fantasmas de Dos Mundos*. Barcelona: Editorial Seix Barral, S.A.

Véliz, C (1980). *The Centralist Tradition of Latin America*. Princeton: Princeton University Press.

Warrell, M (2014). Learn, Unlearn and Relearn (3 February 2014). *Forbes*.

Williamson, E (2009). *The Penguin History of Latin America*. London: Penguin Books.

World Bank (2011). *Latin America and the Caribbean's Long Term Growth: Made in China?* Washington D.C.: September.

Yergin, D and J Stanislaw (1998). *The Commanding Heights*. New York: Simon & Schuster.

Zea, L (1976). *El Pensamiento Latinoamericano*. Barcelona: Editorial Ariel,.

Zoellick, RB (2012). Globalization: Made in the Americas (7 June 2012). *30th Anniversary Celebration of the Inter–American Dialogue*. Washington D.C.

Zweig, S (2004). *Conscience contre Violence*. París: Le Castor Astral.

MAP OF LATIN AMERICA